MARITIME UNION IN POLITICS AND LAW

UNDERSTANDING CANADA

MARITIME UNION IN POLITICS AND LAW

THE CONSTITUTIONALITY OF UNITING CANADIAN PROVINCES

Donald A. Desserud

UNIVERSITY OF TORONTO PRESS
Toronto Buffalo London

INSTITUTE OF PARLIAMENTARY AND POLITICAL LAW
INSTITUT DE DROIT PARLEMENTAIRE ET POLITIQUE

Irwin Law
An imprint of University of Toronto Press
Toronto Buffalo London
utppublishing.com
Printed and bound by CPI Group (UK) Ltd, Croydon, CR0 4YY

ISBN 9781552217344 (paper)   ISBN 9781487571054 (EPUB)
                                    ISBN 9781552217351 (PDF)

Library and Archives Canada Cataloguing in Publication
Publication cataloguing information is available from Library and Archives Canada.

Cover image: Adobe Stock

We wish to acknowledge the land on which the University of Toronto Press operates. This land is the traditional territory of the Wendat, the Anishnaabeg, the Haudenosaunee, the Métis, and the Mississaugas of the Credit First Nation.

University of Toronto Press acknowledges the financial support of the Government of Canada, the Canada Council for the Arts, and the Ontario Arts Council, an agency of the Government of Ontario, for its publishing activities.

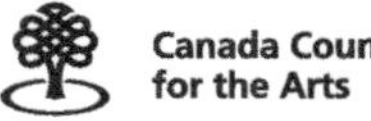

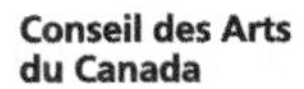

You could no more induce Nova Scotia, New Brunswick and Prince Edward Island to drop their identity than you could get Rhode Island, Connecticut and New Hampshire to join together. Such communities are particularly tenacious of their autonomy. It is a respectable sentiment and one which must be recognized.

Prime Minister Wilfrid Laurier (1906)

Contents

Foreword

In the geographic space between the western shore of the northern Atlantic Ocean and the eastern boundary of the valley of the St. Lawrence River, French and English explorers founded settlements, made claims on behalf of their respective monarchs, and displaced previous peoples' governing authority. The initially sparse populations eventually became settled and self-governing colonies, with both sovereignty and boundaries shifting according to the global power struggles of colonial empires and local political and economic circumstances. Each regime added a layer to the local legal systems. Maps became more stabilized when the northeastern border of the United States was fixed at the eastern edge of Maine and especially with the adhesion, first of Nova Scotia and New Brunswick, and later with the joining of Prince Edward Island and ultimately of Newfoundland with Canada. There were reasons, even by then rooted in history, for each jurisdiction to join Canada as a separate political entity. The reality is that those reasons survive today and appear likely to remain.

Ever since 1867, geopolitical circumstances have engendered a question. From a distance, the characteristics of the three Maritime provinces, and alternatively of the four Atlantic provinces, are seemingly similar. Would it be wise for some or all of them to unite into a single jurisdiction within Canada? Bearing in mind the possibility of both economy of government and prosperity of economy, would such a change be useful? Could it even be feasible? Historical comparisons do not guide us. The union of many, but not all, German-speaking jurisdictions into Germany, and of many, but not all, Italian-speaking jurisdictions into Italy, each in the latter nineteenth century, are irrelevant to our question. Similarly, we cannot find guidance by recollecting efforts to merge certain American states. Looking in the opposite direction, the 1979 carve-out of the new Canton of Jura from the Canton of Bern, within Switzerland, is equally inapplicable. The possibility of Maritime Union is a singularly Canadian matter.

Professor Desserud first combines the factual, namely the social diversity of the peoples and politics in the Maritimes, with the visceral love of autonomy of each community. This leads him to note that Maritimers are notionally related to each other but are not identical. Such considerations are the first ones to colour the entire discussion. They demonstrate the reality that local public opinion could, and probably would, frustrate political moves in the direction of union. A further and not insignificant factor in the debate of, or planning for Maritime Union, is the rigidity of the Canadian Constitution, especially in relation to amendment. The *British North America Act* was planned to enable the incorporation into Confederation of additional parts of the continent, not the union of jurisdictions once inside the country. In this context, the author raises several challenging questions as to both the constitutional and political processes that Maritime Union would require. One of these is the legal question of whether such a development would require each uniting province to be abolished and a single, entirely new province be brought into legal existence. Reading the scholarly opinion on the relevant *Constitution Acts* leads to very different conclusions. Another is the political difficulties that would ensue trying to determine what model of representation the new province would need to adopt. There is also the question of the impact of Maritime Union on the general amending formula found in the *Constitution Act, 1982.*

Through a blend of social study and history, then constitutionalism and law, finally through political analysis, the author captures the specificities of the issue in a masterful way and thereby contributes to our better understanding of Canada. By contrast to a superficially good idea, the weight of history is on Professor Desserud's side of the analysis. Whatever one's perspective on the question, and whether one reads this from the perspective of life and/or study in Edmundston or Edmonton, this book is most useful.

Gregory Tardi, DJur.
Editor, *Understanding Canada* collection
January 2024

Preface

What are we going to do, form our own country? That's absurd. Stay as a part of a fractured Canada? A good possibility but that's all. Or be part of the United States? There's no choice.

Nova Scotia Premier John Buchanan,
18 April 1990[1]

On the one-year anniversary of their party's landslide victory in the 1993 federal election, Liberal delegates from across the country met in Ottawa to celebrate. But the delegation from the Maritime provinces was unsettled. The new Parliament might have had a large majority of Liberal Members of Parliament (MPs) but it also seated fifty-four members of the separatist party the Bloc Québécois (BQ) who now formed the Official Opposition. The Parti Québécois had won the provincial election in Quebec just a month before and now the BQ joined their provincial counterparts in a position of significant power. A referendum on separation was already being planned. Quebec separation was a real and pressing danger.

The Maritime delegates worried that Canada would fall apart if Quebec left Confederation. What would the Maritimes do then?[2] Would the Maritimes, as a now former premier of Nova Scotia had said recently, be forced to join the United States?

Doug Young was then the Minister of Transport and the MP for Acadie-Bathurst, a riding in northern New Brunswick. I attended a meeting that Young held in Ottawa with the Maritime Liberal delegates. At the time, I was writing a newspaper column in New Brunswick and I wanted to speak to different politicians about what they thought would happen to the Maritimes if Quebec separated. I soon got one answer. At Young's meeting, a delegate asked him the million-dollar question: if Quebec separates, will the Maritimes be forced to join the United States?

"Never!" shouted Young. "If Quebec separates, the Maritimes will not join the United States!" Everyone cheered. But Young wasn't finished and the new minister thought to have some fun with his partisan audience. "If Quebec separates," he continued, "we'll join Quebec!" I was then treated to the sight of a room filled with people all frozen in mid-clap.

After the meeting was over, I paid a visit to Suzanne Tremblay. Tremblay was the Bloc MP for Rimouski-Témiscouata (now Rimouski-Neigette—Témiscouata—Les Basques), a Quebec riding on the New Brunswick border. Among her responsibilities in the Official Opposition, Tremblay was the critic for francophone affairs outside Quebec which included Acadians living in the Maritime provinces. She was sympathetic but not optimistic about the fate of Acadians and their culture in a Canada without Quebec. At one point in our discussion Doug Young's name came up. Young, born and raised on New Brunswick's Acadian peninsula and fluently bilingual, had been sparring with Tremblay in the House of Commons.

"I do not like that man!" she said, shaking her head. "He has no respect for Quebec's needs."

"Well," I replied, "Doug thinks more highly of Quebec than you may know." I told her the story of Young's speech, ending with Young's cry, "If Quebec separates, we'll join Quebec!" Madame Blanchard grew visibly pale. "Oh, my God," she said, "we never thought of that!"

I am sure she did not. I also doubt she really gave much thought to the fate of the Acadians or the Maritimes in general were Quebec to separate. But in 1994 Maritimers were thinking of precisely this.

A referendum on separation did take place the very next year, in 1995, and the Yes vote in favour of separation came perilously close to a majority.[3] University of Prince Edward Island political scientist David Milne wrote that in the immediate aftermath of that vote: "Fear was compounded by embarrassment when Atlantic Canadians openly speculated about whether their region might even be wanted by other Canadians."[4] It is difficult to imagine this reaction in any other part of the country.

Maritimers are profoundly aware of their position, often precarious,[5] in Canada and for that matter in North America. Robert Finbow writes: "The region least equipped to deal with the breakup of Confederation is Atlantic Canada."[6] National unity matters to Maritimers and threats to national unity are always a grave concern. Donald Savoie explains:

> It is no coincidence that the issue of Maritime political union or cooperation will surface on the public policy agenda only when national unity is threatened. In 1964, it was Quebec's Quiet Revolution and the pressures of the mid-twentieth century that accounted for Louis Robichaud's call for a "serious" look at political union of the four Atlantic provinces. The issue again gained currency immediately after the Parti Québécois came to power in Quebec in 1976. Frank McKenna issued a call for greater regional cooperation in the aftermath of the failed Meech Lake and Charlottetown constitutional accords. The point is that outside forces, not those from within, have put Maritime union on the public policy agenda.[7]

At the time of writing, no such external forces are present or at least are not apparently present. However, consider the prospect of Quebec separation or Western separation. Both these movements are real threats and do deserve to be take seriously but they are not immediate threats — at least not in 2024. But will this always be the case? Likely not. Events happen, things change, and just as Quebec separation will certainly return someday as a real possibility, or just as someday Western separation might become a real possibility, so too might Maritime Union be back on the table. When it does, certain questions will need to be answered.

The near win of the separatist forces in Quebec in 1995 resulted in a reference case which asked, basically, if and how the Canadian

Constitution could deal with a province determined to separate.[8] The Court's ruling, still debated today,[9] established a refined jurisprudence concerning how constitutions can deal with profound change. Maritime Union would also profoundly change the Constitution. Such a change would not be traumatic, I do not believe, but it would be far-reaching. And so it warrants our attention.

Yet another question needs answering: what are the chances that someday the Maritime provinces will unite? That's not an easy question to answer, but frankly I would say not strong at all. It is true that to some it just seems obvious that Nova Scotia, New Brunswick, and Prince Edward Island should be one province. Some of those people even live in the Maritimes. However, there are not too many such people and at present no one in the Maritime provinces' political leadership endorses Maritime Union. If they do, they keep it a secret because it would not be well received by voters. For most Maritimers, union means giving up a lot for an uncertain little. What Dalhousie political science professor J. Murray Beck wrote in 1969 holds true today: "Clearly it is essential to demonstrate that substantial positive good is likely to result from Maritime Union before incurring the wastage through ill will and conflict that will inevitably follow any attempt to effect it."[10]

So why, then, write a book on Maritime Union? That's a good question, and a good a place to start.

Acknowledgments

I would like to begin by acknowledging my intellectual debt to Donald Savoie and Charles McMillan. While they may not agree with all of my conclusions, their work on the politics and economics of the Maritime Provinces – particularly on Maritime Union and regional economic integration – has significantly shaped my thinking and analysis. I am also grateful to the series editor, Greg Tardi, whose encouragement led me to undertake this book. Most importantly, I wish to express my deep gratitude for the unwavering love, support, and encouragement I have received and continue to receive from my life partner of the past 30 years, Robin Sutherland.

The Perennial Topic of Maritime Union

The leaders of the maritime colonies had planned to meet at Charlottetown in the fall to discuss the perennial topic of maritime union.

Reference re Secession of Quebec[1]

Why a Book on Maritime Union?

At the time of writing there is no political party[2] nor any provincial leader in the region who advocates for the unification of Canada's three Maritime provinces; that is, Nova Scotia, New Brunswick, and Prince Edward Island. A few years ago, three senators banded together to call for Maritime Union, but that initiative went nowhere[3] and in any case, after 2024 none of these people will still be in the Senate.[4] Nor is there significant popular support for Maritime Union. Shortly after the three senators made their call for Maritime Union, Innovative Research Group (IRG) conducted an opinion poll to gauge popular support for the initiative. The telephone poll only surveyed one province — Nova Scotia — but 54% of the respondents opposed Maritime Union, with 34% being strongly opposed.[5] The limited nature of this poll (it did not survey New Brunswick or Prince Edward Island) and the fact that it is one of a very few public opinion polls taken over the past fifty years that has asked this question is an indication that the topic is not one of pressing concern in the Maritimes.[6] Even those academics in the region who have supported Maritime Union have come to accept that the idea has no traction.[7]

So why write a book on Maritime Union? Three reasons: (1) the "perennial debate" in support of or against Maritime Union has yet to be settled and may never be. Understanding why this is the case will help us better understand the nature of Canadian federalism; (2) there is a need for greater clarity over constitutional reform in Canada, particularly at the provincial level. Have we entrenched too rigid amending formulae?; and (3) regionalism and identity are words used far too loosely in studies of Canada. The Maritime provinces do constitute a unique region with a regional identity, but not a homogeneous region: the Maritimes also house many sub-regional and sub-provincial identities and that matters.

The Three Reasons

1) The Perennial Debate

Two connected arguments in favour of union dominate the debate surrounding Maritime Union. One is economic, the other political. Both can be summed up this way: with Maritime Union, the region would prosper and as a prosperous, larger province it would have more "clout." The economic argument claims that Maritime Union would save money through realized efficiencies, provide benefit from economies of scale, and allow for economic synergies. Maritime Union would harmonize regional industrial policy and put an end to the current practice by which two and sometimes all three provinces try to outbid each other with tax concessions and relocation grants to attract businesses. Maritime Union would eliminate inter-provincial trade barriers in the region, which constitutionally should probably not exist but do anyway. A unified transportation policy would allow for a pooling of resources and the creation of a single, efficient grid coordinating highway, rail, air, and marine transportation thereby lowering costs. A single code of regulations for the movement of products, both imports and exports, would be more efficient and less expensive. A union would provide efficiencies of scale, particularly in the provision of health-care services but also more generally in the provision of all government services. Some claim that Maritime Union would reduce the number of people employed in the civil service; where there are now three people doing a certain job, with union there would only need to be one (a dubious claim, as much of civil service staffing is determined by caseloads). Similarly, the new province would require fewer elected members and fewer Cabinet ministers than now exist in the aggregate, which would also save money. Of course, having fewer elected members is assumed to be a good thing.

Do these arguments that a united Maritimes would be economically prosperous stand up to scrutiny? They are based on an assumption, which is that the economic malaise of the Maritimes is because they are separate provinces. Is this in fact true? Considering these economic arguments carefully will help us better understand the nature of economic disparity in Canada.

The second related argument in the perennial debate is that a unified Maritime province would have far more influence and political clout in the federation. Size and wealth matter when it comes to inter-provincial and federal-provincial relations: Ontario and Quebec are large; therefore, they have clout. Ontario and Alberta are wealthy; therefore, they have clout. A Maritime province would have a combined population of just under two million.[8] As such, it would be larger than Newfoundland and Labrador, Manitoba, and Saskatchewan.[9] As a relatively large province with a strong(er) economy, a Maritime province premier would be able to flex political and economic muscles both in dealing with the federal government and with other provinces. This argument oversimplifies just what political and economic influence is; nevertheless, considering whether a united Maritimes would be more influential will help us better understand inter-governmental relations in Canada.

I deal with the arguments both for and against Maritime Union in Part Three, but here are some things to consider: much of the economic benefits that union would generate could also be achieved through greater regional cooperation without losing political autonomy and much-valued provincial identities. The assumption that a united Maritime province would have more national clout, and that such clout would be significant enough to matter, is assumed rather than verified and in any case the new-found clout of a united Maritimes would still be far less than the clout of Ontario, Quebec, Alberta, or British Columbia. As well, Prince Edward Island has long worried that union with the other Maritime provinces would reduce, not increase, its clout as the interests of the other two provinces would dominate. Clout for whom, then, is a question that would need to be answered, as is the question whether moving up a step or two on the pecking order would be worth the costs.

2) Clarifying Constitutional Reform

The second reason for a book on Maritime Union is the one that I believe is the most compelling. Were the Maritime provinces to unite, a series of far-reaching constitutional amendments would need to be completed. The several amending formulae, found in the *Constitution Act, 1982*,[10] Part V, only came about after what Peter Russell has famously called a "Constitutional Odyssey"[11] and that only after a Supreme Court decision which is still debated and has yet to be accepted by the Province of Quebec.[12] The result is a multi-step, cross-listed set of formulae that seem to thwart any ambitions for constitutional reform before they even start.[13] Adam Dodek writes:

> Constitutional amendment is almost always difficult. Such is the nature of a constitution as higher law that it endures over generations, perhaps centuries. Although the requirements for amending a constitution are usually demanding, they are often straightforward and clear. Such is not the case in Canada, where constitutional amendment is not only difficult; it is also exceedingly complicated.[14]

Mind you, not all of the amendments would be difficult, at least not constitutionally speaking. For example, among the changes that would need to be made would be amendments to the three provincial constitutions. As Erin Crandall points out, "The formal amendment procedure for the Constitution of Canada is one of the most difficult in the world. By contrast, the formal amendment procedure for the constitutions of Canadian provinces, which requires a simple majority of a provincial legislature [i.e, Constitution Act, 1982 [CA 1982], sec. 45], is one of the easiest."[15] Of course, Professor Crandall means that from a strictly legal standpoint amending a provincial constitution is easy because it can done unilaterally. But she goes on to explain that provincial constitutions are notoriously elusive and there is considerable "ambiguity that surrounds what is and is not part of a province's constitution."[16] As a result, Crandall argues, provinces are likely amending their constitutions without even knowing that they are.[17]

This raises a whole other question. To effect Maritime Union, figuring out what the provincial constitutions are and which amendments affect only these constitutions will be complicated. But surely this is a project worth doing. Constitutional ambiguity cannot be healthy. The prospect of Maritime Union, even if only hypothetical, provides us with an opportunity to add a little more clarity to the question of just what a provincial constitution is,[18] and also to provide a useful case study into just how complicated and difficult such an amendment to the Constitution would be. Or, for that matter, might not be. Perhaps, once we work these things through, we will realize that complicated is not the same as impossible.

Related to the question of constitutional amendment is the question of the impact of Maritime Union on Canada's federal system which in turn has a stated goal of protecting provincial (not just regional) autonomy. This might seem an odd point, as no one is contemplating unifying the Maritimes against the will of the three Maritime provincial governments. If all three were to agree to a union, then surely the protection provided by the principle of federalism would remain intact. However, as the Quebec

Secession Reference has shown us, government actions that would fundamentally alter the constitutional position of a province require more than just the decision of a provincial government, and for that matter the federal government. The secession of a province would require, at the outset, a clear majority vote on a referendum asking a clear question. But what would constitute a "clear question" on the proposed union of several provinces? How would such results be interpreted and assessed? What would constitute a clear majority? What would happen if a referendum on union passed with a clear majority but with a very low turnout? What would happen if results (and turnout rates) were very different province-by-province?[19]

I am, therefore, approaching this subject in the manner in which certain court cases, particularly those involving the Constitution, use hypothetical scenarios. As the Supreme Court of Canada has explained (albeit in a different context), "reasonable foreseeable hypotheticals are an accepted and appropriate analytical tool."[20] Is Maritime Union reasonably foreseeable? I would argue that it is, at least to a point. As I have said, at present the likelihood of Maritime Union is practically non-existent and certainly not imminent. But it is not entirely non-existent. A future Canada dealing with issues at present unimaginable or barely foreseeable may indeed prompt Maritimers to embrace the concept of a unified province. The prime motivations for union in the past had to do with such concerns as American expansionism, which prompted Confederation in 1867, and the threat of Quebec separation, which prompted the Maritime Union movements of the 1960s and 1970s. Basically, profound threats to the region's viability have generated calls for union. Such threats will likely occur again, perhaps not in the immediate future but certainly in the distant future. If such threats occur again, certain profound constitutional questions would be raised. These constitutional questions are important even if they are only hypothetical. The value of hypothetical scenarios is that they allow us to examine or re-examine our Constitution and politics in ways which we may not have thought of otherwise. As such, we gain a better understanding of our Constitution, including our federal system, our regional identities, and our provincial governments.

3) Regional and Subregional Identities

The final reason for examining Maritime Union is the "regional" argument. That the Maritimes remain separate provinces perplexes many Canadians, at least those who live outside the Maritimes. It is less perplexing for those of us who live in the Maritimes. One problem is that the identification of a region, like beauty, is in the eye of the beholder. And perhaps as well, the further the beholder is away from the region, the more cohesive and homogenous it appears. As Cochrane and Perrella write, "There is little agreement . . . about what causes these regional divisions or, indeed, about where the lines of regional division should be drawn."[21] Or to quote Lachlan MacKinnon, "Region is a slippery idea."[22]

Richard Simeon writes:

> But we need to be a good deal more systematic both in how we conceive of the phenomenon "regionalism" and in how we describe its dimensions and effects. We must first recognize that in no sense is it an explanatory variable: by itself it doesn't explain anything; nothing happens because of regionalism. If we find differences of any sort among regions, it remains for us to find out why they exist; regionalism is not an answer. In this sense, regions are simply containers, whose contents may or may not differ. And how we draw the boundaries around them depends entirely on what our purposes are.[23]

In other words, the fact that the Maritimes — or for that matter Atlantic Canada — can be identified on a map as a region does not mean by itself that these provinces constitute a homogenous or even coherent sub-national unit. Over the years, several area leaders have voiced the bromide: "As Maritimers we have much more which unites us than separates us."[24] This is no doubt true, but it is in itself not an argument for full political union.

Regionalism, specifically regional integration theory, was a hot topic in the years following the Second World War.[25] Many scholars believed, for example, that the creation of international organizations such as the North Atlantic Treaty Organization (NATO) and the European Economic Community (EEC) would transfer citizens' allegiances away from their national country to these supranational units: their economic and physical security now in the hands of such organizations would mean nation-states were no longer relevant or not as relevant. Of course, this did not happen, and at about the same time as Maritime Union was being discussed in the 1960s and 1970s, regional integration theorists were reconsidering just from where such things as identity and allegiance came.

On a smaller scale, despite significant incentives to do so and despite a long list of regionally integrated programs and inter-provincial agencies, the three provinces still stand and show no indication of abandoning their provincial statuses. Claiming that I can provide a definitive answer as to why this is the case would be an ambitious claim indeed. But I do think I can provide some insights into why provincial identities matter and why regional identities fail to supplant them, or perhaps more accurately, why provincial, regional, and sub-provincial identities co-exist.

In 1969, Murray Beck wrote: "In 1713 the Treaty of Utrecht decreed that Acadia was to be British. More than two hundred and fifty years later — in 1969 — the number of political entities that is most appropriate for administering the original Acadia is still subject for study and debate."[26] More than half a century later, these words are still true, albeit without the intensity that accompanied this debate in 1969. Nevertheless, consider this: if the territory we call Canada were a blank slate and had no provinces, would federalists tasked with dividing the country into provincial units consider assigning provincial status to the present-day New Brunswick, Nova Scotia, and Prince Edward Island? Prince Edward Island might claim its island status as a reason to be its province, but Vancouver

Island is larger both in size and population and it is not its own province.[27] By most objective measures, Canada's three Maritime provinces should not be separate provinces: their small size, shared geography, and common history would strongly suggest they form a single unit. However, the origins of these provinces and the fact that they have never united — despite several serious initiatives to do so — is not a story about optimizing the administrative division of responsibilities, but instead is a tale of complex identities and a visceral love of autonomy. And while people over the years have argued that the three provinces should join as one, some others have even argued that the appropriate number of provinces for this region might well be four or even five, with — for example — a separate Cape Breton and a new province for the Acadian population of New Brunswick.

The idea that the three provinces should be, or could be, one province has been around for a long time. Indeed, at several times in its history, the region has been united into one political unit. At one time, the entire region (albeit with poorly defined borders) was the single colony of Nova Scotia. New Brunswick and Prince Edward Island were severed from Nova Scotia in the late eighteenth century. Prior to the British occupation of the region, the colony was known as Acadie and was under French rule. And prior to that, it was — and still is — the home of several First Nations: the Mi'kmaq, the Maliseet or more properly the Wolastoqiyik, and the Passamaquoddy or Peskotomuhkati. These nations were culturally and linguistically related but were not identical. Yet they were allied under a compact known as the Wabanaki Confederacy, an alliance which dates back at least to 1680. The British recognized and signed treaties with the Confederacy, particularly the Treaty of Boston (1725) and Mascarene's Treaty (1726). These treaties are still Canadian law[28] and have been referenced in various court decisions.[29] The treaties provided a division of powers and responsibilities that would be quite familiar to students of Canadian federalism. Writing in the wake of *R v Marshall*,[30] James [Sákéj] Youngblood Henderson explained:

The eighteenth-century Mikmaw treaties with the British sovereign arose under the parties' respective jurisdictions surrounding foreign affairs. The treaties illustrate the mutually embracing authority of both British and Mikmaw sovereignty and the ability of both nations to establish a new legal order that both affirmed the existing Mikmaw order and generated new legal rights and obligations. The treaties apportioned ultimate decision-making authority concerning fundamental law between the two parties. They delegated some subject matters to the British sovereign, while reserving other inherent Aboriginal rights and tenure to the Mikmaw as vested treaty rights. Thus, the treaties created a new division of jurisdictional authority between the two nations.[31]

But there is still much we do not know about the Wabanaki Confederacy, and it is but one story of many regarding the first peoples that deserves more attention than I am able to provide here.[32] John Ralston Saul has told us that we owe a considerable intellectual debt to the First Nations: their social and political structures had a profound influence on the development of Canada's current political system. He is not writing specifically about the Maritimes, but what he writes applies well to this region: "The francophones and anglophones who came here found a complex web of First Nations and learned to live as part of that web of dozens and dozens of different nations and cultures."[33] Yet, writes Saul, we have largely forgotten the debt we owe to the First Peoples. This is quite true in the Maritimes as well.

Nor can I do justice to the rich history of *Acadie* and its people, a people who once again share a common culture and geography, but yet also present a complex identity and diverse origins. France was their country of origin, but some were Basque, some Breton, and some from Normandy. Although the Acadian story still has much to be completed, we now have a robust literature on Acadia before and after the British conquest in 1710. What we have learned about Acadie and its material culture has revised our understanding of the sophistication of those communities.[34] While I wish we knew more about the internal governance of Acadian communities and their system of selecting delegates to deal with the British governors, that body of knowledge is growing as well.[35]

The constitutional history of the Maritime provinces as British colonies begins in the early eighteenth century. Prince Edward Island and New Brunswick were split off from Nova Scotia; Cape Breton annexed to Nova Scotia, then split off, then re-annexed.[36] This constitutional history is also important and is referenced several times throughout this book. Unlike Acadian and First Nations history, we have a considerable amount of knowledge and archival material covering the Planters and Loyalists and basically the British colonial presence in the Maritimes. But decisions had to be made about where to start and what to include in this text. The references supplied here are a good place to start for those interested in eighteenth century Maritime provinces constitutional history.[37]

I have chosen to begin my story in the late eighteenth century, a time of considerable change in North America and its division into the United States of America and British North America — what would eventually become Canada. I see some interesting parallels between what was happening in the Thirteen Colonies and what was happening in what was then the colony of Nova Scotia. Michael Lienesch's study of the ideological origins of the American constitution argues that both the Federalists and Anti-federalists were "founders" but just "different kinds, holding fundamentally different definitions of founding." The Federalists had an audacious agenda — a new, radical, republican constitution — and they believed that the time to act and create such a republic was fleeting. Failure to act and act now would doom the new nation to ruins. The Anti-federalists opposed the idea but were as much concerned about the imprudence of the Federalist agenda as they were of its ultimate goals. The Anti-federalists were not against change; as Patrick Henry said of his fellow Anti-federalists, "Every man says that something must be done." It was just that the Anti-federalists cautioned prudence in counter to the Federalists' "audacity." "At heart," writes Lienesch, "Antifederalists were conservative reformers."[38]

I would argue that this also describes many of those who have engaged in Canada's Confederation debate and also the Maritime Union debate, then and subsequently. In fact, the events leading up to Confederation such as the campaign for Responsible Government established a culture of pragmatism and caution that has influenced Maritime Union discussions ever since: perhaps a Maritime expression of Horowitz's Tory streak.[39]

Attempts to unify the Maritimes invariably end up asking the same questions, articulating the same complicated and often contradictory arguments for and against, and inevitably seeing the initiative dissolve like sandcastles in the wake of the tide. "We are a region," pro-union advocates claim, "therefore the Maritimes should unite." "But are we really?" ask the sceptics. "And what is a region, anyway?" To borrow a phrase from Kenneth McRae (describing Quebec sovereignty movements), Maritime Union has been a movement of "genuine indeterminacy."[40] However, this was and still is a product of a Maritime preference for prudence and moderation in all things. Like Maritime Union, the problems that Confederation were meant to solve were many and Confederation offered an opportunity to address these. But it was never precisely clear how Confederation would solve these problems, nor was it certain that Confederation would not simply replace one set of problems with a new set. This, to put it bluntly, is the overarching concern of Maritime Union: would it solve problems or create new ones? Would the gains outweigh the losses?

PART ONE

Leadership, Adaptability, and Maritime Union

A Vision of Union

*So many petty states as now exist in the Colonies, having the power of legis-
lation ill defined & as badly executed, govern'd by persons whose small sal-
aries and emoluments are inadequate to support the dignity of the Kings
[sic] representatives or to uphold the authority of the Mother country . . .
diminishes [sic] the authority of the British Government & place those who
should support it in a state of dependence.*
Richard Uniacke, Attorney General of Nova Scotia, 1806[1]

Over the years, there have been a number of attempts to unite or
reunite the Maritime provinces. However, not a single initiative
came about as the result of a popular movement, not in the nineteenth century, not in the twentieth century, and certainly none
exist today. Confederation in 1867 generated popular opposition to
the new federal union in both Nova Scotia and New Brunswick and
several attempts, including a "repeal election" were made to reverse
the decision to join with the Province of Canada. But there was no
popular movement for union, either Maritime or of British North
America. The Maritime Rights movement in the 1920s, discussed
below, had some characteristics of a popular movement, but it is not
clear whether it was a pan-Maritime movement or was a collection
of isolated factions.

Instead, most Maritime Union initiatives were the project of a specific person: a leader in the region who had a vision. That vision was usually fuelled by a frustration that the region, blessed with so much, continued to struggle, a struggle which was invariably economic. None of the Maritime Union initiatives argued that the Maritimes should unite to preserve a pan-Maritime culture or identity or to further a nationalistic cause. Often, identity was used as a justification or as an argument as to why union could succeed, but preserving and promoting identity was never the goal.[2] In this way, Maritime Union initiatives have been very different than Quebec sovereignty movements. Because the Maritime Union initiatives focused primarily on the economic benefits or necessities of union, they have tended to be regarded as strictly pragmatic exercises. There is certainly a pragmatic current involved in all of them, but there is more than pragmatism in play.

One such visionary leader was Richard Uniacke (1753–1830), who among other things was the attorney general and also Speaker of the Nova Scotia Legislative Assembly.[3] He is responsible for the first compilation of Nova Scotia statutes, commonly known as "Uniacke's Law," which can still be found in law libraries.[4] Uniacke believed that the Maritimes should be united, or reunited as he would have it. After all, the region was at one time the single British colony of Nova Scotia and prior to that it was the French colony, *Acadie*. Uniacke, who also spoke Mi'kmaw and French, would no doubt have also known that the region's First Nations, ethnically and culturally akin but unique nevertheless, formed alliances and cooperative governing structures such as the 1680 Wabanaki Confederacy[5] (the boundaries of which, of course, bear little relationship to today's provincial boundaries).[6]

With the Treaty of Utrecht (1713) and later the Treaty of Paris (1763), all of what we now know as the Maritime provinces came under British colonial rule. Cape Breton had not been included in the Treaty of Utrecht, but was covered by the Treaty of Paris and thereby annexed to Nova Scotia that same year (1763).[7] Two years later, Cape Breton was separated from the mainland province and became its own colony.[8] In 1769, St John's Island or Isle Saint-Jean — today's Prince Edward Island — was also separated from Nova Scotia, followed by New Brunswick in 1784. Uniacke thought this dissection of the colony was a mistake. The result was too many "petty states" that spread the available leadership talent too thin and created unnecessary and inefficient competition.

Over the years, Uniacke underwent a remarkable change in views on just what the Maritimes' position in North America and in the British Empire should be. He began by wanting Nova Scotia to be the "fourteenth colony" in the American rebellion against the British, so in 1776 at the age of twenty-three years he joined forces with Colonel Jonathan Eddy in a misguided attempt to seize Fort Cumberland on the Chignecto Peninsula that connects Nova Scotia with New Brunswick. Apparently Uniacke and the others were under the mistaken assumption that once the fort fell, Washington's Continental Army would come to their aid and finish the job of securing Nova Scotia's independence.[9] The fort did not fall, and regardless Washington showed no interest in enlisting Nova Scotia in the revolutionary cause.

Meanwhile, Uniacke was quickly disillusioned by the ineptitude of the disingenuous rebels under Colonel Eddy, a crew Cutherbertson describes as "a motley force of fewer than a hundred men, who were more interested in plunder than in bringing liberty to Nova Scotians."[10] Nevertheless, Uniacke was marched back to Halifax in chains and charged with treason. However, his wealthy Irish family connections saved him, and he received a pardon without even a trial (agreeing to give King's evidence didn't hurt).[11] After a brief sojourn back in his native Ireland, Uniacke returned to Nova Scotia where he was elected to the Legislative Assembly. He then rose through the ranks as solicitor general, then attorney general and Speaker.[12]

Some may call Uniacke an opportunist and there is no question that he recognized opportunity and seized it when he could. He may also be seen as a pragmatist rather than an ideologist.[13] But Uniacke's adaptation to changing circumstances also demonstrates prudence and an understanding of the need to moderate one's views, a philosophy of which he was well aware.[14] Moderation is pragmatic, but it is not just pragmatism. Moderation, the essence of Montesquieu's political philosophy,[15] is a principle that can be traced back to the origins of the Maritimes as a British colony and before, when neutrality was the preferred response both by Acadians, the "Neutral French," and then by the "Neutral Yankees," the Planters who replaced the expelled Acadians in Nova Scotia, arriving in the years just prior to the American Revolution.

In 1806, Uniacke presented a memorandum to the Rt Hon William Windham, Secretary of State for War and the Colonies in the Lord Grenville government. Upper and Lower Canada[16] were still separate colonies in 1806: Lord Durham's *Report on the Affairs of British North America* (1838) and the subsequent *Act of Union* of 1840[17] were still some years away. Uniacke proposed that the two Canadas unite and that New Brunswick, Prince Edward Island, Cape Breton, and Nova Scotia unite as well, or as he wrote, these other Maritime colonies "should be *reunited* with N. Scotia." British North America would then comprise just two provinces. These two unions were essential to protect the "British colonies" from the draw of the United States: "British capital and talents are every day transferred to the pestilential & factious cities of America to which they are tempted by the advantages which the deranged state of European commerce has afforded."[18]

Uniacke's proposal went nowhere but this did not stop him from trying again some years later. However, by 1826 and with the War of 1812 still a fresh memory, Uniacke had abandoned the idea of the two unions and instead campaigned for a full federal union ("a Confederation") of all British North America.[19] He was now seventy-three years old. In this memorandum,[20] Uniacke now recommended that Nova Scotia reabsorb Cape Breton and Prince Edward Island but leave New Brunswick intact. Upper and Lower Canada would also remain apart. This would mean that there would be four provinces (Newfoundland was not included) but still united in a federation. A new constitution would be created, containing provisions to accept or create provinces in the rest of the land as required, but protections for "Indians" in the territories would also be included. The federation would be a free-trade zone. A dispute resolving mechanism would be set up to handle federal-provincial conflicts. All of this, plus much more, was necessary to resist American expansionism and to firmly entrench the British presence in North America.

In some ways — politically at least — Uniacke was an exemplar for the leaders who followed him in the Maritimes; leaders who, thankfully, did not foment rebellion but who nevertheless brought forward radical ideas that they then had to adapt to changing circumstances. These changing circumstances were often forces having an impact on the Maritimes from outside the region as well as changes in the internal dynamics within the region as provinces sought to protect their own identities and interests. We see this again and again over the years as Maritime leaders continue to struggle with finding a solution to a problem, but striving to do so without making the situation worse.

For example, in the mid-nineteenth century (and like the rest of British North America), there were movements in the Maritimes advocating for Responsible Government, primarily in Nova Scotia and to a lesser extent in Prince Edward Island (although barely at all in New Brunswick). The fight for Responsible Government also provides a useful template for understanding Maritime political behaviour, particularly the tendency in the Maritimes for leaders to adopt a pragmatic agenda. Responsible Government, a constitutional pillar in Canada, refers to the principle that the executive can only govern if it enjoys the support (known as the "confidence convention") of a majority of the elected branch, that is, the Legislative Assembly. Nova Scotia was granted Responsible Government in 1848; Prince Edward Island in 1851; and New Brunswick in 1854.[21] Many of the leaders of the movements became key figures in the Confederation debates that would follow a decade or so later. George Coles in Prince Edward Island and Joseph Howe in Nova Scotia were not enthusiastic supporters of Confederation, although they would eventually come around. But one reason (among many and discussed below) for their reluctance was their concern that the democratic gains they achieved with Responsible Government would be undermined or at least tempered by joining a larger union whereby their own provincial representatives would have considerably less influence over the executive branch of government. Responsible government may not have been a popular movement manifested by street demonstrations — not in the Maritimes, anyway — but neither was it a project imposed by colonial masters. It was reform effected within the political system, not through protests or rebellion.[22]

Leaders like Coles and Howe have often puzzled scholars who have wondered why such powerful figures would oppose something as obviously beneficial as Confederation. As a result, such people have been labeled "pragmatists" when the biographer is being kind; "opportunists" when they are being critical (opportunism is simply pragmatism but toward a goal with which one does not agree).[23] This assumes that pragmatism is something to be either justified or dismissed: leaders must be visionary if they are to be accepted in the pantheon of Canadian history. But idealism refers to the vision of the goal; pragmatism to how the goal is to be achieved. And in politics, that involves coordinating a number of moving parts, most of which are moving in different directions.

Frank McKinnon's classic study of the government of Prince Edward Island was not speaking of Maritime Union when he described the "inconsistency" of party politics on the Island, but his words apply well to the various Maritime Union movements:

> [P]arties change from generation to generation to adjust themselves to trends in an ever varying public opinion; the events and circumstances with which they deal do not remain stationary; and their whole nature must change with the personnel of which they are composed.[24]

In the chapters that follow here in Part One, I will attempt to show that the practicality and logistics of Maritime Union invariably undermined the philosophy and idealism of the concept. Time and time again, Maritime Union or some variation is looked upon as a solution — some would say a panacea — to the problems that have plagued and continue to plague the region. But time and time again, the difficulties of finding the balance between mutual benefit and loss of identity and autonomy thwarted efforts. The problem is not that the logistics were difficult: difficulties can be overcome. The problem is that when these logistics are discussed, the questions of identity and autonomy loom large.

CHAPTER TWO

Confederation and the Great Compromise

Our best policy would be to keep out until Canada, in her eagerness to include us in the union, should offer to treat with us on fairer terms; and then, should we find that we were suffering by keeping out, self-interest might induce us to accept the best terms we could get.

Frederick Brecken, Prince Edward Island (1866)[1]

The Charlottetown Conference took place in the first week of September in 1864. Ostensibly, the conference was held to discuss the union of Nova Scotia, New Brunswick and Prince Edward Island. Each province agreed to send delegates and Prince Edward Island agreed to host. Enthusiasm for the Maritime Union project was somewhat disjointed and not everyone agreed what the project even was. Some — perhaps most — of the delegates were quite pessimistic whether an agreement could be reached at all. The delegates representing Prince Edward Island were the least enthusiastic expressing what Father Francis Bolger has described as a "policy of exclusiveness."[2] Indeed, Fredericton or Saint John were the original choices for the meeting, but Charlottetown was picked instead so Island delegates would have no excuse not to attend. Even that was not a sure thing as the coincidence of a travelling circus in town (Slaymaker & Nichols' Olympic Circus), set up just three blocks away, attracted considerable attention. When the delegates from the Province of Canada arrived on the second day of the conference, many of the Prince Edward Island delegation opted to attend the circus rather than meet their colleagues as they made their way ashore.[3]

Scholars have long argued about why the Maritime delegates were so easily distracted from Maritime Union in 1864. The most common explanation claims the arrival of the Canadian delegates overwhelmed the discussions concerning Maritime Union and imposed their own agenda through beguiling rhetoric, deception, and bribery.[4] If so, the Maritimers did not put up much of a fight and were quick to adopt the new agenda. In fact, writes historian P.B. Waite, "It is clear that it was only by Canadian initiative — interference perhaps — that the Charlottetown Conference was held at all."[5] In other words, at least according to Waite, this was a Canadian project from the get-go.[6] As D.C. Harvey wrote in 1933, "Thus, it is seen that the subject of Maritime union was never seriously discussed in the one conference that had been called to consider it."[7] This may well be, but the fact that the Canadian delegates proved persuasive — at least to New Brunswick and Nova Scotia — does not mean that everyone was in lockstep. Desmond Morton may have put it best when he wrote that "it was not conservatism but a sense of dangerous, uncontrollable choices that hung over the Confederation debate in the Maritimes."[8]

There were as many different perspectives on Maritime Union and on Confederation as there were Maritime delegates. Some wanted the Maritimes to unite but not join in federation with the Province of Canada; some argued for a united Maritimes but within Confederation; and some wanted the Maritime provinces to remain separate yet also within Confederation. Some, particularly those from Prince Edward Island, wanted to wait and see how the new arrangement worked first. But the Islanders did not close the door on the idea of either Maritime Union or Confederation.

Two positions articulated by Maritime delegates regarding Confederation are quite germane to our discussion of why Maritime

Union movements have invariably failed. The first was the argument that the Maritime provinces should first unite and then join Confederation as a single province. The second was that the Maritimes should join Confederation but remain separate provinces. Each of these arguments raises a crucial point which will return again and again: the power of a united province in the federation versus the desire to preserve provincial identity. But before we can discuss these two arguments, we should review why Nova Scotia and New Brunswick agreed to join Confederation in the first place, with Prince Edward Island eventually coming on board six years later in 1873. This is but a brief survey of yet another complicated issue.[9]

First, there were a number of economic factors that convinced most Maritime leaders that some sort of arrangement had to be found to mitigate the end of Reciprocity with the United States and the growing economic power of the Province of Canada, the latter now threatening to out-compete Maritime businesses. It was also becoming clear that the Maritime economy was itself in need of a refit as traditional industries such as shipbuilding were not keeping pace with modernization.[10] Maritime shipyards dominated world shipbuilding then;[11] however, industry was still dependent on "wood, wind and sail"[12] and the region had not embraced the new technologies of "iron, coal and rail."[13] Confederation offered an opportunity to ensure that Maritime prosperity continued by providing new infrastructure, such as the Intercolonial Railway, which would in turn spur on modernization.[14]

Those who supported Confederation were optimistic the Maritimes could compete successfully with their Canadian rivals. While it was true that Toronto and Montreal were bigger than Halifax and Saint John, they were not that much bigger: no more than "half as large," according to one estimate.[15] Both Halifax and Saint John in 1864 were "capable of matching the productive capabilities of central Canadian 'metropoles.'"[16] The Province of Canada's mineral wealth, including even petroleum — despite the fact that the age of the automobile had yet to arrive — was seen as the future. But the Maritimes had mining potential as well. Coal was still a valuable resource, and an article from Nova Scotia reprinted in Edward Whelan's *The Examiner* in Charlottetown confidently (and extravagantly) predicted that Maritime coal would be in demand in Canada for "hundreds, probably for thousands of years to come."[17] While the huge mineral deposits of iron, lead, zinc, and copper in northern New Brunswick were yet to be discovered, Maritimers, quite correctly as it turned out, "believed that their colonies possessed vast, untapped mineral resources."[18] Furthermore, the Maritime economies were mature and had considerable manufacturing strength. As member of the Legislative Assembly James McDonald of Nova Scotia put it, "Give us the population of four million[19] that union will give, strike down the hostile tariffs, . . . and you will have the market for manufacturers that is now wanting. Why should not Halifax be the Boston of British North America?"[20]

Economic reasons were not the only arguments made in favour of Confederation, and possibly they were not even the most persuasive. The need for stronger and mutual defence in the wake of the Civil War in America was a powerful incentive. American expansionism was already a concern.[21] Although the traditional date for the first Fenian raids is 1866,[22] the Fenian threat was recognized much earlier. Toronto's *The Globe* reported on 20 December 1864 that the Fenians were planning on invading: "Canada to be invaded by 50,000 Fenians," read the headline.[23] But not all of the Fenians coveted Old Canada.[24] One faction, led by John O'Mahony and Bernard Killian planned instead to invade the land "north of Maine" with a goal of establishing the St. Lawrence River as the northern border of an expanded United States.[25] Such a border would have excluded what is now Ontario but would have included southern Quebec sweeping east through the Eastern Townships and the Gaspé Peninsula. More to the point, it would have encompassed all of the Maritimes.[26] Meanwhile, British policy of defending its North American colonies consisted primarily of rhetoric and pressure for the colonies to unite for their own protection.[27]

Ambition was another reason for embracing Confederation. Many Maritime leaders were frustrated — or claimed they were — by the small-minded nature of their own provinces and the deep-seated divisions over language and religion that just seemed to be rehashed over and over. As F.R. Scott wrote, "the pettiness of the politics and of public life in the individual provinces, the inefficiency of their local economies, the scant opportunity they offered to men of ability and ambition, were constant themes in the addresses on Confederation."[28] A larger union would help end this factionalism and give greater scope to ambition.

Lest this be seen as mere ambition, it is also true that some leaders were quite taken with the nation-building opportunity that Confederation offered. Phillip Buckner provides solid evidence of the "dominion from sea to sea" vision of leaders like Nova Scotia's Charles Tupper, New Brunswick's Samuel Leonard Tilley, and Prince Edward Island's Colonel John Gray. At the Quebec Conference that followed the Charlottetown Conference in 1864, Gray said that it "has been the dream of my life to be one day a citizen of a great nation extending from the Great West to the Atlantic seaboard."[29]

Much of the positioning either for or against Maritime Union at this time ended up entangled with the Confederation debate as proponents and detractors saw Maritime Union as either a step toward Confederation or a detour away from it.[30] As stated above, among those in favour of Confederation some preferred a united Maritime province within Confederation and some preferred that the provinces join but retain their autonomy.

Some argued for the first and then changed their minds. Nova Scotia's James Johnston[31] was such a person. Although Johnston was not a delegate in Charlottetown or in Quebec, he was an influential figure in Nova Scotia and premier prior to Charles Tupper. On 28 March 1864 in the Nova Scotia House of Assembly, Johnston argued that the "union of the lower provinces [i.e., the Maritimes]" was "a step toward a larger one. . . . What we want is to produce a real unity — make the parts that are now separate a homogeneous whole — give them a oneness of existence and purpose."[32]

Tupper's initial argument in favour of Maritime Union was that a united province would be an equal province, or at least closer to being equal, in Confederation. A united Maritimes "would present a sufficient area, population, and resources to exercise no small amount of influence in the scale between the two sections in which Canada is divided."[33] But in the aftermath of the defeat of the Tilley government in New Brunswick in 1865 and the rejection of the Quebec Resolutions in the Prince Edward Island legislature that same year, Tupper was concerned that Nova Scotia would follow suit. So, he tried to calm things down by reproposing Maritime Union as a soft option. Beck explains:

> On the one hand, he hoped to prevent a frontal attack on Confederation; on the other hand, he felt the resolution would not be displeasing to the Canadians and also go some way towards meeting the views of the Maritime critics of Confederation that the three small colonies could not hold their own in a union with Canada.[34]

As Beck continues, "the debate on Tupper's resolution was somewhat farcical" and no one was fooled. Nevertheless, the resolution passed without division.

George Coles of Prince Edward Island was an early advocate for Confederation, but he wanted the provinces (well, Prince Edward Island anyway) to remain intact.[35] Yet he recognized that a larger union was not only advantageous but was essential to the Island's survival, and he thought Confederation was a means by which the Island could both avail itself of the benefits of British North American union without losing its uniqueness.

In 1864, Coles was leader of the Opposition and was one of the Prince Edward Island delegates to the Charlottetown Conference. A few weeks prior to the conference, Coles wrote a letter to *The Examiner*. In his letter, Coles explained that he was initially opposed to even meeting with the other Maritime provinces as he saw no advantage and much harm to Prince Edward Island were it to accept Maritime Union. However, when he realized that the conference would give him an opportunity to advocate for a broader union, "a Federal Union of all the Provinces from the Atlantic to the Pacific," he changed his mind and agreed to attend.

"[B]y accepting the appointment, my long wished-for desire may be obtained."[36]

Coles believed that with such a federation, the British North American provinces would be finally free from interference from the Colonial Office and allow for Responsible Government to at last fulfill its role. Coles thought that the Province of Canada should be divided, but not — as everyone else thought — back into Upper and Lower Canada; rather, Coles suggested that that the new federation would be better served were Canada to be divided into three, so Upper, Central, and Lower Canada. This is an interesting proposal, as one insightful concern of the Maritime delegates and particularly those from the Island was that the Old Canada, even divided into two, would dominate the new federation.

Coles also called for each province to have a bicameral legislature with both chambers elected, as had been the case in Prince Edward Island since 1862. But he did not want an upper house at the national level. Each province's lieutenant governors would also be elected under Coles' scheme, but the Governor General would be appointed. Oddly, he also recommended that all provincial legislation be first approved "by the Federal Assembly"; however, he proposed this as an improvement on what was then the practice of disallowance by "the Colonial Minister of the day."

Coles also hoped that Confederation would finally solve the "Land Question," an issue that haunted Prince Edward Island politics since its beginnings as a colony of Britain. In essence, the original plan for settling the Island involved dividing the land into lots for proprietors who were to pay quickrents, which were to be used for development. They would in turn rent out the land to farmers. But the farmers would not have title to the land, and the landowners over the years lost interest and many were absentee. Consequently, generations of farming families could still not obtain title to their property, but neither was there any funds available for development.[37] When the Land Question did not emerge in the conference debates, Coles became disillusioned with the project, and subsequently campaigned against Confederation.

Support or opposition to Confederation on Prince Edward Island crossed party lines and divided families. When the Island delegates returned from the Quebec Conference, any pretext of unity was abandoned. Gray and Pope resigned from the Executive Council; Pope's brother, J.C., became premier. The motion to agree to the terms of Confederation set out in Quebec City was made by W.H. Pope; the motion to amend and so reject it by his brother. In New Brunswick and Nova Scotia, similar divisions occurred and while supporters of Confederation eventually won the day in those provinces, it was not without encouragement and coercion from the Colonial Office.[38] Popular opinion in all three provinces was mostly against and in both Nova Scotia and New Brunswick, the anti-confederate forces won convincing electoral victories in 1865 and 1867. In New Brunswick, in 1865 "every delegate to Quebec who was a member of the house lost his seat."[39] In Nova Scotia, the first post-Confederation provincial election was held 18 September 1867. William Annand's Anti-Confederation Party won thirty-six seats. Hiram Blanchard's Confederation Party won two. In the first federal election, anti-confederates won eighteen of Nova Scotia's nineteen seats.

CHAPTER THREE

Maritime Rights and Buyers' Remorse

I know that if official action was taken now in the direction of Maritime Union we could get no aid from the Governments of New Brunswick and Prince Edward Island. The island Government is Tory, the New Brunswick Government is timid. If we make application to the Tory Government of England for release of Nova Scotia we shall as the case now stands almost certainly receive a flat refusal.

Premier of Nova Scotia William Fielding (1886)[1]

Nova Scotia's 1886 Repeal Election

There was quite a bit of "buyer's remorse" in all three Maritime Provinces in the years immediately following Confederation. Some even spoke of requesting annexation by the United States.[2] Others, such as Joseph Howe, were initially opposed but came to see Confederation as the lesser of several evils. While serving as a federal Member of Parliament (Hants), Howe led a delegation in 1868 to London asking for a repeal of the *British North America Act, 1867* (BNA 1867). But he was summarily rebuffed. Howe, who would soon become a Cabinet minister (President of the Queen's Privy Council for Canada, 19 January 1869), was apparently disillusioned both by the indifference of the British government to

Nova Scotia's concerns, and by the "unpatriotic" reaction to Confederation by those in Nova Scotia arguing for annexation. Some historians believe that these two concerns convinced him that working within the Macdonald government would better Nova Scotia's chances for improvements.

Yet the Maritimes were not the only provinces raising concerns about Confederation. All the provincial governments, including and especially Ontario and Quebec, began to chafe under the authority of the new federal government, particularly as they realized that their revenue sources were now quite limited and they no longer had "the fiscal capacity to match their constitutional responsibilities."[3] In an attempt to deal with what the provinces saw as inequities, Quebec's premier Honoré Mercier invited Prime Minister John A. Macdonald to meet with the premiers at a conference to be held in Quebec City in 1887. Macdonald refused to attend. However, including Mercier, five of the country's seven premiers did attend. The others were the premiers of Manitoba, Ontario, New Brunswick, and Nova Scotia. But Prince Edward Island and British Columbia both declined the offer.

In Pope's *Correspondence of Sir John Macdonald*, he writes that Mercier's purpose was to gather the Liberal[4] premiers of the country "with an eye to embarrass the Dominion Government, which they had signally failed to defeat at the polls, and now sought to entangle in controversy, thus presenting the spectacle of the larger provinces arrayed in hostility to the Central Government as the common enemy of all." But, Pope continues, Macdonald did not fall for the trap and questioned the very constitutionality of the event. "He therefore declined to take part in this conference or to recognize it, on behalf of the Dominion Government, in any form."[5]

This may well have been true, in part anyway: the provincial opposition did have a flavour of Old Canada politics. Oliver Mowat was the Liberal premier of Ontario and Mercier the Liberal premier of Quebec. This was the Grits and Rouges once again ganging up on the Macdonald's Tories and Bleus.[6] Indeed, the first few such conferences made it obvious that these events were to be an Ontario-Quebec alliance against the federal government: it was "agreed" that Ontario and Quebec would always be the hosts. The other provinces were there as the supporting cast.

But one premier — William Fielding of Nova Scotia — had other ideas. Fielding, who was premier of Nova Scotia from 1884 to 1896, thought that the costs of Confederation outweighed the benefits to the Maritimes. Anti-confederation movements in the Maritimes were, once again, on the rise and in 1886 Fielding's Liberals won twenty-nine of the province's thirty-eight seats on a platform that called for a repeal of Nova Scotia's agreement to join Confederation. In fact, the 1886 election is known as the "repeal election."[7] The issue, which crossed party lines, was (once again) the terms of union and whether Confederation had been a mistake.[8] The "repealers" argued that Nova Scotia and the Maritimes in general had lost their ability to trade with their "natural markets" in the south. The new National Policy did not open up new markets in Ontario and Quebec; instead, it "turned the Maritimes into a 'slaughter market' for Central Canadian suppliers."[9] This was a secessionist movement that "developed logically out of a regional ideology that attempted both to explain and to remedy the area's declining economic fortunes."

This regional ideology, although never a coherent body of thought, was an amalgam of the following elements: a belief in a pre-Confederation Golden Age; a conviction that Confederation itself was responsible for the region's decline; a feeling that the financial terms of Confederation needed revision; a belief that prevailing national policies were detrimental to the region; a feeling that closer commercial ties with the United States were desirable; and a conviction that the Maritimes could prosper as independent states if left to their own devices. In coming to terms with political secessionism, therefore, it is important to keep in mind its relationship both to economic decline and fiscal disability, and to this broader and more comprehensive ideology.[10]

Initially, Fielding was not inclined to attend the 1887 conference and told Mowat that while his Nova Scotia election win was "of course a victory for the Liberal Party," it was in fact "much more." "The repeal issue goes beyond the question of better terms," Fielding wrote. "On the repeal issue we can expect no aid or cooperation from your Province [Ontario]."[11] In the end, Fielding was persuaded to attend but found his efforts in vain. With Macdonald refusing to attend the 1887 conference, and with Mercier and Mowat dominating the agenda, Fielding was unable to make a credible case for Nova Scotia's grievances.

But Fielding's real problem was that he could not convince his fellow Maritime premiers to join with him. It also didn't help that, despite Fielding's convincing anti-confederate win in 1886, Macdonald's Conservatives won fourteen[12] of Nova Scotia's twenty-one seats in the federal election, which immediately followed in 1887. Macdonald had brought Sir Charles Tupper back from his post as High Commissioner in London to lead the Conservative and pro-Confederation forces and Tupper's political skills once again carried the day. Nevertheless, Fielding understood that a united Maritime voice was necessary if the Maritimes were to counter the prevailing forces of Old Canada and the rising influence of the newly settled West. But it was not to be, and instead Fielding and for that matter the other Maritime premiers changed tack and now focused on provincial rights within the federation.

Maritime Rights Movement

While the provincial rights movement encompassed all provinces in various degrees at one time or another, the movement manifested itself in the Maritime provinces in its own unique way. This was the Maritime Rights Movement (1919–1927),[13] rumblings of which could be heard at the turn of the twentieth century when national economic policies were accused of pulling capital and industries out of the Maritimes and into southern Ontario and parts West.[14] With the Maritime Rights Movement came renewed interest in Maritime Union.

Some scholars have argued that the emergence of the Maritime Rights Movement was a defining period in Maritime history as it marked the emergence of a coherent Maritime identity. The movement and the emergence of a Maritime identity went hand-in-hand, but according to this argument the Maritime Rights Movement was only possible because there *was* a pan-Maritime identity. It is certainly true that in the first few decades of the twentieth century, there were several calls for Maritime Union: one analyst, writing in 1906, claimed that "[i]n recent years the question of the union of the Maritime Provinces has been so frequently mentioned that it looks as if it had come to stay until dealt with in some decisive manner by the electorate."[15] In 1919, the *Atlantic Leader* published an editorial calling for Maritime Union. The Halifax *Evening Mail* printed excerpts, calling the editorial one of the most remarkable and "fearless" articles ever published on the subject. In the article, the *Atlantic Leader* writer made the claim that the Maritimes had a common identity and that full political union was the only way to harness this identity for the common welfare:

> For we are the East. We have those functions of the East to justify and execute. And, people, Eastern Canada does not begin with Amherst and end with Louisbourg. Eastern Canada, insofar as our functions are laid down, is MARITIME CANADA. The Canadian Atlantic country is our territory. And always remember that Maritime Canada is bounded on the north by Bay Chaleur and Quebec, on the south and east and west by Maine and the waters of the Atlantic Ocean. Maritime Canada is NEW BRUNSWICK, NOVA SCOTIA and PRINCE EDWARD ISLAND — and the functions of any part of that whole are merely functions within functions.[16]

Even those who did not call for full union recognized the need for the Maritimes to band together, primarily to offset the growing political and economic power of the West.[17]

But we need to take a step back to understand the complexities of the Maritime Rights Movement. The crucial issue was whether it was in fact a coherent movement, or was nothing more than a blanket term for several disassociated pockets of protest. We can begin by looking back at the years just after Confederation and to the foundations of the Maritime provinces' economies.

In 1870, writes T.W. Acheson, the Maritimes "probably came the closest to any region to representing the classical ideal of the staple economy."[18] Timber, lumber products, fish, and the construction of the ships that transported these goods dominated the region's industrial sector. But things began to change and change rapidly as overseas markets dried up and new technologies made some traditional industries redundant or at least highly inefficient. Macdonald's National Policy, designed to restrict imports and realign Canada's industries so they were focused on inter-provincial rather than international trade, was at first "embraced by much of the Maritime business community" as it had the potential of opening up new and aggressive markets in central and western Canada. As Acheson reports, "This development was so significant that between 1881 and 1891 the industrial growth rate of Nova Scotia outstripped all other provinces in eastern Canada."[19] However, all was not rosy in the Maritimes. Industrial growth was unevenly distributed: some centres like Halifax were booming, others were in decline. The region lacked a comprehensive economic strategy or even strong provincial strategies, and industrialization was left in the hands of a small number of prominent families. This had the effect of entrenching conservative business practices and often hindered modernization. But it also became apparent that the National Policy, once seen as a lifeline, now imposed systemic barriers: transportation headed the list as the transcontinental railway project, designed to unite the country from sea to sea, now was focused on connecting Montreal to the West coast. As Stephen Tomblin explains, the purpose of the railway was primarily to ensure that British Columbia was securely connected with the Dominion.[20] Meanwhile, the Intercolonial Railway connecting the Maritimes to central Canada was underutilized with central Canadian industries preferring to export goods and resources through

Portland and Boston rather than Saint John and Halifax.[21] Freight rates on the line increased by as much as 216%.[22]

> The impact of the National Policy was surprisingly quick. In 1885, the region contained eight of the twenty-three Canadian cotton mills — including seven of the nineteen erected after 1879 —, three of five sugar refineries, two of seven rope factories, one of three glass works, both of the Canadian steel mills, and six of the nation's twelve rolling mills.[23]

By the time the First World War broke out in 1914, most of these were gone: closed down or relocated.[24] The region's banks suffered the same fate with Maritime banks merging and relocating to Montreal or Toronto. This not only pulled venture capital out of the region, but it undermined local investment expertise. Halifax industrialist John F. Stairs wrote to William Robertson, president of the Union Bank of Halifax (14 July 1902):

> [T]he acquisition by the larger banks of the Upper Provinces of our smaller local banks must prove disastrous to the interests of our Provincial manufacturing, industrial and trading concerns, and prejudicial to the general commercial interests of these Maritime Provinces, inasmuch as the control of the amalgamated bank must necessarily in such case be in Montreal or Toronto, and the natural result will be to withdraw the bank deposits and capital from these Maritime Provinces to be used in Quebec and Ontario, to the neglect and injury of the business men of these provinces, who should have the use of the capital owned here.[25]

Published in 1926, Alexander Paterson's *The True Story of Confederation* claimed that "time has more than justified practically every point raised in opposition to Confederation by Maritime Anti-Confederates. Confederation has been for the Maritimes one of the worst commercial disasters ever experienced by an Anglo-Saxon country."[26] Paterson, described as "a self-taught 'expert'" with "unorthodox ideas,"[27] advanced a hyperbolic claim, but many during this time would have agreed with him as a cascading number of economic problems now plagued the region. Economist Robin Neill succinctly summarizes Maritime grievances:

> In 1867 the British North America Act had denied the Maritimes the instruments it needed to conduct economic policy. Trade and commerce, elements of the power to tax, and jurisdiction over the fisheries had been transferred to the Dominion government. Expansion into the west with railroads and settlement conferred no benefits on the east coast. Ontario and Quebec benefited from the acquisition of new territories. Montreal benefited as a transcontinental railway terminal. The Maritimes had contributed to an expansion that had drained its resources and exposed it to competition from central Canadian manufacturers expanding behind a tariff wall that the Maritimes did not want.[28]

Because of these issues, as the twentieth century moved along many Maritimers now found common cause that perhaps a new deal was indeed necessary. This, according to Ernest Forbes, was significant. According to Forbes, by the 1920s a consensus emerged that the Maritimes had finally coalesced into a coherent region:

> Previously, popular loyalties had been focused upon larger imperial or national entities or upon smaller political, cultural or geographical units. The shift was dictated by a growing realization of the need for co-operation. Co-operation was essential if the three Atlantic Provinces [sic] were to counteract the eclipse of their influence which resulted from the rise of the West and the growing metropolitan dominance of Central Canada.[29]

This sense of regional identity respected none of the traditional or newer cleavages in Maritime political culture: not language, not party partisanship, not economic or social class. Forbes quotes New Brunswick premier P.J. Veniot, who in 1923 wrote to Mackenzie King "that, after looking 'carefully into the [Maritime Rights] movement,' he had found it was 'purely non-political and embraces [the] efforts of all classes[30] to obtain what is sincerely considered fair play for [the] Maritime Provinces."[31]

So what happened? Why did this movement peter out? The question, crucial to our understanding of why the Maritimes have yet to unite, boils down to this: was the Maritime Rights Movement truly a pan-Maritime movement? Or was it just the chimera that Murray Beck refers to when speaking of Maritime identity? In his contribution to *Eastern & Western Perspectives*, Beck challenged Forbes's view that the movement was in fact a regional response.

> By demonstrating Prince Edward Island's minuscule part in the Maritime Rights movement and the *de facto* existence of two largely independent movements in Nova Scotia and New Brunswick, [Forbes's] book adds corroboratory evidence that the provinces do not meet the rigorous conditions for a region as defined in my article. That the Maritimes did not even fully appreciate their disadvantaged position until after World War I, that it took, in addition, their failure to recover from the post-war recession to produce a movement that was anything but "grass roots" in character, and that the old-line parties could easily turn it into channels that constituted no danger to their existence, all support the view I have taken of the provinces' political cultures.[32]

Whatever the reason, the apparent regional solidarity did not last. The reasons could be that the movement never really existed, not as a coherent force. Still, the federal role in undermining the movement cannot be ignored.

In 1926, Prime Minister Mackenzie King established *The Royal Commission on Maritime Claims* under the chairmanship of Sir Andrew Rae Duncan. The Report, a slim forty-five pages, echoed claims that the promises made to the Maritimes were unfulfilled "whereas the doubts and fears that the Maritime Provinces themselves entertained at the time of Union have been justified by events." The Commission was tasked with "finding 'practical solutions' to economic problems," and avoided looking for "palliatives for the dissatisfaction and political unrest which have been prevailing in that part of the Dominion." The Commission got much right. It zeroed in on the dilapidated condition of the region's railways, particularly in Prince Edward Island. The entire question of federal subsidies, which had been the focus of the 1897 Premiers' Conference and was still an issue more than thirty years later, was addressed and recommendations were made for increases. Other issues were dealt with tactfully, perhaps too tactfully. Recognizing that there was no consensus among the Maritime provinces with regard to tariffs and duties, the Commission recommended that the Tariff Advisory Board deal with the Maritime claims.[33]

However, the Commission did not believe that Confederation was the source of the Maritimes' problems, and while it acknowledged that the federal government had not done all it could, the real problem was the Maritimes' own failure to "adjust themselves to changing conditions," which in turn was a product of their age. The Maritimes were "old-established colonies, with a great measure of growth and settlement behind them," and therefore did not possess the nimbleness of the newer provinces to the west.

But the Duncan Commission did not recommend Maritime Union as a solution. Focusing specifically on the argument that economies of scale would be realized with a union, the Commission stated that "we are not seriously impressed with the argument that any financial saving which would arise could materially affect the present condition of their finances, even if Maritime Union would produce the other advantages which it is alleged would result."[34]

In the end, the Report did not do much except, as Forbes writes, give the King government an opportunity to turn the recommendations "into a program for political pacification."[35] "Each region," writes Anthony Careless, "had to agree to the prime minister's cash solution of specific claims of other regions before he would accept the settlement of their own."[36] This pacification, according to Forbes, deflated the Maritime Rights Movement.

Did the strategies of the Mackenzie King government indeed defeat the movement? Perhaps. Yet as several commentators have pointed out, it seems unlikely that even a prime minister of Canada could defeat such a movement unless it lacked a strong base and rationale in the first place. In other words, Forbes's thesis might need to be turned upside down. He claims the movement would not have succeeded unless the Maritimes were a region; the corollary is that the movement failed because the Maritimes were not. And so once again, we have the enigma which is the Maritimes: sometimes a coherent region, sometimes not. Somewhere between the Forbes' thesis and Beck's lies the true picture of the Maritimes.

One positive result of the Maritime Rights Movement was an increase in formal cooperative measures, such as the creation of the Maritime Transportation Commission in 1925. The commission's mandate was to lobby for changes to, and relief from, the freight rate differential between the Maritimes and the other provinces. A Maritime trade commission office was set up in Toronto in 1928. The Timber Commission of Eastern Canada — now the Maritime Lumber Bureau — was established in 1934.

Of course, the Great Depression in the 1930s had a profound impact on the Maritimes, although, somewhat ironically, this impact was not equally felt. Prince Edward Island, for example, already in an economically depressed state and lacking an industrial base, did not suffer a traumatic drop in living standards or at least not as traumatic as what happened elsewhere.[37] Nevertheless, the reliance on a staples economy and the lack of infrastructure and resources necessary to alleviate the worst effects of the Depression, the Maritimes once again realized that Confederation was not going to be the safety net many had thought. As Forbes writes:

> Canada's initial ventures in social welfare discriminated against poorer provinces by making their participation conditional upon their ability to match federal contributions. In those provinces unable to do so, the system often translated into harsher treatment for those requiring aid.[38]

The result was yet another call for constitutional reform, not just from the Maritimes but from politicians across the country.[39] For that matter, the Dominions around the world — albeit for very different reasons — called on the British Parliament to renounce its legal hold over their constitutions. Britain was happy to oblige, having enough to do at home, and so the *Statute of Westminster* was passed 11 December 1931.[40] Famously, Canada's inability to find federal-provincial agreement on an amending formula meant that the statute had to include an exception so that the Parliament of the United Kingdom could nevertheless amend the several British North America acts if so requested by Canada.[41]

1935 Dominion-Provincial Conference

A New Brunswick premier, after winning an election with the largest landslide in that province's history is the lone holdout to a proposal, led by the province of Quebec, for a package of constitutional amendments supported by the federal government and all the other provinces, one that proponents hoped would solve Canada's constitutional malaise once and for all. No, this was not Frank McKenna and the Meech Lake Accord in 1987, but Allison Dysart and the 1935 Dominion-Provincial Conference.

In 1935, Mackenzie King returned as prime minister of Canada. By now, the Great Depression was in full force. While there was a slight recovery in 1934, 1935 saw setbacks which contributed to the defeat of the Bennett Conservative government. R.B. Bennett, a descendant of New Brunswick Loyalists, had defeated Mackenzie King in the 1930 election winning 135 seats to King's eighty-nine. But Bennett's "dictatorial" style alienated voters,[42] nor was he particularly popular among the premiers. At the 1934 Dominion-Provincial conference, Bennett managed to offend both the Maritime premiers and the Western premiers, telling each caucus that their individual provincial status was costly and inefficient. The "cost of government in the west was too high," and three separate governments in the Maritimes for "so small a population was anomalous."[43] Furthermore, Bennett had made an unqualified promise to end the Depression.[44] That did not happen; Bennett's aggressive tariff policies were no match for the impact of the collapsing world economy. In 1935, voters made Bennett's Conservatives the scapegoat for their economic misery reducing the party to just thirty-nine seats. At the time this was the worst showing in the party's history.[45]

With the return of Mackenzie King and his Liberals came a new zeal to seize control over the Canadian constitution and so a Dominion-Provincial conference was convened on 9 December 1935. There were seven items on the agenda: financial concerns occupied items two through seven and included "questions relating to financial relations between the Dominion and the provinces, and to taxation" as well as "questions relating to unemployment and relief." But the first item was "questions relating to the procedure which should be followed in amending the British North America Act."[46]

Ten Men in a Room

The headline in the *Vancouver Sun* read "Ten Premiers in a Room Reshape a Nation." The subheading was optimistic: "Fathers of Confederation look down on historic scene – picturesque figures will mould Canada's destiny." But the accompanying editorial cartoon struck a more cautious note. Titled "The Bug Bear Overcome," the cartoon showed a hungry bear carrying the name "constitutional limits" and emerging from hibernation in a den made up of a rolled document titled "B.N.A. Act." The bear, with a bandage on its neck, has been through some scrapes. Drooling, the bear now looks to the arrival of the premiers, one of whom carries a banner reading "Dominion and Provinces Conference" to which a standard is attached reading "expedition to a better constitution." However, the bear's lair is surrounded by bones, "previous attempts at national action," and the skeleton of a beast — possibly a sacred cow or beaten dead horse — bearing a sign reading "earlier expeditions." Previous attempts at national action had all been defeated by a bugbear. Who would be the bugbear stymying collective efforts this time?

Eight of the ten first minsters at the 1935 conference were Liberal: Mackenzie King, who chaired the conference, was joined by Ontario premier Mitchell Hepburn, Quebec premier Louis-Alexandre Taschereau, Nova Scotia premier Angus Macdonald, New Brunswick premier Allison Dysart, British Columbia premier T.D. Pattullo, Prince Edward Island premier W.M. Lea, and Saskatchewan premier W.J. Patterson. Manitoba premier John Bracken (Progressive) and Alberta premier William Aberhart (Social Credit) were the only non-Liberals. The largest delegation came from Ontario, with sixteen official delegates. The federal government had fifteen, but that didn't include the small army of senior civil servants who were also in attendance. The third largest delegation came from New Brunswick, with fourteen. Quebec was next with twelve.

The size of the New Brunswick delegation is surprising. Allison Dysart and his Liberals were fresh off a landslide victory, having defeated the Conservative incumbent Leonard Tilley on 27 June 1935. Tilley, the son of Father of Confederation Samuel Tilley, had succeed Charles Richards as premier of New Brunswick upon Richards's appointment to the Supreme Court of New Brunswick in 1933. Like governments across the country,[47] Tilley's Conservatives bore the brunt of the blame for the Great Depression and so Dysart's Liberals won forty-three out of forty-eight seats, with every Cabinet minister including Tilley defeated in their own ridings. Still, perhaps Dysart thought he needed all the support at the conference that he could get. After all, he would have to hold his own in the company of some formidable colleagues, many — like Bracken, Aberhart, and Hepburn — would go on to be figures of national prominence. Hold his own he did, and the "bugbear" at the 1935 conference would turn out to be, not Ontario or Quebec or even Alberta, but little New Brunswick.

Ostensibly, reforming the Constitution was to be the focus of the 1935 Conference, and most provinces agreed that changes had to be made to the BNA 1867. The financial concerns were connected to the call for constitutional reform, simply because the provinces recognized that without amending the division of powers between the provinces and the federal government, the federal government could not provide the assistance they were requesting.

As the *Globe* reported, revision was required "to make [the BNA 1867] more suitable for the modern age." At first, things looked promising. Quebec's premier Taschereau, reported the *Globe*, was now "in favour of harmonious consideration of necessary amendments" having won the agreement from the other premiers to "guarantee the traditional rights and privileges of the French-speaking Canadians in respect to language and religion."[48] However, the *Globe* reporter was overly optimistic.

Much of the 1935 conference was devoted, not surprisingly, to the need for relief from the ravages of the Depression, with several provinces calling on the federal government to provide more assistance. Concerns were raised by the policy of matching funds under which aid was provided to municipalities. Under the system then, grants were provided in the form of matching funds, so that wealthier cities and towns received far more than poorer ones. But not all provinces were asking for handouts, or not just handouts. Prince Edward Island premier Walter Lea pointed out that Confederation had radically altered the Island's traditional trading patterns:

> Previous to this we traded with the east. The Province of Nova Scotia supplied our industrial needs, while they in turn took the agricultural products of Prince Edward Island. Partly as a result of Confederation, but largely because of the evolution of business, the industries that formerly supplied our needs were moved to the central provinces and the long railway haul has prevented our sending the products of our farms to exchange for the goods we need. . . . In nearly every case we must send real money to the central provinces of Canada. One of the reasons they are so much more wealthy than we are, one of the reasons why we should be given certain things, is the $8,000,000 or $9,000,000 of unfavourable trade balance against us.[49]

New Brunswick's delegation also wanted something more than relief: specifically, it asked for help creating jobs.[50] In fact, Dysart was concerned that the availability of federal relief — the dole, as he called it — encouraged people to accept welfare rather than seek employment. This seems to be an odd argument for a Liberal to make but it was not so odd in 1935:

> People who had never stepped into the ranks of those on relief, and never dreamed of going on relief, immediately looked upon this vast sum [$20,000,000][51] as something of which they could claim a portion. This mentality developed overnight, and it is still with us. A changed psychology, a changed outlook, a changed viewpoint are absolutely necessary.[52]

Then Dysart made an odd comment: "We are all in Canada, whether we like it or not, and we have to remain here, and our problems, municipal, industrial, provincial or federal, weigh upon the taxpayers." I can only speculate what Dysart meant by "whether we like it or not." Did this mean he did not like it but was resigned to New Brunswick putting up with being a province in Canada? Of course, it might have just been a throwaway phrase, said without much thought or said in jest. Or perhaps it spoke to the premier's frustration with the current constitutional situation. Regardless, this is where New Brunswick parted ways with the other provinces. The others all wanted what we now call a "patriated" constitution; that is, one that could be amended without recourse to the British Parliament. Speaking on behalf of Ontario's Premier Hepburn, Attorney General Arthur Roebuck summarized the "almost unanimous conclusion" of the Committee on Constitutional Questions,

> that the British North America Act imperatively requires amending both in the present and undoubtedly in the future, and that that amending should be done in the Dominion of Canada rather than across the seas.[53]

The one holdout was New Brunswick. Dysart's chief advisers on constitutional affairs were his minister without portfolio, Alexander Paterson, the author of *The True Story of Confederation* (quoted above), and John B. McNair, his attorney general.[54] Paterson argued that no changes to the Constitution were necessary; Ottawa simply needed to fulfill its constitutional obligations.[55]

In the end, it was agreed that a committee[56] of "representatives of the Law Departments of the Provinces" and "Dominion constitutional experts" would be appointed to come up with an amending formula. That committee gathered 28 January 1936 and concluded their deliberations 11 February 1936. (A week before the committee met, King George V died and was succeeded on the throne by Edward VIII.) But the New Brunswick delegation feared the consequences of a "new constitution," particularly one "hastily" composed.[57] The province's concerns and its assertion of its own status as a province were spelled out by Attorney General John McNair. While a rejection of Maritime Union was not the point here, it is worth noting his reference to "legislative union" option in 1867:

> [McNair] predicted that, under the plans, New Brunswick would lose her status, enjoyed since her foundation in 1784, as a Province of Great Britain, and would become simply a territorial division of Canada; that her sovereignty would disappear, and that the Confederation established in 1867 would cease to exist.
>
> "In other words," he declared, "we would find the Province in new legislative union, a system which the original Provinces rejected in 1867 in no uncertain terms."[58]

New Brunswick would support a full study of the BNA 1867, including a review of sections 91 and 92, but the province would not agree to anything that brought about "the subordination of the provinces." Meanwhile, the federal government did agree to "substantially" increase the provincial grants, although no specific amount was specified.

That Dysart, Paterson, and McNair opposed federal encroachment on provincial rights and independence may seem to have been against their best interests and perhaps today seems counterintuitive, considering how the Maritimes in general have long been seen as manifesting a culture of dependency on federal largesse. However, such an assumption ignores the efforts of so many to find a local solution to the economic problems of New Brunswick and the region in general. Recall that this was also the time of the great cooperative movements such as the Antigonish Movement led by Father Moses Coady out of Saint Francis Xavier University, and the

Acadian cooperative movement in both northern New Brunswick and Prince Edward Island.[59]

The Rowell-Sirois Report

Following up on the 1935 conference, the King government executed an order-in-council to establish a royal commission in 1937. The first hearings were in Fredericton. New Brunswick's submission to the commission was by Paterson who argued that Confederation was a compact under which provinces gave up certain rights — that is, jurisdictional powers — in return for certain benefits. However, if these benefits were no longer forthcoming, then the provinces had the right to retrieve those rights. After all, the very preamble of the BNA 1867 made it clear that the purpose of Confederation was "to conduce to the welfare of the provinces and promote the interests of the empire." Corey Slumkoski elaborates:

> As they told the Commission, if a province "is not able to provide for its people the same privileges which are enjoyed by those in other provinces," then Dominion assistance is required to ensure "that living conditions be on par with those obtaining elsewhere." Although New Brunswick did not advocate "a redistribution of all the wealth in Canada," the province did believe that "the burden [of providing the money for fiscal need grants] should fall upon those provinces which have profited most" in Confederation.[60]

The commission's report (*Report of the Royal Commission on Dominion Provincial Relations*), commonly known as the Rowell-Sirois Report, was delivered in 1940,[61] the same year that King managed to have the BNA 1867 amended so that unemployment insurance now fell under section 91.[62] In addition to recommending just that, the report called for a radical reorganization of federal-provincial fiscal relations, including a comprehensive program of equalization payments and a national pension plan.[63] As far as the Maritimes were concerned, many of these issues had been raised before by the

Duncan (1926),[64] Jones (1934),[65] and White (1935)[66] commissions. However, if the issues were the same, the recommendations were sometimes not and while provinces like Nova Scotia were pleased with many of the Rowell-Sirois recommendations, other measures were condemned "as a trampling of provincial rights."[67] It should not have come as a surprise, but it became clear that the result of any new program involving federal assistance was further centralization of power in Ottawa.

In any case, and despite the regard with which it is held today, the Rowell-Sirois Report was not popular at the time. Harold Innis, for example, had difficulty finding much of value in the report.[68] When King attempted to gather the premiers again in 1941 to discuss the report, enough premiers expressed their overall dissatisfaction that the meeting adjourned without discussion. Of course, in 1941 the Second World War was also a preoccupation.[69]

Dysart's health would force him to resign in 1940, although not until suffering the humiliation of having the banks refuse to refinance New Brunswick's bond issues unless their officials could "assist" Dysart with his budget (which he agreed to). Dysart's attempt, perhaps quixotic, to articulate provincial rights was the last gasp of the Maritime Rights movement. Subsequent events consolidated federal power and the Maritime provinces, "literally on the edge of bankruptcy" no longer had the strength to oppose centralization.[70] As Savoie writes, referencing W.L. Morton, the next fifteen years was a period that saw the revival of national power. This included a massive restructuring and centralization (again) of the Canadian economy. Savoie explains:

> C.D. Howe, for example, favoured either private monopoly regulated by government controls or Crown corporations to create a strong manufacturing sector. Howe's decision during the Second World War to locate the bulk of wartime production in central Canada speaks to the underlying goal of the country's economic development policy. It also had serious implications for the Maritime provinces.

Furthermore:

The decision to locate all Crown corporations in Ontario and Quebec during the Second World War and the construction of the St Lawrence Seaway, which served to undercut the superb Maritime ports, strengthened the economy of central Canada, often with serious implications for the Maritime region.[71]

One example of the effects of wartime centralization was in transportation. Obviously a crucial sector for a wartime economy, Canada's transportation system was regulated by the Wartime Prices and Trade Board. However, in 1946, the federal government handed over regulation of the railways back to the Board of Transport.

The *Maritime Freight Rates Act, 1927* (MFRA) was a product of the Duncan Commission, which had concluded that freight rates for goods travelling from the Maritimes to Montreal were indeed unfair and recommended that they be reduced by 20 percent. The MFRA did that. Over the years, and particularly during the Second World War, the transportation infrastructure in Canada evolved and as more and more roads were paved, trucking competed with rail for transport markets. In 1947, the Railway Association of Canada (RAC) requested that freight rates be increased by 30 percent. This would be across the board, and so affected the Western provinces as well. The RAC cited competition from the trucking industry but also the need to deal with deferred maintenance. The Commissioners on the Board of Transport fundamentally agreed with the railways but thought an increase of just 21 percent was a reasonable compromise.

The provinces disagreed. Such an increase would be devastating to the Maritime manufacturing industry, and so an effort was made to lobby against the proposal. But it soon became apparent that the Maritime provinces lacked a coherent institution to do this. On the other hand, the Maritimes in 1948 did have three Liberal premiers and the Liberal Party of Canada was about to choose a new leader. So, the Maritime premiers came up with a scheme:

New Brunswick premier J.B. McNair would nominate [Nova Scotia's] Angus L. Macdonald for the leadership, with Prince Edward Island's Walter Jones seconding that nomination. McNair, Jones and Macdonald — who was expected to decline the nomination — would each take the stage to denounce Ottawa's indifference to the needs of the Maritimes and to call for a royal commission on transportation.[72]

Macdonald got cold feet and the Maritime cabal never did make their grand stand, and the Liberal Leadership Convention proceeded without incident, choosing Louis St-Laurent as Mackenzie King's successor. But the threat did prompt the federal government to appoint yet another commission, tasked with reviewing transportation policy in general. Justice W.F.A. Turgeon of Saskatchewan was appointed as chair. The other two commissioners were Harold Innis and Henry Angus, the latter an economist from the University of British Columbia who had served on the Rowell-Sirois Commission (which must have made for interesting conversations between the two, given Innis's disdain for the Rowell-Sirois Report). The Turgeon Commission did agree that the increase in freight rates was excessive and that the rates established by the MFRA should be maintained, but not much else requested by the provinces — not just the Maritimes — made its way into their final report, and the Commission rejected any suggestion that Confederation created a contractual right for equalization for the country's poorer regions.[73]

Nevertheless, the consequence of this experience for Maritime leaders was the recognition that the region needed a more coherent voice and the regional institutions created in the 1950s were a direct result.[74]

An Atlantic Revolution?

New Brunswick will be destined for years to come to remain the hewer of wood and the drawer of water that it has [been] for years past. But . . . this province is no longer content to remain one of the weakest links in Confederation. If need be, we will fight for our place in the economic sun.
New Brunswick Premier Hugh John Flemming (1955)[1]

In 1957, historian W.S. MacNutt thought to label the 1950s in Atlantic Canada as the "Atlantic Revolution" decade.[2] The term was an optimistic overstatement — more significant changes took place in the next decade — but regardless, MacNutt saw a profound change in attitude in Atlantic Canada with regard to "the ongoing federal-provincial struggle," manifesting in a movement away from the provinces' former strategies, which had been too long focused on "'better terms,' 'repeal,' and 'Maritime Rights.'" Now the focus was on regional cooperation and self-sufficiency.[3] While it could be argued that this spirit of cooperation and self-reliance still has yet to catch on, in the 1950s Premier Hugh John Flemming of New Brunswick was instrumental in promoting this ethos, working to facilitate Maritime (and Atlantic) cooperation and economic integration. Much was indeed accomplished during this decade, but not without frustration and setbacks.

The years following the Second World War were kind to Canada and by 1949 the country was flush with optimism.[4] Looking ahead to the new year, a *Globe and Mail* editorialist claimed there was no reason why 1949 should not continue Canada's tremendous success of 1948, a year "in which bountiful crops were harvested, trade and industry flourished, employment was high and the country went ahead."[5] Other editorialists agreed. *The Financial Post* predicted continued investment growth and a billion-dollar increase in the country's GDP.[6] Everything pointed to a very bright future for Canada. *The Globe and Mail* editor outlined Canada's potential:

> Measured statistically [1948] was indeed a banner year. The number of Canadians at work reached an all-time high. The national income . . . passed fifteen billion dollars. Total exports and import trade approached six billion. Wages were good and industry was little disturbed by strikes. The national treasury collected a huge surplus of revenue over expenditure.[7]

Immigration was booming as well: "more people came to Canada to live in 1948 than in any year since 1930."[8] Not just people, but British industries were also arriving at a steady pace. The editorialist did caution that the Canadian economy was becoming too dependent on the American dollar, and some industries like gold mining had been allowed to "languish." But the writer was confident that the country was nevertheless in good hands, pointing to the fact that the Liberals and the PCs[9] had both held national leadership conventions the year before, the first time Canada saw both major parties hold leadership conventions — still a relatively rare event — in the same year. The editorialist predicted that with refreshed leadership would come new vision and vitality.

One of those new leaders was Louis St-Laurent, the affable Secretary of State for External Affairs who replaced Mackenzie King as Liberal leader and prime minister in 1948. In the federal election campaign that followed (held 27 June 1949, which the Liberals won in a landslide), St-Laurent claimed that Canada was now an "une nation adulte."[10] What he was referring to, however, was not economic prosperity but constitutional independence. Several significant constitutional amendments had been made in the years following the end of the Second World War. In 1947, Canada passed its own *Citizenship Act* (*Canadian Citizenship Act, 1947*),[11] becoming the first Commonwealth country to do so.[12] Also in 1947, the Governor General's *Letters Patent* were revised and now, as St-Laurent explained in the House of Commons, under the "new letters patent, the Governor General is authorized to exercise, on the advice of Canadian ministers, all of His Majesty's powers and authorities in respect of Canada."[13]

Late in 1949 (10 December), the Parliament of Canada passed a revision to the *Supreme Court Act*, which completed the process by which the Supreme Court of Canada would become the final court of appeal for Canada.[14] The Judicial Committee of the Privy Council (JCPC), which until then still heard appeals on civil and constitutional matters, had ruled in 1947 that the *Statute of Westminster, 1931* provided Canada with the constitutional authority to assert its own highest court as the final court of appeal[15] (the JCPC had stopped hearing appeals in criminal cases in 1933).

St-Laurent wanted to continue what he saw as an evolution toward complete Canadian sovereignty and thought to do so by amending the *British North America Act, 1867* (BNA 1867) so that Canada could amend its Constitution without the need for the British Parliament to be involved.[16] The result, which of course did not accomplish this goal, was the *British North America Act (No. 2), 1949*.[17] This did give the Parliament of Canada the power to amend the Canadian Constitution, but only concerning matters not already under the exclusive jurisdiction of the provinces. What jurisdictions were exclusively provincial was, just as today, still a subject of some disagreement.[18]

The prime minister did not consult the provinces before requesting the amendment and this did not go over well. However, some scholars have speculated that this was a tactic: St-Laurent wanted to spur the provinces into finally agreeing on amending formulae and with that in mind promised to convene a Dominion-Provincial conference to decide on what we would now call a "patriation" procedure.[19] If so, the tactic failed and the provinces all took the position that this was an unprecedented attempt to undermine provincial constitutional authority.

The Dominion-Provincial conferences held to deal with the BNA (2) 1949 took place in 1950; there were three in all. The first two were on the Constitution, and the third, held in December, was meant to focus on federal-provincial fiscal issues such as taxation, old-age security, and pensions. These issues were all jurisdictional concerns that, if resolved, would require constitutional amendments; another incentive for provincial consensus.[20] However, the complexities involved in just figuring out an "old age" pension plan ended up dominating the conference and the other issues were dropped. Nevertheless, the conference did produce the Old Age Security program.[21]

The 1950 conferences were the first involving Newfoundland, which had joined Confederation in 1949 with the passage of the *British North America Act (No. I), 1949*[22] and so finally fulfilling Canada's motto, *A mari usque ad mare* (from sea to sea). Newfoundland's presence at the First Ministers' table changed the dynamics, at least concerning the Maritimes. Margaret Conrad writes that Joey Smallwood "was an inspiration to Maritime premiers."[23] But the provinces were still working as independent actors. Corey Slumkoski explains that, while Newfoundland's entry into Confederation in 1949 was treated as an opportunity for the Maritime provinces to leverage greater resources from the federal government, regional rivalries still dominated:

> The limited gains promised by the Maritime Rights movement gave way to the harsh realities of the Great Depression, the Second World War, and the protracted negotiations around dominion–provincial relations that privileged provincial needs rather than regional ones. By the end of the Second World War the regional front of the 1920s was a distant memory, with each Maritime province using Newfoundland's pending entry to champion schemes

that would largely help itself, and reluctant to endorse development plans in a neighbouring province that would not bring corollary benefits.[24]

This appeared to change in the mid 1950s and it was at this time that MacNutt's "revolution" became apparent. By the mid-1950s, Maritime premiers began looking for ways to work together, particularly through programs and institutions that would foster economic integration. In part, the incentive for this change in tack came about, not so much because of dissatisfaction with the federal-fiscal reforms that were now in place — the equalization program was certainly popular — but with the realization that these programs came at a cost and by the mid-1950s the initial optimism that this would be a decade of great prosperity began to fade:

> By 1955, per capita income in the region had dropped to 33 per cent below the Canadian average. In other words, the decade following the war's conclusion saw per capita income in the Maritimes drop from 76 per cent to 67 per cent of the Canadian average. Moreover, the net value of secondary manufacturing in the Atlantic Provinces was only $94 per person, far below the national average of $405.[25]

Coincidentally, the fortunes of the federal Liberals were also fading. The 1953 federal election saw the St-Laurent government remain in power, but with a reduced majority. The Progressive Conservatives were gaining confidence both federally and provincially. In New Brunswick, the Liberals' stretch of electoral victories came to an end, when in 1952 Hugh John Flemming's PC Party won thirty-six seats to the Liberals' sixteen. A sense that change was coming was also apparent in the other provinces. In 1953, both Prince Edward Island and Nova Scotia had Liberal governments that had been in power for some time, but in a few years hence they would be defeated as well: in 1956 Robert Stanfield's PCs would win in Nova Scotia and in Prince Edward Island, a little late in the game, Walter Shaw's PCs would win in 1959.

St-Laurent, realizing that his party was weakening in the eastern and western regions, established *The Royal Commission on Canada's Economic Prospects* under the chairmanship of Walter Gordon, which began its deliberations in 1955. The Gordon Commission, as it was known, travelled the country and in October of that year, held meetings in Fredericton. Premier Hugh John Flemming met with the commission and made the case for yet another economic development program for the region. Massive deposits of copper, lead, zinc, silver, and sulphates had been discovered in northern New Brunswick, but without the necessary infrastructure — primarily "cheap hydro"[26] and a better rail system — New Brunswick would "become no more than an ore digger" and the minerals would be taken away to be processed elsewhere. "But," said Flemming, "this province is no longer content to remain one of the weakest links in Confederation. If need be, we will fight for our place in the economic sun."

Flemming pointed out that the economic principle of Confederation was east-west trade, replacing north-south trade, but that in turn was dependent upon a railway link that was designed "to form a new nation and not as a mere dollar-and-cents proposition." He proposed a program in which the federal government would support power projects and transportation links, such as the Trans-Canada Highway and the railway as well as a "new transportation policy in which the Maritimes would be restored to the favorable freight rate position they had on the old Intercolonial Railway."[27]

From April 1955 through to March 1956, three Dominion-Provincial conferences were held. Unemployment insurance, natural resources development, health and welfare, hospital insurance, and general "federal-provincial fiscal relations" were the topics discussed and at each one, concerns were raised by the Maritime premiers about their economic plight and why the federal government had a duty to do something about the situation. For that matter, all the premiers except for Maurice Duplessis of Quebec called on the federal government to do something about the country's rising unemployment rate, with Saskatchewan's Tommy Douglas and British Columbia's W.A.C. Bennett calling for a federal unemployment insurance program.[28]

New Brunswick's Premier Flemming called for a review of federal transfers to the province arguing that the significant grants of land with the expansion of the other provinces over the years gave them an economic advantage unavailable to New Brunswick or the other Maritime provinces. Nova Scotia premier Henry Hicks worried about the imminent collapse of the province's coal industry, primarily situated in Cape Breton. Without assistance from the federal government, the collapse of this industry "could make unemployment of such magnitude that he doubted the Provincial Government could cope with it."[29]

A rather remarkable request came for Prince Edward Island's Alexander Matheson at the October conference, who pointed out that his province was educating workers at public expense who were now employed in Ontario and the Western provinces and helping those provinces prosper. This was a "debt owed by other provinces to PEI," and Matheson called on the federal government to fund provincial education programs:

> If the young Canadians now growing up in Prince Edward Island are to make a contribution to the productive capacity of Canada, they must have a proper start in life. This will be possible only if the Federal Government recognizes its responsibility to equalize educational resources across the country.[30]

Then, on 24 April 1956, Prime Minister St-Laurent addressed the inaugural meeting of the Canadian Labour Congress in Toronto. After congratulating organized labour on the creation of their new association, St-Laurent thought to send a message to the Atlantic provinces. This was, to say the least, an odd venue to choose for such a message but the prime minister nevertheless let the provinces know that any improvement to the Atlantic economy had to begin with them and challenged the provinces to produce "the initiatives and ideas" that were needed themselves.[31] "It will be then for us elsewhere to co-operate and help make such ideas and efforts fruit-ful in providing better opportunities for workers in those areas."[32] However, it does not seem that St-Laurent was thinking of Maritime Union. The Canadian Labour Congress was formed through the union of the Trades and Labour Congress and the Canadian Congress of Labour. St-Laurent also expressed his concern this merger was the result of an unfortunate modern tendency to assume that bigger was better. "There seems to be some inherent tendency towards large organizations in our present say life — it shows in government, in business, and in associations of many kinds."[33]

Meanwhile, the PC government in New Brunswick was facing an election (which would be held two months later, on 18 June 1956). Flemming saw St-Laurent's remarks as an opportunity and on 30 April 1956 invited his fellow Atlantic premiers to come to a conference in Fredericton for 9 July 1956, which would be just a few weeks after his provincial election, which he was confident he would win.[34]

Flemming believed that the provinces could and should build on the positive steps toward greater cooperation had already begun with the creation in 1955 of the Atlantic Provinces Economic Council (APEC).[35] Spearheaded by Nova Scotia's Henry Hicks, this was "the first Canadian experiment in extensive economic cooperation on a regional basis."[36] The Atlantic Premiers' Conference, established in 1956, was a natural next step and Flemming predicted that the new organization would mean "the resumption of a certain order of business which was interrupted in the city of Charlottetown in the year 1864."[37] Although lacking a formal infrastructure, from this date the Atlantic premiers began meeting yearly. Donald Savoie reports that at the first meeting, the premiers "agreed to study jointly the following themes:"

- the advantages of collaboration in securing better federal-provincial financial agreements;
- the possibility of cooperating to achieve cheaper electric power;

- the desirability of a joint drive to locate defence industries and place defence orders in the Atlantic provinces;
- the means to attack jointly the effects of the tariff on the regional economy;
- the possibilities of cooperation in the marketing of fishing and agricultural products; and
- the possibilities of maintaining joint trade representatives in the United Kingdom and elsewhere.[38]

Much progress toward regional cooperation did occur in the years that followed, but much did not as well. Initiatives that began with great fanfare eventually petered out, as one province and then another would withdraw to go it alone. It would not be until the mid-1960s that a more comprehensive effort to unite the Maritimes would emerge, and that effort came primarily from Louis Robichaud, New Brunswick's first Acadian to lead a party to an election win[39] and at the age of thirty-four years then the youngest premier ever elected in New Brunswick.

CHAPTER FIVE

Maritime Union Movement: 1960s and 1970s

There was music in the cafés at night /
And revolution in the air

Bob Dylan, "Tangled up in Blue" (1974)

Except for the negotiations that eventually led to Confederation in 1867, the Maritime Union movement that began in the 1960s and continued briefly into the 1970s was the one that presented the greatest opportunity for union and the one that came closest to succeeding. Even so, the support was tepid. As the *Canadian Annual Review for 1970* suggested, the concept of a Maritime Union (and for that matter "One Prairie Province") had "reached the stage of semi-serious discussion"[1] by the end of the decade. But perhaps not much more.

Still, if Maritime Union ever had a chance to succeed, it was in the mid- to late 1960s. This was one of the very few times that three Maritime premiers were at least willing to seriously consider Maritime Union, if only fleetingly. But for that brief time, Maritime Union looked like a dream that would soon be realized. Public opinion appeared to be onside with approximately two-thirds of respondents favouring union.[2] Actual policies and institutions were put in place that were meant to allow for incremental integration so that eventually Maritime Union would seem an obvious and easy step. It didn't happen. Maritime Union was an idea that fit well into the ethos of the 1960s but it floundered when the decade ended.

The 1960s in Canada, like in much of the Western world, was a time of great optimism and a flourishing of protests and counter-culture. Big ideas — revolutionary ideas — were taken seriously. They had a traction that we have not seen since. "The 1960s," writes Della Stanley, "was a pivotal decade."

> The growing importance of new technologies stimulated change throughout the western world. As part of a long period of economic growth, the decade saw substantial improvements in Canadian living standards. Faith in material progress was accompanied by an optimistic and egalitarian idealism that encouraged concern for the plight of minorities and the poor, the questioning of traditional values, and new attempts to define national goals and aspirations.[3]

While Quebec's Quiet Revolution was transforming that province, the Maritimes were experiencing their own radical changes. One premier who stood above the others for implementing brave new reforms was Premier Louis Robichaud of New Brunswick (1960-1970). Stanley describes the Liberal leader as the driving force behind regional cooperation in "virtually all the major economic, political, educational, and social programs on the regional agenda."[4]

In 1964, at the Federal-Dominion "Centennial" Conference marking the one hundredth anniversary of the Charlottetown Conference, Robichaud called upon his fellow Atlantic[5] premiers to fulfill "the dream" that began in 1864. Echoing the remarks of Flemming a decade earlier, Robichaud claimed that the Maritime Union initiative of 1864 had been sidetracked by the arrival of the Canadian delegates:

> Perhaps, however, Premiers Stanfield, Smallwood and Shaw and I may get together today and, on this centennial of that first meeting in Charlottetown, decided to reduce the number of

Canadian Provinces from ten to seven. Should that occur, the focal point of progress and activity in the nation would unquestionably and rapidly take a marked shift to the east.[6]

The reaction to Robichaud's call was decidedly mixed, at least within the region. "Local public response was polite and slight. National reaction was quite the opposite."[7] Smallwood was sceptical and countered with his own idea of union: not of Atlantic Canada, but a union of the country's two "island" provinces, Newfoundland and Prince Edward Island. This of course ignored the obvious fact that Newfoundland includes Labrador, which is certainly not an island. Regardless, no one in the Prince Edward Island government expressed any interest with Smallwood's proposal — nor, it seems, Robichaud's proposal either — and Smallwood quickly dropped the idea. He was already involved in another project that would occupy his time: the development of the Churchill Falls hydroelectric project.

Nova Scotia's premier Robert Stanfield also expressed his reservations: it would be a tough sell in Nova Scotia, he is reported as saying.[8] Nevertheless, Stanfield did acknowledge that the idea was at least worth exploring, and so he and Robichaud went back to their respective legislatures with a proposal that a commission be established to study the idea. Resolutions were passed unanimously in New Brunswick and Nova Scotia the very next February.[9]

True to form, Prince Edward Island dragged its feet. However, with the election of Alex Campbell and a Liberal government in 1966, Prince Edward Island did eventually come on board, although not without a few false starts. The 1968 Speech from the Throne (22 February 1968) promised to establish a "Secretariat" to "to further encourage and facilitate the co-operative efforts of the Atlantic Provinces in dealing with regional problems of mutual concern," but did not call for a study on full union, nor was any such secretariat ever created. Premier Campbell did join the other premiers in making a statement to their respective legislatures announcing the sponsoring of what we now know as the Maritime Union Study under the supervision of the principal of Queen's University Dr. John J. Deutsch, together with F.R. Drummie, then economic adviser to the New Brunswick government who would serve as executive director.[10] Deutsch had previously been engaged by the Robichaud government to recommend reform of the province's post-secondary education system.[11] Drummie, another New Brunswick Rhodes Scholar, was a senior policy adviser to Premier Robichaud. The Maritime Union Study (*Commission d'étude de l'union des Provinces Maritimes*) delivered its multi-volume report in 1970.[12]

Was it the case, then, that Premier Robichaud was, alone among his fellow premiers, a Maritime Union visionary? This is not clear. Richard Wilbur, writing in the *Canadian Annual Review for 1964*, considered Robichaud's call for union at the Centennial Conference "jocular" and another example of the premier's "shrewd" talent for publicity.[13] Robichaud's biographer Della Stanley agreed and writes that "Louis' purpose was to gain some publicity, more than to achieve union itself."[14] Although not without a grain of truth, I consider these characterizations unfair (and perhaps now dated). Robichaud may not have been the sole architect of Maritime Union, or Equal Opportunity for that matter, but there is no question that Robichaud was open to new and big ideas and knew how to move them along. Michel Cormier's biography, quoting Don Tansley, might have summed up Robichaud best: "Louis was not necessarily a man of ideas, but he knew how to recognize an idea he liked."[15]

Maritime Union was just such an idea. Yet there was a pragmatic side to Robichaud's call for union. He knew that his government would have huge problems implementing the massive reforms recommended by the New Brunswick Royal Commission on Finance and Municipal Taxation, known as the Byrne Commission.[16] This 1,000-page report called on the government to completely reorganize the province's education, public health, hospital services, social welfare, and even justice system. Gone would be the old county system of raising taxes for local services, a system that was clearly antiquated and near collapse. In some cases, it had collapsed: the same day as the Report came out (5 February 1964) Gloucester County announced that they had run out of money and could no longer pay teachers.[17]

Robichaud was also a tireless defender of French-language rights in New Brunswick and was successful in passing legislation establishing New Brunswick as an "officially" bilingual province. This legislation would eventually become the basis for New Brunswick's constitutional entrenchment of language rights.[18] Bilingualism was and continues to be a controversial issue in New Brunswick and is either at the forefront or just behind most policy issues in the province. As Michael MacMillan writes, "Analysis of public opinion on language equality reveals the puzzling patterns that anglophones in New Brunswick accept a policy of bilingualism, but not one of language equality."[19] Indeed, when the Program for Equal Opportunity was first announced, an anonymous letter to the editor in Fredericton's *The Daily Gleaner* described it as "robbing Peter to pay Pierre." Richard Wilbur writes, "The anti-French overtones of that letter unleashed a torrent of invective and resentment."[20]

The Maritime Union Study (1970)

The Maritime Union Study comprised twenty slim volumes on topics ranging from provincial-municipal relations to public finances. The longest, the collection of public submissions, is 300 pages.[21] Most volumes are between 100 and 200 pages, although *Region-Wide Policies for Higher Education* is a terse six pages.[22] Only one was written in French and even it was originally written in English,[23] something that could not happen today particularly given that all the studies were published in New Brunswick. A public opinion poll was also commissioned in which 64% of respondents indicated support for Maritime Union.

Not surprisingly, much of what the commission found concerned the economic relations of the three provinces. The summary report explained, "Time and time again in the past, changes in the outside environment — in the rest of Canada, in the United States and overseas — have dominated the course of events." Economic growth and development in Canada were characterized by: "a powerful trend toward urbanization" together with "an increasing concentration of industrial and service activities in the St. Lawrence Valley — Southern Ontario region." This was attracting manufacturers who wanted to be near "large mass consumer markets." The Maritimes were not keeping pace. If they hoped to, they had no choice but to "establish immediately a method of co-operation which would envisage the attainment of full political union as a definite goal."[24] Somewhat disingenuously, the commission assured the Maritimes that they could, of course, reject union and maintain their "local attachments, local diversities, local autonomies, small scale relationships, and the existing structure and pace of life."[25] Although the authors generously conceded that neither choice was more "virtuous" than the other, it was also true that the Maritimes could not have the best of "both worlds." Despite the disclaimer, it is evident that the commission saw no other choice for the region than full political union.

So how to establish "a method of co-operation which would envisage the attainment of full political union as a definite goal"? The commission understood that union sprung on the Maritimes would likely fail. Instead, it recommended three institutions be established that would acclimatize Maritimers into embracing their regional identity, and therefore come to support union as an obvious step. The three institutions were to be the Council of Maritime Premiers, the Maritime Provinces Commission, and a Joint Legislative Assembly.

The Council of Maritime Premiers was created and still functions although it has been largely superseded by the Council of Atlantic Premiers. The three Maritime provinces all passed legislation establishing that council in 1971.[26] However, the other two institutions were never established, nor has there ever been a joint assembly of Maritime legislators. The idea of the other two institutions is intriguing but now appear to be arcane products of another time. The Maritime Provinces Commission, for example, would "consist of five full-time members appointed by the Council of Premiers." "Needless to say, all these persons should have out-standing qualifications,"[27] the Report says baldly. This commission would have very broad mandate to basically provide a road map to full union, which would then be presented to the Joint Legislative Assembly, a body comprising all the MLAs of the provinces which would in turn have "the duty of determining the method by which the final step of ratification of the union would be accomplished, i.e. whether by referendum, constitutional convention, or by some procedure in the Joint Assembly itself."

Writing ten years later, J. Murray Beck — himself a contributor to the Maritime Union Study — threw cold water on the Maritime Union Report, arguing that there was "little hard evidence . . . to demonstrate the kind of consciousness that the sociologist posits for the existence of a region, or the existence of any meaningful sense of identity."[28] As for the 64 percent support for union reported by the public opinion poll, Beck pointed out that the "survey provided no inkling of the intensity of the respondents' feelings towards political union."[29] Nor did the poll provide any details of what union would entail, such as where the new capital would be. Would any province give up having a capital city? But Beck saved his most severe criticism for the "Special Advisor" and the executive director:

> Perhaps it was inevitable that the Deutsch commission should go astray since its leading members were an outsider who did not fully appreciate grass-roots attitudes in the Maritimes and a technocrat with an exaggerated view of the goodness of his finely laid plans.[30]

That Beck considered Deutsch an outsider who wouldn't appreciate something Beck called Maritime grassroots attitudes (on the assumption that Maritimers shared these common attitudes) is interesting and perhaps ironic. It does seem that Maritimers quickly develop a common identity the moment they perceive someone from outside the region is criticizing them or telling them what to do. Beck went on to point out that without the benefit of legislative union, the Maritime provinces already participated in a vast network of cooperative enterprises, with "virtually every field of provincial

activity . . . involved in one or more Maritime interprovincial relationships."[31] More than 180 active organizations were influenced by
cooperative activity, and quoting Guy Henson, Beck wrote that this
"whole complex of voluntary provincial activity . . . constitutes an
identifiable, distinctive, and apparently unique regional life of the
Maritime or Atlantic Provinces."[32] Apparently, this "unique regional
life" is not a chimera.

That the region is already cooperating at significant and even
heroic levels is an argument that is often made to counter the Maritime Union project. Why unite when the region is already doing all
that it can to cooperate? Perhaps, because clearly even this level of
cooperation has not solved the problems that have been identified
over and over. Either a lack of cooperation is not why the region
struggles, or cooperation alone — or what passes for cooperation
— is not enough to solve the problems.

PART TWO

Maritime Union and the Canadian Constitution

CHAPTER SIX

The Constitutional Processes

[T] he constitutional processes employed would have to abolish the three exist-
ing provinces and their governmental structure, and fix the terms upon which
the new province and its residents would continue as an integral part of the
federal structure of Canada.

B.L. Strayer (1970)[1]

The general discussions on Maritime Union and the lead up to the Maritime Union Study generated conversations in other parts of the country as well, particularly in Western Canada. The University of Lethbridge and the *Lethbridge Herald* co-sponsored a conference titled "One Prairie Province? A Question for Canada," in May 1970, several months before the Maritime Union Study released its own report. Like the Maritime Union question, this conference asked whether the three Prairie provinces (Manitoba, Saskatchewan, and Alberta) would be better off as one province, and if so, how this would come about. Of course, this was well before the patriation of the Constitution in 1982 and so any significant changes would have to be enacted by the British Parliament.

One participant was the late Hon Barry L. Strayer, then a professor of constitutional law at the University of Saskatchewan.[2] Strayer's conclusion was that the only way to unite the three provinces would be to abolish all three and then create a new province. The offices of three lieutenant governors would also have to be abolished and replaced with a new office of a lieutenant governor for the united province. Under the (then) *British North America Act* (BNA 1867), section 92(1), this was beyond the constitutional competence of the provincial legislatures.

> By Section 92 (1) of the BNA Act, 1867, [the provincial legislators] have the power of "amendment . . . of the constitution of the province, except as regards the office of Lieutenant-Governor." It seems unlikely, however, that the power to amend a provincial constitution includes the power to abolish the province and its government (necessarily including the office of Lieutenant-Governor).[3]

While there are provisions in the *Constitution Act, 1982* (CA 1982) for the establishment of a new province and the adjustment of a province's boundaries (sections 42(1) e and f; 43(a)), there is no provision in either the *Constitution Act, 1867* (CA 1867) or the CA 1982 that deals with the abolition of a province or its government (or, for that matter, for a province leaving the federation). The office of the Lieutenant Governor can be altered under the CA 1982, section 41(a), but only through use of the "unanimity formula"; that is, "by proclamation issued by the Governor General under the Great Seal of Canada only where authorized by resolutions of the Senate and House of Commons and of the legislative assembly of each province." Section 41 replaces the reference to the office of the Lieutenant Governor found in BNA 1867, section 92(1), while the powers of a province to amend the constitution, including its own, are now covered by CA 1982, sections 38, 41, 42, 43, and 45, with the latter providing for unilateral amendments of a provincial constitution. Section 92(1) of the BNA 1867 is thus repealed by the CA 1982.[4]

When Strayer was writing, the British Parliament still had final authority over amendments to Canada's Constitution and so he rightly concluded that the British Parliament and only the British Parliament would have the authority to unify the three Prairie provinces. Only that parliament had the constitutional authority to abolish a province and the office of the respective lieutenant governors. Now that the Constitution has been patriated, the office of the Lieutenant Governor can be changed without the consent of the British Parliament, but only through unanimous consent of the Parliament of Canada and the legislative assemblies of all the provinces — a difficult task to say the least. Even more difficult, however, would be the initial abolishment of the three provinces, at least if we follow Strayer's logic. There appears to be no competent authority within the present constitution to abolish provinces. This, then, would seem to doom any attempt to unite the Maritime provinces.[5]

Perhaps, however, we need to re-examine the premise. With due respect to the learned professor and judge, I am not convinced that merging three provinces is the same as abolishing three and creating a new one. Neither am I convinced that the merging of the offices of the three lieutenant governors is the same as abolishing those offices and creating a new office.

When the provinces of Canada, Nova Scotia, and New Brunswick joined together to form the new Dominion of Canada, the constituent provinces were not considered to have been first abolished and then newly constituted as provinces of a federation. Two of them, Nova Scotia and New Brunswick, retained their provincial constitutions (BNA 1867, s 88). Since Confederation in 1867, three British North American colonies have joined the federal union: British Columbia in 1871, Prince Edward Island in 1873, and Newfoundland in 1949. Like Nova Scotia and New Brunswick, these colonies had their own constitutions that predated Confederation. All these constitutions were retained upon joining Confederation. So, it is not the case that joining together with other provinces necessarily requires the deletion of a province's constitutional past.

Of course, the new Dominion was a federation, which assumes that its constituent states or provinces continue to function as semi-autonomous units. K.C. Wheare's definition of the federal principal is "the method of dividing powers so that the general and regional governments are each within a sphere co-ordinate and independent."[6] Nevertheless, what would happen when two or more provinces join together? Would this be so constitutionally different than joining a federation?

An interesting pre-Confederation example of uniting provinces involves Nova Scotia and Cape Breton, but it is problematic as a model for unification. Both Cape Breton and Prince Edward Island (Ile Saint-Jean) had been French possessions but were formally ceded to the British following the Treaty of Paris in 1763. Both were initially annexed to Nova Scotia, with PEI becoming a separate colony in 1769 and Cape Breton in 1784. But Cape Breton was then re-annexed in 1820. Murray Beck's *The Government of Nova Scotia* (1957) states that Cape Breton had had a "troublous history" since 1763. Basically, the constitution of the colony (the Instructions),

> permitted the Governor and Council to make rules and regulations for the peace, order, and good government of the Island until conditions were ripe for the calling of an Assembly, but forbade them to do or pass anything which affected the life and liberty of the subject, or imposed a duty or tax.[7]

Cape Breton was not, then, a fully-functioning colony (although this was strongly disputed by its inhabitants). In any case, Cape Breton's union with Nova Scotia was the product of an annexation, not a merger of two colonies. The constitutional question that this raised — whether the Crown had the constitutional right to re-annex the island — was debated well into the nineteenth century. In 1883, the Lieutenant Governor of Nova Scotia, Adams Archibald, reported to the House of Commons that "it may be assumed that the Constitution of Nova Scotia, whatever that may be, is also the Constitution of that part of Nova Scotia [i.e. Cape Breton] which was formally a separate Government."[8]

A better pre-Confederation example would be the (re)unification of Upper and Lower Canada in 1840, followed by the "severing" of those two provinces into Ontario and Quebec with Confederation in 1867. The Province of Canada had its own constitution in 1867, but the BNA 1867 did not create new constitutions for these new provinces. Since Ontario and Quebec corresponded to the old colonies of Upper and Lower Canada, the constitutions of those provinces are considered to be part of the constitutional history of Ontario and Quebec.[9] Indeed, even in its time as the Province of Canada, Canada West (Upper Canada/Ontario) was governed under common law while Canada East (Lower Canada/Quebec) was under the *Civil Code*, and both had their own attorney general.[10] Note that BNA 1867, section 6 states that the Province of Canada "formerly constituted respectively the Provinces of Upper Canada and Lower Canada" and that with the passing of the Act were now "deemed to be severed" and renamed Ontario and Quebec. Hence these two provinces were not newly created by Confederation; rather their previous status was restored.[11]

That the BNA 1867 restored the old division of the original constitutions that existed prior to 1840 means that the old constitutions had not been erased. From a constitutional standpoint, Confederation did not create two new provinces; it restored two provinces. But then, by the same logic, neither did the unification of Upper and Lower Canada in 1840 mean that both were abolished. They were merged. Were they abolished, their constitutional history could not have been restored — what else could be "severed" with Confederation than two legally-constituted bodies?

What, then, are the constitutional provisions for uniting provinces? We can begin by examining the amending formulae found in CA 1982, Part V (Procedure for Amending the Constitution of Canada). The pertinent sections that would apply to the unification of the provinces, and ignoring for the time being the implications for and effects on other parts of the Constitution (which I address later), are sections 41, 42, 43, and 45. I will begin, however, with another Act entirely, the *Constitution Act, 1871*, which was once the *British North America Act, 1871*.[12] For reasons which should become apparent, I am leaving CA 1982, section 41 for last.

CHAPTER SEVEN

Sections 42 and 43 (and the Constitution Act 1871)

[P]arliament was also authorised, with the consent of any of the provinces concerned, to increase, diminish, or otherwise alter, provincial boundaries and to legislate for any territory not included in a province. Should provinces so desire, they could be amalgamated pursuant to this subsection.

W.H. McConnell[1]

[T]he extension of provinces and the establishment of new provinces requires no amendment of the Constitution of Canada.

Peter Hogg[2]

Canada's motto is *A mari usque ad mare*, which every Canadian student knows (one hopes) means "from sea to sea." The motto, so the story goes, was first suggested by New Brunswick's Samuel Tilley. Tilley took the words from the King James version of the Bible: Psalm 72, "A Psalm for Solomon," where he found this line: "He shall have dominion also from sea to sea, and from the river unto the ends of the earth." From this psalm came the motto and the proposed name for the newly federated country: the Dominion of Canada. This, it seems, was regarded as less threatening to the United States than the original title, the King-dom of Canada.[3]

The motto sums up nicely the vision that the Fathers of Confederation had for the new country. Although in 1867 the four constituent provinces occupied but a fraction of the North American land mass north of the US border, the plan was to expand and do so quickly. This expansion involved the implementation of four strategies. One was to admit existing colonies into the federation as provinces. Another was to annex territories. A third was to carve out new provinces from some of these territories. And the fourth was to extend the boundaries of the provinces, including the new provinces.

The first and second were covered by the *British North America Act, 1867*, section 146.[4] Under this provision, Prince Edward Island would join Confederation in 1873.[5] However, there was some confusion over whether the Parliament of Canada had the authority to accomplish the third and fourth strategies. As Paul Gérin-Lajoie wrote in his *Constitutional Amendment in Canada* (1950), "The Constitution of 1867 contained no express provision empowering Ottawa to create provinces."[6] The first test came when Manitoba was created through an act of Parliament in 1870, and so to clear up this confusion the British Parliament passed the *British North America Act, 1871* (now the *Constitution Act, 1871*).[7]

The British North America Act, 1871

The year 1871 was a significant one for the new Dominion. Manitoba had just been created, albeit under questionable constitutional authority. British Columbia was admitted to Confederation in 1871 under the terms of the BNA 1867, section 146. That province also passed its own *Constitution Act, 1871*, a piece of legislation that has fascinated constitutional scholars ever since.[8] The Treaty of Washington was signed and ratified in 1871 settling several outstanding claims that the United States had with the United Kingdom regarding the latter's role in the American Civil War (particularly over the CSS Alabama). Other issues included American access to the Grand Banks, reparation to Canada over Fenian raids, and apparently a demand from the American commissioners — at least some[9] — that the United Kingdom cede Canada to the United States. Many Maritimers were no doubt grateful not to be ceded to the United States but were less enthusiastic about the settlement of the fisheries. Nevertheless, the existence of the new Dominion was now on firmer ground than it had been for some time, and so it was time to grow.

The Canadian population was on the rise. The first national census was conducted in 1871, under the authority of BNA 1867, section 8 and the *Census Act* (12 May 1870). Including estimates for British Columbia, Manitoba, and the North-West Territories, the census put the Canadian population at 3,689,257. New Brunswick (285,594) and Nova Scotia (387,800) had a combined population of 673,394 or 18% of the total Canadian population.[10] Prince Edward Island, just two years away from joining Confederation, conducted its own comprehensive census. That census revealed that the Island had a population of 94,021. When added to the populations of Nova Scotia and New Brunswick, the Maritimes constituted 21% of the total population or one-fifth (today that percentage is just over 5%).

Yet, the Maritime economies were now noticeably in decline. David Alexander reports that "between 1871 and 1941 the Canadian rate of growth was 1.64 per cent per annum. In the Maritimes it was only 0.55 per cent."[11] One reason was the national focus on expansion to the West and the North, and that was enabled by the BNA 1871, now the CA 1871.

The Macdonald government had thought to request that the United Kingdom pass the BNA 1871 without going first to the Canadian Parliament, but that initiative was quickly thwarted.[12] The Member of Parliament for Gloucester (New Brunswick) Timothy Anglin[13] called on the government to remember that "our constitution was too sacred a thing to be altered without being fully discussed by the representatives of the people," by which he meant the members of the House of Commons. A resolution was then passed that hereafter, any requests to amend the Canadian

Constitution had to come from the Parliament of Canada, and not just the Cabinet. However, Anglin and the House of Commons in general seemed unconcerned with the need to consult the provinces.[14]

The preamble to the Act explains that "doubts have been entertained respecting the powers of the Parliament of Canada to establish Provinces in territories admitted, or which may hereafter be admitted, into the Dominion of Canada." To alleviate such doubts, the Act confirms that the "Parliament of Canada may from time to establish new Provinces in any of the territories." A caveat was also included: the territories referred to are those that are a part of the Dominion of Canada, "but not included in any Province thereof."[15] Until the patriation of the Constitution in 1982, this Act provided the constitutional authority for altering borders or admitting new provinces (other than those already covered by BNA 1867, section 146). There were several restrictions. Parliament could not establish a new province out of land already within a province (section 2). Any changes to borders (limits) of a province, either increases, decreases, or alteration, could only take place with the consent of the affected provinces (section 3). The full text of the germane clauses in the Act are as follows:

> Sec. 2: The Parliament of Canada may from time to time establish new Provinces in any territories forming for the time being part of the Dominion of Canada, but not included in any Province thereof, and may, at the time of such establishment, make provision for the constitution and administration of any such Province, and for the passing of laws for the peace, order, and good government of such Province, and for its representation in the said Parliament.

> Sec. 3: The Parliament of Canada may from time to time, with the consent of the Legislature of any province of the said Dominion, increase, diminish, or otherwise alter the limits of such Province, upon such terms and conditions as may be agreed to by the said Legislature, and may, with the like consent, make provision

respecting the effect and operation of any such increase or diminution or alteration of territory in relation to any Province affected thereby.[16]

The word "otherwise" (*"otherwise* alter the limits of such Province") found in section 3 may carry a lot of weight. However, to be clear, despite the broadness of "increase, diminish, or otherwise alter the limits of such Province," I am not suggesting that the 1871 Act anticipated the union of provinces. These provisions were clearly intended to allow for the expansion of Canada across the West and to carve provinces out of these territories, as well as to expand those provinces as needed. It was under the authority of this Act that Saskatchewan and Alberta were created, and Manitoba's provincial status confirmed.[17] Manitoba, Ontario, and Quebec's boundaries were extended under this Act as well. Since Confederation all but the three Maritime provinces have so extended their boundaries.[18]

Nevertheless, the CA 1871 is important to our discussion because its presence in the Schedule of the CA 1982 means that it is still a valid part of the Constitution. However, whether the entirety of the Act is still valid (that is, whether some sections have been made redundant), as well as whether the Act allows for, not just the creation of new provinces (carved out of territories), but the merger of provinces, is uncertain. To try to answer these questions, we need to first examine the sections of the CA 1982 that interact with or replace sections of the CA 1871. We can begin with CA 1982, sections 42 and 43.

Constitution Act, 1982, Sections 42 and 43

Section 42 falls under those amendments that must be accomplished through the "General Procedure," so CA 1982, section 38(1), while section 43 is known as the bilateral formula and refers to those amendments which affect only some of the provinces. Because these two sections deal with overlapping amendments dealing with Maritime Union, I will discuss them together.

Section 42(1) reads:

An amendment to the Constitution of Canada in relation to the
following matters may be made only in accordance with subsection
38(1):

(a) the principle of proportionate representation of the provinces
in the House of Commons prescribed by the Constitution of
Canada;

(b) the powers of the Senate and the method of selecting Senators;

(c) the number of members by which a province is entitled to be
represented in the Senate and the residence qualifications of
Senators;

(d) subject to paragraph 41(d), the Supreme Court of Canada;

(e) the extension of existing provinces into the territories;
and

(f) notwithstanding any other law or practice, the establishment
of new provinces.

Section 43 reads:

An amendment to the Constitution of Canada in relation to
any provision that applies to one or more, but not all, provinces,
including

(a) any alteration to boundaries between provinces,
and

(b) any amendment to any provision that relates to the use of
the English or the French language within a province, may
be made by proclamation issued by the Governor General
under the Great Seal of Canada only where so authorized by
resolutions of the Senate and House of Commons and of the
legislative assembly of each province to which the amendment
applies.

Section 42(1)(a) and (c) would be affected by the union of the
Maritime provinces (or, rather, a unified Maritime province would
have an effect on these sections) and are discussed below. However,
clauses (a) and (c) are not clauses that would need to be invoked

to unify the provinces. Clause (e) would not apply, as it refers only to the expansion of a province into "the territories," which now obviously and specifically means Yukon, the Northwest Territories, and Nunavut. The history of this clause has a bearing on the question of Maritime Union, but otherwise, the operative clause in section 42(1) as far as Maritime Union is concerned is 42(1)f.

Section 43 is different than section 45. The latter section, 45, allows provinces to unilaterally amend their own provincial constitutions, while the former section, 43, requires resolutions from both the Parliament of Canada and the legislative assemblies of the affected province or provinces. Hogg argues that the presence of section 45 implies that section 43 applies "only to those provisions of the Constitution of Canada which, although applicable to only one province, do not come within the phrase the 'constitution of the province.'"[19]

It is not entirely clear where the line is drawn between an amendment which affects only, say, New Brunswick and one that affects only New Brunswick's provincial constitution. In fact, what precisely section 43 means by "[a]n amendment to the Constitution of Canada in relation to any provision that applies to one or more, but not all, provinces" is sufficiently obscure to prompt the Supreme Court, in describing section 43, to note that "the determination of its scope and of the effects of its interaction with other provisions of Part V presents significant conceptual difficulties."[20] It seems that the effect of the change is restricted to something that has an impact on the Constitution rather than simply the province.

For example, the Terms of Union for Prince Edward Island were amended by the Constitution Amendment, 1993 (Prince Edward Island) which provided for the construction of the "fixed link" (Confederation Bridge) between Prince Edward Island and New Brunswick. The original Terms of Union for PEI contained guarantees that the "Dominion Government" would "assume and defray all the charges for" (among other things) "Efficient Steam Service" connecting PEI to the mainland. The 1993 amendment allowed the bridge ("a fixed crossing") to be substituted for the steam service. However, although Confederation Bridge links PEI to NB, the latter province's approval was not required for the 1993 Constitution Amendment. PEI had a constitutional guarantee of a service connecting it to the mainland; NB did not have a constitutional guarantee connecting it to PEI.

Although they are not meant to be exclusive, section 43 does provide two examples of changes that would thus not fall under section 45: alteration of boundaries and the use of French or English in a province. Both also have implications for Maritime Union; however, I discuss the language issue, which primarily concerns New Brunswick, in a separate chapter below.

Constitution Act 1982, Section 42(1)(f) "notwithstanding any other law or practice, the establishment of new provinces"

Section 42(1)(f) means that the establishment of a new province — either by admission or by the granting of provincial status to a territory — can only be accomplished by following the amending procedures of section 38(1), the General Amending formula. Would union of the Maritime provinces, then, mean that a new province was being created and therefore require an amendment under the General Formula? This is not clear. Two questions arise. The first is: does uniting three provinces into one mean that a new province is being created, at least in the meaning of this section? The second is: how completely does the notwithstanding proviso in (f) negate other constitutional acts?

To repeat, section 42(1) reads: "An amendment to the Constitution of Canada in relation to the following matters may be made only in accordance with subsection 38(1)"; while clause (f) reads: "notwithstanding any other law or practice, the establishment of new provinces." Although this provision does not explicitly refer to the CA 1871, at first glance this seems to be what this entire section, and section 43 as well, has in mind. Indeed, that is the interpretation many if not most constitutional scholars[21] provide: the extension and alteration of provincial boundaries and the establishment of new provinces — other than those referenced by the CA 1867, section 146 — was formerly covered by CA 1871. However, CA 1982, section 42(1)(e) and (f) now supplant and make redundant CA 1871. The "notwithstanding any other law or practice," then, includes CA 1871. By this reading, regardless of what CA 1871 said, the establishment of a new province now requires the use of the General Amending formula.

Constitution Act 1982, Section 43 (a)
"any alteration to boundaries between provinces"

But unifying the Maritime provinces is not so simple. Consider section 43(1)(a) on the alteration of boundaries. Altering boundaries between provinces is not the same as extending the boundaries of a province. For two or more provinces to alter their shared boundary requires the approval both of Parliament and of the affected provinces' legislative assemblies. This provision is different than section 42(1)(e), as that refers to the expansion of a province into a territory.

It is likely that the framers of the CA 1982 imagined the future possibility of, say, the City of Lloydminster deciding that it should be wholly in either Saskatchewan or Alberta, or perhaps they recalled the difficulties leading up to the *Canada (Ontario Boundary) Act, 1889*[22] or even the uncertainty of the British Columbia-Alberta border and the issues confronting the surveyors in 1913.[23] They may even have considered the far more contentious question of the Labrador-Quebec boundary, which has yet to be completely resolved.[24] However, were the Maritime provinces to unite, the boundaries between New Brunswick, Prince Edward Island, and Nova Scotia would be erased, not merely altered.[25] I doubt the framers imagined boundaries being erased. What, then, does "alteration" mean in this context, and how broad is "any alteration" meant to be? Is the word "any" meant to carry the weight of the CA 1871's "increase, diminish, or otherwise alter the limits of such Province"? We can return to CA 1871, section 3.

W.R. Lederman, writing for the 1970 Maritime Union Study, stated that section 3 of the CA 1871 "contemplates the continuance of each such Province, albeit with altered boundaries, and *not* the union of two or more Provinces" [emphasis in original]. Indeed, Lederman explains, the BNA 1949 (2), which added a new section 91(1) to the BNA 1867, contemplates "the continuance of the existing Provinces," and as such, the "very existence of each Province . . . is secured by the B.N.A. Acts and other Constitutional Acts."[26]

However, W.H. McConnell's interpretation of the BNA 1871 states that this Act's section 3 does not only authorize Parliament "with the consent of any of the provinces concerned, to increase, diminish, or otherwise alter, provincial boundaries and to legislate for any territory not included in a province." The Act allows provinces, should they so desire, "*to be amalgamated pursuant to this subsection*."[27] If McConnell is indeed correct, then the constitutional authority for the Maritime provinces (or for that matter the Prairie provinces) to unite is found in the BNA 1871, now the CA 1871. What is required under CA 1871 is consent of the provinces concerned, and the consent of the Parliament of Canada. No other provinces are involved. The question now is whether or not the CA 1871 survived the CA 1982, and if so, which parts (if not all)?

Bayard Reesor maintains that section 42(1) (e) and (f), and particularly the notwithstanding proviso in (f), renders at least section 2 of the CA 1871 "inoperative."[28] Parliament can no longer carve out provinces from the territories, not without triggering the General Amendment formula of CA 1982, section 38(1). But Reesor does not comment on whether CA 1871, section 3 is also inoperative, and we are not speaking here of carving out provinces from territories.

Steven Scott points out that CA 1982, section 52(3), "imposes a condition upon the validity of amendments by providing that '[a]mendments to the Constitution of Canada shall be made only in accordance with the authority contained in the Constitution of Canada.'" However, "the term 'Constitution of Canada' is broader than merely "Part V of the Constitution Act, 1982" [for example, the several amending formulae]. Hence:

Section 52(3) leaves open the possibility that pre-existing rules of law admittedly forming part of the "Constitution of Canada" may be altered by processes outside the confines of Part V; and this is so, even though that Part gives the general appearance of an exhaustive scheme.

The example Scott provides of such a procedure is the CA 1871, section 3, albeit only in "a limited operation."[29]

Finally, Peter Hogg argues that *all* of CA 1871 is still in effect. Hogg notes that the BNA 1871 (CA 1871) was neither repealed nor amended and by renaming it in the Schedule to the CA 1982 (section 53), the Act is now entrenched in and so a part of the Constitution of Canada. It is, he maintains, still legally in force and as such its provisions "can still be operated without any change in the Constitution of Canada."[30] Section 42(1) refers to amendments to the Constitution of Canada, so changing the provisions of CA 1871 would constitute an amendment, but employing the provisions would not. Therefore, "it is probably wrong to treat these paragraphs (for example, CA 1982, section 42(1)(e) and (f)) as requiring the seven-fifty formula for the extension of existing provinces or the establishment of new provinces."[31] As for the "notwithstanding" proviso in clause (f), Hogg considers it "obscure."[32] However, Hogg does not refer to the amalgamation of provinces and under the terms of CA 1871 "new provinces" quite explicitly mean provinces created out of territories. But if we follow McConnell's analysis, amalgamation of provinces is authorized under CA 1871, section 3, not section 2, so the question of territories is irrelevant.

Charlottetown Accord 1992

Another approach to understanding whether CA 1871 is still in effect is to examine the interpretation of this Act by the framers of the Charlottetown Accord. The Charlottetown Accord was a failed attempt to gain public approval through a national referendum of a comprehensive set of amendments of the Constitution of Canada meant to address the problems with the previous failed attempt to so amend, known as the Meech Lake Accord.[33] A conference was convened and tasked with coming up with a proposal. Two "final documents" were produced: one was the text with explanation of the proposed amendments (the "Consensus Report"), the other the "Legal Text" of these same amendments. Oddly, they are not the same. Nevertheless, both deal in part with the CA 1871. However, the Consensus Report implied that the CA 1871 should be reinstated (and so assumed it was not operative), while the Legal Text seems to conclude that the CA 1871 was still in effect and just needed to be amended to accomplish the goal of the Consensus Report. It seems that while the authors of the Consensus Report did not believe or did not know that the CA 1871 was still operative, the legal drafters did. Once it was referred to them, corrections were made. Compare the two versions.

Section 58 of the Consensus Report:

Establishment of New Provinces

The current provisions of the amending formula governing the creation of new provinces should be rescinded. They should be replaced by the pre-1982 provisions allowing the creation of new provinces through an Act of Parliament, following consultation with all of the existing provinces at a First Ministers' Conference. New provinces should not have a role in the amending formula without the unanimous consent of all the provinces and the federal government. Territories that become provinces could not lose Senators or members of the House of Commons.

The provision now contained in Section 42(1)(e) of the Constitution Act, 1982 with respect with the extension of provincial boundaries into the Territories should be repealed and replaced by the Constitution Act, 1871, modified in order to require the consent of the Territories.

The Legal Text notes that the proposed amendments would affect the CA 1867, CA 1871, the Alberta Act, and the CA 1982. It contains a section (21) titled "Constitution Act, 1871" and provides for the amendment of both sections 2 and 3 of that Act. Section 2 is amended to include "at the request of the territory," but also that a new province so created under this section would require a

First Ministers Conference "take into account the views of the provinces."[34] The text of section 3 was to remain as it was, but renamed section 3(1) and a new subsection added:

> (2) The Parliament of Canada may not, pursuant to subsection (1), alter the limits of any territory forming for the time being part of the Dominion of Canada, except with the consent of the legislative authority of the territory.

The Legal Text did not provide for a repeal of CA 1982, section 42(1)(e) as recommended by the Consensus Document because it did not need to. Nor did it prepare for the reinstatement of CA 1871, because it did not need to do that either. CA 1871 is, at least according to the drafters, still operative and needed only tweaking.

Where does that leave us with regard to the Maritimes? In a nutshell, there is no evidence that these sections of the Constitution anticipated the union of provinces. Rather, they were concerned with the conversion of the territories into provinces and the impact that adding new, additional provinces would have on the federation. Nevertheless, if McConnell is correct that CA 1871, section 3 allows for the "amalgamation" of provinces solely with the consent of those provinces and the Parliament of Canada, it is quite possible that this would be at least in the initial stages constitutionally sufficient. Union in principle would not require unanimous consent nor the General Formula, nor could other provinces block such a union. However, there would still be consequences for other parts of the Constitution were the Maritimes to unite. These consequences would also require or would at least make desirable other amendments, under which the other provinces would have a stake.

I still have yet to answer the question of whether the union of the Maritime provinces actually creates a new province, in the constitutional sense of these provisions. Clearly, these provisions — explicitly in CA 1871 and implicitly in CA 1982, section 42 — are concerned with converting territories to provinces. CA 1982, section 42 may even be thinking back to Newfoundland's admission into Confederation and wondering if such an event with another island might still happen in the future.[35] The key seems to be what the phrase "any alteration" means and how courts would interpret it. I am not aware of, nor could I find, legal commentary on the Constitution's use of the word "alteration." Scholars who have studied the amending formulae do not focus their attention on this wording and assume it means that a boundary between two provinces would be adjusted, so moved one direction or another. Therefore, I am unsure what a court would do if the Maritime provinces attempted to use this section of the Constitution to erase their borders.

Possibly, a court would consider what *Black's Law Dictionary* says about alteration as a "change of a thing from one form or state to another; making a thing different from what is was *without destroying its identity*."[36] Or, similarly, they could consider what a United States court ruled when it said that to alter something is "to cause to become different in some particular characteristic . . . without changing into something else."[37] So it is possible that a court would thus consider the erasure of a boundary as going beyond alteration, and so not coming under this provision. On the other hand, section 43(1)(a) says *any* alteration, which could mean even trivial changes or, at the other extreme, complete changes, such as erasure.

In any case, if it is true that an alteration means a change but not so drastic that something new is in its place, could one not argue that the unification of the three Maritime provinces, with their provincial constitutions now melded but historically still in place, means that a united Maritimes was not a new province but merely an altered one? Would that not mean that the approval of the three provinces together with Parliament would be constitutionally sufficient to at least form a united Maritime province in principle?

CHAPTER EIGHT

Section 45

Who will seriously say that the legislature of the beautiful province of Prince Edward Island, with its thirty members consisting of fifteen Councillors and fifteen Assemblymen, is a Parliament in the same sense as the Dominion Parliament which is now managing war affairs in the nine provinces, and the great Parliament of the United Kingdom, whose long arm reaches the mighty Empire on which the sun never sets.

Arthur Beauchesne (1944)[1]

The brevity of *Constitution Act, 1982* (CA 1982), section 45, belies the underlying complexity of this amending formula. The section reads, simply, "Subject to section 41, the legislature of each province may exclusively make laws amending the constitution of the province." The first thing to note is that this section refers to the "legislature," not the Legislative Assembly. The other amending formulae involving the provinces all refer to the Legislative Assembly of the province (similarly, section 44 refers to Parliament, not the Senate and House of Commons). Connected to this is the fact that no specific procedure is specified, while in the other formulae (save section 44) the assemblies are required to pass "resolutions" followed by a "proclamation issued by the Governor General under the Great Seal of Canada."

This may be because both sections 44 and 45 are in effect the replacements for *British North America Act, 1867* (BNA 1867), sections 91(1) and 92(1), and such was the procedure recognized under those sections. Nevertheless, some scholars consider the difference significant. By specifying the "legislature" and not a "resolution of the legislative assembly," etc., an amendment to a provincial constitution can take the form of a bill rather than a resolution, and as such need not declare itself as an attempt to amend the provincial constitution.[2] As Erin Crandall points out, provincial legislatures may not be even aware that their legislation is a constitutional amendment to a provincial constitution. But this is all moot, as an amendment attempting to unify provinces would be obviously a constitutional amendment and could hardly be accomplished, to use Crandall's clever analogy, "by stealth."

Another interesting point to consider is whether an amendment to a provincial constitution made under CA 1982, section 45, and as such a product of ordinary provincial legislation, would be subject to disallowance as provided by CA 1867, section 90. Probably not. As the Supreme Court said (and seemed to concur) in the *Reference Re Quebec Secession of Quebec* case, the federal power of disallowance as provided by CA 1867, section 90, is considered by "many"[3] as having been abandoned. In any case, this is not likely to be an issue with Maritime Union.[4]

Regardless of all this, a bigger question remains: What is a provincial constitution? As we will see below, in 1887 when the Maritime provinces were asked by the House of Commons for copies of their constitutions, they reported that no such document or documents existed. In 1992, Nelson Wiseman made a similar request, this time to the attorneys general of all the provinces, asking them "what documents their departments/ministries considered to be part of their provincial constitutions." But he had no better luck. The attorneys general, Wiseman reported, "were not sure where their provincial constitutions began and ended."[5]

But this is not to say that provincial constitutions do not exist; it is just that their full and complete form is not precisely known. We know many things that are included in the definition of a provincial constitution, but the list is not exhaustive. Stephen Scott provides a succinct definition, but qualifies it: "roughly speaking," he writes, the constitution of a province "is the body of law governing the provinces' executive and legislative institutions."[6] Erin Crandall's definition is a bit more inclusive albeit no more specific as to where the constitutions begin and end. She writes: "Provincial constitutions are found in multiple sources, including portions of the Constitution of Canada, ordinary provincial legislation, common law, and the unwritten constitutional conventions typical of Westminster-style governing."[7]

In *Ontario (Attorney General) v OPSEU*, the Supreme Court defined an amendment to a provincial constitution as an enactment bearing on

> operation of an organ of the government of the province, provided it is not otherwise entrenched as being indivisibly related to the implementation of the federal principle or to a fundamental term or condition of the union, and provided of course it is not explicitly or implicitly excepted from the amending power bestowed upon the province by s. 92(1), such as the office of Lieutenant-Governor and, presumably and *a fortiori*, the office of the Queen who is represented by the Lieutenant-Governor.[8]

Note that the Court was referring, not to CA 1982, section 45, but to the BNA 1867, section 92(1).[9] That section read: "The Amendment from Time to Time, notwithstanding anything in this Act, of the Constitution of the Province, except as regards the Office of Lieutenant Governor." Section 92(1) was repealed by the CA 1982.[10] Section 45 replaces the first part, while restriction on amending the office of the Lieutenant Governor is now found in section 41. Hogg considers the following to be amendments within the competence of a province acting unilaterally:

- abolition of a province's upper house
- the public service of a province
- the powers and privileges of the legislative assembly
- the term of the legislative assembly.[11]

An odd, but nevertheless useful debate took place in the 1940s with regard to just what amending power provinces had. In the introduction to Beauchesne's third edition of *Parliamentary Rules and Forms*, he argued that the provincial legislatures were not "parliaments" as defined by the Canadian Constitution. The significance of this distinction, according to Beauchesne, was twofold: first, the power of disallowance over provincial legislation granted to the Parliament of Canada under (then) BNA 1867 sections 56 and 90, was neither moribund nor spent; and second, that the unilateral right of a province to amend its own constitution was quite limited. In fact, Beauchesne questioned whether provinces even had a constitution in the formal sense of that word. The use of the term "legislatures" in the BNA Act 1867 was meant, argued Beauchesne, to affirm the "inferior" position of the provinces vis-à-vis the Parliament of Canada.

Beauchesne's arguments were refuted by Louis Pigeon, who would become a Supreme Court of Canada justice but at the time (1943) was a law professor at Laval University.[12] Pigeon pointed out that in *Hodge v The Queen*[13] the Judicial Committee of the Privy Council made it clear that provincial legislatures are not subordinate to the Parliament of Canada and within their constitutionally-defined powers are sovereign assemblies. But Beauchesne was not convinced, and his response was published a few months later. Here he argued — somewhat speciously — that the scope of powers and duties carried by the Parliament of Canada were so much more significant than those of the provinces, and therefore the provincial legislatures could hardly be seen as equal in any sphere.[14]

Beauchesne's arguments were convoluted and even contradictory. He argued that court decisions that upheld the autonomy of provincial constitutions were in error; those that limited provincial autonomy were authoritative. The constitutional power of the Parliament of Canada to disallow provincial legislation was real and not bound by convention; however, the similar power of the Parliament of the United Kingdom to do the same had existed only in theory as convention dictated otherwise, a convention now codified in the Statute of Westminster.

Remarkably, Beauchesne claimed that the Statute of Westminster did not just assert the independence of the Dominions from the UK Parliament; it also *removed* any rights provinces previously held with regard to their own constitutions. Beauchesne referred to a case in 1892, in which a "Mr. Thomas" was found in contempt of the Nova Scotia Legislative Assembly and imprisoned for forty-eight hours. In 1896, the Judicial Committee of the Privy Council (JCPC) ruled on the appeal of this decision, finding that the Nova Scotia Assembly did indeed have such power as this ancient feature of *lex et conseutudo parliamentari* was possessed by the Assembly through its original constitution and that constitution was carried forward with Confederation as per the BNA 1867, section 88. As well, the JCPC ruled that the *Colonial Laws Validity Act* (1865)[15] gave the Nova Scotia legislature "the power to prevent and punish obstruction to its legislative business."

This was all, wrote Beauchesne "hard to understand" because Nova Scotia had no [formal] constitution; its Lieutenant Governor had reported to the Parliament of Canada as such in 1882 [actually 1887].[16] Therefore, there was no constitution to survive Confederation and any constitutional powers Nova Scotia had, began and ended with those provided by the BNA Act 1867. Furthermore, Nova Scotia could not now rely on the powers provided to them by the *Colonial Laws Validity Act* because, by virtue of sections 2 and 6 of the Statute of Westminster (1931), the *Colonial Laws Validity Act* no longer applied. "It seems therefore that, if the legislature had any such powers it has lost them by the passage of the Statute of Westminster. It is in a worse position than it was."[17]

This is, to say the least, an odd reading of the *Colonial Laws Validity Act* because that Act was meant to place (or clarify) limits on the autonomy of colonial legislatures. While the colonial legislatures had significant autonomy under the Act, nevertheless they could not pass legislation repugnant to "a [U.K.] statute extending to the colony." But the Statute of Westminster released the provinces and the Parliament of Canada from those limits; it did not remove any rights the provinces once held.[18]

Although Beauchesne overstates his arguments and reaches extreme and dubious conclusions, he does make some valid points. First, the unilateral right of a province to amend its own constitution is limited to those powers the province has been assigned by the BNA 1867. In other words, a province cannot amend itself to being more than it is, a restriction some premiers in other Canadian provinces might want to carefully consider. A province does not have the unilateral right to amend CA 1867, section 92. Another restriction is the fact that a province cannot legislate extraterritorially, so its amendments cannot impede the constitutional authority of another province.[19]

What then can a province constitutionally amend, unilaterally? Apparently, a lot. Bayard Reesor's *The Canadian Constitution in Historical Perspective* claims that there have been "many amendments to provincial constitutions over the years."[20] This is no doubt true, but it is not easy to determine just what sort of changes were amendments to a provincial constitution or were instead examples of ordinary restructuring. Possibly, they were both. As Erin Crandall explains, some of these "restructuring" changes are in fact constitutional amendments but are "amendments by stealth." Either provincial governments making such changes do not realize these actually are constitutional amendments, or the province hopes to avoid public and opposition scrutiny which might overly complicate the matter or sink the initiative.

An example of an amendment to a provincial constitution (which may or may not be seen as a stealth amendment) is Prince Edward Island's sometime amendments to its *Executive Council Act*. Under this Act, the Executive Council (Cabinet) is limited to the premier and no more than eleven members. The minimum number is seven.

However, the upper limit was not always eleven. Frank MacKinnon writes in *The Government of Prince Edward Island* (1951) that "The executive has consisted of nine members since 1784, and this number, which was originally specified in the instructions to colonial governors and later maintained by custom, is now provided by statute."[21] The instructions MacKinnon refers to are the 1769 Royal Instructions to Lieutenant Governor Patterson. MacKinnon states that this instruction to the colonial governors remains a part of Prince Edward Island's provincial constitution. However, that statute has been revised and now reads:

> There shall be an Executive Council of the province consisting of the Premier, who may be President of the Executive Council, and not less than seven or more than eleven other persons appointed by the Lieutenant Governor on the advice of the Premier.[22]

The revision was completed unilaterally and under the authority granted to provinces to amend their own constitutions; in this case, BNA 1867, section 92(1).

Another example, albeit a hypothetical one, would be the ability of a province to change its electoral system. Over the years some provinces, British Columbia and Prince Edward Island being the most noteworthy examples, have held plebiscites on electoral reform. In the case of Prince Edward Island, three such votes have been held: one in 2005, another in 2016, and finally one conducted in concert with a provincial election in 2019. While the 2005 and 2019 plebiscites rejected electoral reform, the 2016 vote — using a preferential ballot with five different choices — resulted in the Mixed-Member-Proportional-Representation (MMPR)[23] option winning out. In the end, the Liberal government declined to accept the results, citing the poor voter turnout (just over 36%) but promising to hold another in conjunction with the next election. The 2019 plebiscite, now called a referendum, simply asked whether the results of the 2016 vote should be accepted or rejected. Islanders chose to reject.[24]

The results could have easily gone the other way and so Prince Edward Island would have taken steps to change its electoral system from the Single Member, Simple Plurality system (First-Past-the-Post) to an MMPR system. Under the CA 1982, section 45, the province would have the unilateral right to make this change. Yet still, there would be some restrictions, the most important being the principle of Responsible Government. That constitutional principle would nevertheless need to be respected. As the *OPSEU* decision explained:

> The fact that a province can validly give legislative effect to a prerequisite condition of responsible government does not necessarily mean it can do anything it pleases with the principle of responsible government itself. The power of constitutional amendment given to the provinces by s. 92(1) does not necessarily comprise the power to bring about a profound constitutional upheaval by the introduction of political institutions foreign to and incompatible with the Canadian system.[25]

Therefore, the province would not be able to, for example, change the legislative system to one consisting only of hereditary peers or one in which an executive governed without an elected assembly and relied entirely on polling data for its policy decisions.

Would a province have the right to merge its legislative assemblies with those of the other provinces, as would be required by a union of the three provinces? I would argue that they could, as long as the democratic and representative functions of the old provinces were preserved in the new.

Another example that might help our understanding of what scope amending a provincial constitution entails is the successful, albeit protracted, efforts of the Maritime provinces in early years after Confederation to abolish their Legislative Councils. This was perhaps the most significant amendment to provincial constitutions that has taken place.[26] New Brunswick abolished its Legislative Council in 1891; Nova Scotia in 1928. Prince Edward Island, as usual, took a different route. Although it technically did abolish its Legislative Council in 1893 (and, for that matter, its Legislative Assembly), its new legislature was in fact a merger of the two chambers.

The constitutional authority to abolish or significantly alter the provincial upper assemblies was found in BNA 1867, section 92(1), which we have seen is now primarily replaced with CA 1982, section 45. By abolishing their upper chambers, these provinces made substantial changes to the way in which their legislative systems operated. No longer would legislation be subject to the will of two chambers; now it would require the consent of just one. Yet, their new constitutional framework was still similar enough in principle to that of the United Kingdom to be acceptable, no doubt in part because they remained within the federal system which over all — *pace* Dicey[27] — was itself similar in principle to that of the United Kingdom, as per the preamble of the BNA 1867.

In each province, the process took several years, decades even in the case of Nova Scotia. In New Brunswick, several political strategies were employed before one finally worked. In Nova Scotia, the question of whether the province even had the constitutional authority to abolish its Legislative Council was appealed all the way to the Judicial Committee of the Privy Council.[28] From a strict constitutional stance (and frankly, to stretch a point), it wasn't until 1996 that it could be said that Prince Edward Island no longer had legislative councillors.[29] Since New Brunswick was first off the mark, we can begin with that province.

New Brunswick

New Brunswick formally abolished its Legislative Council in 1891 (effective 1892). The premier at the time was Andrew Blair (1883–1896) and he campaigned on a promise to abolish the upper chamber. Blair maintained that Confederation rendered the Legislative Council a frivolous expense: the need for an upper chamber of oversight was now provided by the Parliament of Canada. Furthermore, responsible government was more effective when the executive was accountable to just one assembly.[30]

Recognizing the difficulty of convincing the Council to agree to its own abolishment, Blair was originally content to allow attrition through deaths and resignations to do the job for him. He would simply ensure their replacements were councillors who would support his agenda. But, as Blair complained, his appointees seemed to develop "an alarming independence" once they took their seats. When Blair did get the vote he wanted, the council agreed only on the condition that they be allowed to continue until the next election. "An Act Relating to the Legislative Council" was passed 16 April 1891 containing the provision that:

> This Act shall not come into operation until after the closing of the first Session of the Legislature which shall be holden in the year of our Lord one thousand eight hundred and ninety four [1894], or until the present House of Assembly ceases to exist by dissolution, when this Act shall then have full force and effect.

Blair dissolved the legislature soon after and a provincial election was held in October 1892. Going to the polls early almost cost Blair. He lost his own seat and was forced to run in a by-election in Queens County, courtesy of one of the sitting members, Thomas Hetherington, who resigned to allow Blair to run.[31]

Prince Edward Island

Prince Edward Island abolished its Legislative Council in 1893, twenty years after joining the Dominion in 1873. As was the case in New Brunswick, the question immediately arose after Prince Edward Island joined as to whether the Island still needed two assemblies. A resolution calling on the abolition of the council was put forth the very next year, in 1874.[32] The argument in favour of abolishing the council was similar to that made in New Brunswick but on the Island it focused more on the fact that the Canadian Senate ostensibly represented regions and had a hefty (at the time) property qualification for membership.[33] Furthermore, Parliament had a constitutional power of disallowance. Therefore, Prince Edward Island could count on Parliament and particularly the Senate to protect property owners and their interests, obviously still a pressing concern.[34] In any case, the existing Prince Edward Island Legislative Council had failed in its obligations to do just that, or such was the criticism levelled by some property owners. Colin Grittner quotes the editor of the *Charlottetown Presbyterian and Evangelical Protestant Union* who was writing in 1878: "These Councillors were put in by the property-holders to look specially after their rights of property, and guard against hasty, oppressive or unjust legislation." However, "Every one of them [. . .] grossly violated the sacred trust reposed in them by carelessly and hastily piling on the agony upon the wronged country."[35] Their grievous offence, apparently, was passing legislation allowing for "a poll tax and a real property tax."[36]

Over the years, the debate on whether to keep, reform, or abolish the Legislative Council persisted. In 1879, the Sullivan government made a valiant effort to abolish the upper chamber but the Council, not surprisingly, refused to pass the legislation providing for its own demise. Apparently, however, the Council realized that the writing was on the wall, and what followed were several attempts by the Council at finding compromising reforms that would appease the Assembly. Finally, in 1892 an agreement was reached: both houses would be abolished, and a new legislature would be created in its stead. The Lieutenant Governor, Jedediah Slason Carvell, was unsure of the constitutionality of the move and so requested that the Governor General review the legislation. However, the legislation was deemed to fall within the power of a province to amend its own constitution. A slightly revised version of the Act was passed the next year and given royal assent 20 April 1893. This Act formally abolished the old bicameral legislature and created a new one, in which one half of the members would be elected by the old property franchise of the Council, and the other half by the electorate of the old Assembly.[37] Note that although the means of uniting the two chambers involved formally abolishing each and creating a new assembly, the assumption was that the constitution was retained and continuity preserved.

Prince Edward Island's Legislative Council had been elected since 1862, well before the Island joined the Dominion. When the new legislature was created, its members retained their titles of assemblyman and councillor. They also retained, in modified form, the different qualifications for electing such positions. The Assembly was elected by what was at the time the most widespread franchise in the British Empire. However, a modest property qualification was required to vote for the Council. Furthermore, the property qualification allowed voters to cast ballots in any district in which they owned property. They could only cast one ballot per councillor, but they could cast as many as they were able; Island geography, state of the roads, and means of transportation being the only restrictions. If you could get to another poll in time, you could vote. There are plenty of stories of enterprising fishers offering quick transportation along the coast for anyone eligible to vote in another coastal riding or two. A "modest fee" was charged.

Nova Scotia

Nova Scotia was the last province of the Maritimes (and second last in Canada) to abolish its Legislative Council. It did so in 1928. However, this was after fifty-eight years of efforts to rid the province of what J. Murray Beck called a "travesty on democratic institutions." Every administration after 1878, Beck wrote, "at least professed sanctimonious hopes for its extinction."

> Curiously enough all of them possessed ample power to abolish the Council without their knowing it; it continued to exist simply because no one took the trouble to determine what its constitution actually was, or at least what the courts said it was.[38]

The constitutional authority upon which the Legislative Council existed was prerogative and expressed in Lord Durham's Commissions and Instructions (6 February 1838). Other amendments and embellishments provided by governors over time and subsequent to these instructions were also included. The Legislative Council of Nova Scotia was appointed, but no rules were in place regarding the length of tenure and so life appointments were assumed, although eventually appointments became for ten years. That was in 1924, and the reform of the council included measures to override the council's veto, except for measures relating to the council specifically such as abolishment. Like the other councils, the Legislative Council of Nova Scotia ceased to have any real prestige, or for that matter, any public profile: the real work of government took place in the Legislative Assembly and most regarded the Legislative Council as a "rubber stamp." But this did not stop the Council from periodically making its presence known and not always in a positive way. Various governments tried to ensure new councillors were in favour of abolishment, as Blair had done in New Brunswick. But as W.P.M. Kennedy wrote: "These members supported government measures, but developed scruples about their consent to their own destruction."[39] The council, wrote R. MacGregor Dawson, "displayed an unexpected — and quite unfounded — belief in its own excellence."[40]

By 1926, the Conservative government of Premier Edgar Nelson Rhodes focused its attention on finally ridding the province of the Council. Rhodes had won a landslide victory in 1925, but the Council was solidly Liberal. Rhodes began by trying to encourage councillors to retire by offering generous pensions. This offer was rejected, so Rhodes thought to increase the size of the Council — at that point fixed at twenty-one — and overload it with people (twenty in all) he was confident would support his plans for abolishment. However, this time the Governor General informed Lieutenant Governor James Cranswick Tory that such an expansion might well be beyond the constitutional competence of the province. Finally, a reference question was presented to the Nova Scotia Supreme Court:

(1) Has the Lieutenant-Governor of Nova Scotia, acting by and with advice of the Executive Council of Nova Scotia, power or authority to appoint in the name of the Crown by instrument under the Great Seal of the Province so many members of the Legislative Council of Nova Scotia that the total number of the members of such Council holding their offices or places as such

members would (a) exceed twenty-one or (b) exceed the total number of the members of said Council who their offices or places as such members at the Union mentioned in s. 88 the British North America Act;

(2) Is the membership of the Legislative Council of Nova Scotia limited in number?

(3) Is the tenure of office of members of the said Council appointed thereto prior to the 7th day of May, A.D. 1925, during pleasure or during good behaviour or for life?

(4) If such tenure is during pleasure is it during the pleasure of His Majesty the King, or during the pleasure of His Majesty represented in that behalf by the Lieutenant-Governor of Nova Scotia acting by and with the advice of the Executive Council of Nova Scotia?[41]

The Nova Scotia court did not arrive at an agreement and so the case was appealed to the JCPC. The JCPC held that, basically, the membership in the Legislative Council of any of the councillors who had been appointed solely on the prerogative of the Lieutenant Governor was therefore at the pleasure of the Lieutenant Governor (so basically all those appointed for life would fall under this category). Further, the Lieutenant Governor on the advice of the Executive Council had the right to increase the number of councillors as the Executive Council saw fit. So, under the convention of Responsible Government, the Legislative Council's very existence was in fact "entirely at the mercy of the Executive Council" (that is, Cabinet). Rhodes was thus able to have many of his opponents dismissed and supporters added. The reformed council then passed the Abolition Bill on 24 February 1928.

It is important to consider just how radical a change to the provincial constitution abolishing the legislative councils of these three provinces was, and by extension how broad the powers of a province are to amend its constitution. The JCPC's decision regarding the constitutional authority to take steps to abolish the upper chamber did not limit those steps to simply changing the Legislative

Council. It did not say that the Executive Council had to at least retain the structure of the Legislative Council. Amendment meant complete deletion. Certainly, the entire parliamentary system was not changed into, say, a republican form of government. But the abolishment of the legislative councils was a significant and profound structural change to representative government. The fundamental principle of responsible government was preserved, but the chamber of sober second thought and the vested interests the upper chamber change represented was gone.

Furthermore, this change meant that the Lieutenant Governor no longer had the power to appoint councillors, albeit on the advice of the Executive Council. There was no longer a legislative council to appoint. Would not such a fundamental change to the functions of the Lieutenant Governor constitute a change in the office of the Lieutenant Governor, a power not available to the province as per BNA 1867, section 92(1)?[42] It seems not. The Lieutenant Governor's relationship with the Executive Council and the Assembly remained the same, and as such its fundamental roles was unchanged. Merging legislative assemblies would result in the same situation. However, there would now be only one Lieutenant Governor and that may mean invoking CA 1982, Section 41, under which and amendment to "the office of the Queen, the Governor General and the Lieutenant Governor of a province" falls under the unanimity provision. That change requires some thought and will be dealt with next.

CHAPTER NINE

Section 41

The single most important new element in the situation was that the Supreme Court had abolished the rule of unanimity under which past constitutional conferences laboured and ultimately floundered. "The tyranny of unanimity" . . . could no longer paralyze future efforts.

Roy Romanow, 1982[1]

Despite Roy Romanow's optimistic prediction, it turned out that the "tyranny of unanimity" was not entirely abolished by the Supreme Court in the *Patriation Reference Case*,[2] or at least it re-emerged in Part V of the *Constitution Act* (CA 1982). The amending procedures found under section 41 stipulate that certain features of the Canadian Constitution are protected under this clause by requiring the unanimous consent of the legislative assemblies of all provinces as well as the Parliament of Canada. Specifically:

An amendment to the Constitution of Canada in relation to the following matters may be made by proclamation issued by the Governor General under the Great Seal of Canada only where authorized by resolutions of the Senate and House of Commons and of the legislative assembly of each province:

    (a) the office of the Queen, the Governor General and the Lieutenant Governor of a province;

(b) the right of a province to a number of members in the House of Commons not less than the number of Senators by which the province is entitled to be represented at the time this Part comes into force;

(c) subject to section 43, the use of the English or the French language;

(d) the composition of the Supreme Court of Canada; and

(e) an amendment to this Part.

Section 41(d) would not be affected by Maritime Union, so we can ignore that one. Section 41(c) refers to language rights at the federal level,[3] and is in any case subject to section 43, which in turn deals with those rights at the provincial level (section 43(b)). The latter — language rights at the provincial level — is applicable to Maritime Union; the former is not. Section 41(b) refers to the process for amending *Constitution Act* (CA 1867), section 51A, which ensures that a province has no fewer members of the House of Commons than it does Senators. While it is possible that Maritime Union would precipitate a call for an amendment to this section, it would not be required to do so. The configuration and distribution of seats in the unified province would require adjustment, but the principle could remain the same.[4]

The issue upon which section 41 has the greatest implications regarding the constitutional process of uniting the Maritimes is section 41(a): "the office of the Queen,[5] the Governor General, and the Lieutenant Governor of a province." The question is: would uniting the three provinces into one constitute an amendment to the office of the Lieutenant Governor, and therefore require the unanimous consent of all provinces together with the Parliament of Canada?

Lieutenant Governors are appointed by the Governor General (CA 1867, section 58) on the advice of the prime minister. Once appointed, Lieutenant Governors are subject to the parliamentary conventions of their province and thus they govern on the advice of the respective premiers. Lieutenant Governors hold their office at "the pleasure of the Governor General" but cannot be replaced "except for Cause assigned" before serving five years (CA 1867, section 59):

> A Lieutenant Governor shall hold Office during the Pleasure of the Governor General; but any Lieutenant Governor appointed after the Commencement of the First Session of the Parliament of Canada shall not be removeable within Five Years from his Appointment, except for Cause assigned, which shall be communicated to him in Writing within One Month after the Order for his Removal is made, and shall be communicated by Message to the Senate and to the House of Commons within One Week thereafter if the Parliament is then sitting, and if not then within One Week after the Commencement of the next Session of the Parliament.

The *British North America Act* (BNA 1867), section 92(1) provided provinces with the unilateral right to amend their own constitutions, except for the office of the Lieutenant Governor.[6] Commenting on this section, McConnell wrote: "The provinces were prohibited from enacting laws affecting or altering the office or powers of the lieutenant-governor."[7] And Stephen Scott, writing in 1966, argued that the BNA 1867, section 92(1) precludes "any provincial enactment interfering with the participation of the Crown — or such participation at least as is prescribed expressly or impliedly in the B.N.A Acts — in the legislative process: in particular, the royal assent to, and reservation of, bills, and (perhaps for partly different reasons) the disallowance of Acts."[8] The CA 1982 repealed this section ("Class 1") and replaced it with sections 41(a) and 45. "It is probably safe to conclude," writes Peter Hogg, "that the provincial power of amendment under s. 45 is essentially the same as it was under s. 92(1)."[9] Hogg's conclusion is supported by the Supreme Court in the *Senate Reference Case*.[10]

Erin Crandall writes:

> In the Senate Reference (2014), the Supreme Court was asked to clarify the powers of the federal and provincial legislatures to

unilaterally amend the Constitution of Canada and provincial constitutions via sections 44 and 45. The Court confirmed that these sections fulfill the same basic functions as sections 91(1) and 92(1) of the Constitution Act, 1867.[11]

So obviously the provinces cannot unilaterally amend the office of the Lieutenant Governor, nor can they avail themselves of section 43 (bilateral formula) or even section 38(1) (general formula).

However, would unifying the three provinces in fact constitute an amendment to the office of the Lieutenant Governor? It would certainly affect the person(s) holding the office, as instead of three Lieutenant Governors we would now have one. But is this the same as amending the office?

It comes down to clarifying what precisely the word "office" means in this provision. Note that both Scott and McConnell consider the word "office" to refer to the functions and so powers of the Lieutenant Governor. This is different than the *person* of the Lieutenant Governor. My assumption, then, is that the word "office" is meant to refer to both the power and the function of the position, but not the person in the position. In other words, the provinces do not have the unilateral right to amend the powers of the Lieutenant Governor, nor to reduce or augment those powers. Furthermore, the provinces cannot abolish or fundamentally change the position of Lieutenant Governor. For example, they cannot institute an election for the Lieutenant Governor or create qualifications for the position. Adam Dodek takes this one step further and wonders whether the word "office" is an even narrower term than "power" and so refers only to the "essential features" of the position. Based on the Supreme Court decisions regarding the *Supreme Court Act* and the Senate,[12] Dodek writes that:

> The language and the logic of these two decisions likely could be applied to other subjects in Part V. Thus, it is probable that, in interpreting "the Office of the Queen, the Governor General and the Lieutenant Governor of a province" under section 41(a), a court

would find that this provision protects only the "essential features" of each institution. Thus, the power of a province to amend its own constitution under section 45 should allow it to make changes to the office of the lieutenant-governor so long as it does not impair the "essential features" of the office.[13]

What are those "essential features"? Scott, as stated above, delineated them concisely: the royal assent to, and reservation of, bills, and the disallowance of Acts. To these we need to add the appointment and dismissal of premiers as well as the assembling, proroguing, and dissolution of legislative assemblies. Thus, preserving the essential features of the office of the Lieutenant Governor does not mean preserving all but a shell, but preserving that which is essential to the constitutional function of the office, as well as the office itself.

A union of the three Maritime provinces would mean that a single Lieutenant Governor would replace the three existing Lieutenant Governors. On the face of it, this would seem to affect the office of the Lieutenant Governor as the existing offices would be eliminated and the new office created but in a much larger province.[14] However, the totality of the constitutional powers held by the three Lieutenant Governors would not change; no constitutional powers would be added or subtracted. The *office*, then, would remain unchanged. Two, if not all three, individuals occupying those offices would no longer hold their positions. But there is no constitutional right to hold a position of Lieutenant Governor.

Under the terms found in CA 1867, section 59, two of the three Lieutenant Governors, or all three, could simply be removed by the Governor General — the "cause assigned"[15] being the unification of the three provinces — leaving one as Lieutenant Governor of a larger province, or assigning a new Lieutenant Governor. Or the dates could be calculated so that five years lapsed before the union took place.

Finally, Hogg points out that "s. 41 is confined to the 'Constitution of Canada', while s. 45 is not so confined." Therefore,

> It could be argued that a change in the office of the Lieutenant Governor that did not involve any change in the instruments that form part of the Constitution of Canada would not be caught by s. 4 and would accordingly be open to the province, either under s. 45 or under one of the other heads of provincial legislative power.[16]

Hogg does not provide examples of what such a change would look like. However, the question would be whether merging the three offices of the Lieutenant Governor constituted an amendment to the instruments, which include the Instructions to the Colonies. Given that the original Instructions assumed one province and that subsequently changes were made (and in the case of Cape Breton, unmade), I believe that an argument could be made along the same lines as that made with regard to the number of councillors in Nova Scotia's Legislative Council: that the Instructions were meant to be adapted to the circumstances of the time.

Part V of the CA 1867, "Provincial Constitutions" defines the role of the Lieutenant Governor. Section 58 states: "For each Province there shall be an Officer, styled the Lieutenant Governor, appointed by the Governor General in Council by Instrument under the Great Seal of Canada." Although the CA 1867, section 69 says that there shall be a Lieutenant Governor for Ontario and section 71 specifies that there shall be one for Quebec, the CA 1867 does not specify that there must be a specific Nova Scotia Lieutenant Governor or a New Brunswick or Prince Edward Island Lieutenant Governor.[17] A unified Maritime province would still have a Lieutenant Governor and therefore fulfill the requirement of section 58.

Whether a single Lieutenant Governor fulfilled the requirements of section 64 is another matter. That section, titled "Executive Government of Nova Scotia and New Brunswick," stipulates that "The Constitution of the Executive Authority in each of the Provinces of Nova Scotia and New Brunswick shall, subject to the Provisions of this Act, continue as it exists at the Union until altered under the Authority of this Act."[18] The question, then, is how much weight are we to give to the phrase "The Constitution of the Executive

Authority." This authority is deemed to continue to exist as it did at the Union "until altered under the Authority of this Act." If it means the powers and functions of the office, then I would argue that a unified office would still pass muster. If the provinces have the right to amend their constitutions by unifying, and that such a union does not affect the office of the Lieutenant Governors, then there should be no problem. However, if section 64 means that Nova Scotia and New Brunswick must have separate Lieutenant Governors unless amended by the unanimity formula of CA 1982, section 41, then Maritime Union will be a very difficult project to accomplish.

CHAPTER TEN

Language and the Constitution (Section 16)

The time has come to declare that there exist in New Brunswick not only individual rights but certain collective rights; to affirm that the Legislative Assembly is the protector of those rights; in particular, to make explicit in a declaration of the Legislative Assembly that there exist two official linguistic societies in New Brunswick, the English and the French; to impose a legal obligation on the provincial government to enhance the full development of each and ensure the equality of both. That is the purpose of this bill.

New Brunswick Minister Maurice Simard, on Bill 88 (1981)[1]

In the Supreme Court's decision in *Reference re Secession of Quebec*, the Court made an interesting statement. In pointing out the crucial role that Quebec plays in preserving and protecting French language and culture in Canada, the Court seemed to imply that only Quebec had the constitutional authority to do so, at least within the *Constitution Act, 1867* (CA 1867). While the Court acknowledged that with Confederation New Brunswick (and Nova Scotia) also "affirmed their will to protect their individual cultures," the Court did not see this protection as one of language. Furthermore, while New Brunswick and Nova Scotia affirmed their will to *protect* their culture, it was Quebec that was given constitutional powers to "*promote* their language and culture." The Court wrote:

The federal structure adopted at Confederation enabled French-speaking Canadians to form a numerical majority in the province of Quebec, and so exercise the considerable provincial powers conferred by the Constitution Act, 1867 in such a way as to promote their language and culture.[2]

The Court was not unaware of the presence of a substantial number of francophones (primarily Acadians) in New Brunswick or that *Constitution Act, 1982* (CA 1982), sections 16 to 20 now entrenched New Brunswick's status as a bilingual province. Rather, the Court was recognizing what constitutional powers were provided by the *British North America Act, 1987* (BNA 1867) concerning the protection and promotion of French language at the time of Confederation. In the case of Quebec, quite a bit; in New Brunswick, not very much.

The "considerable provincial powers" to promote the French language to which the Court was referring are found in section 93, "Legislation respecting Education."[3] This section ensures that provinces have full constitutional authority over education and, as well, protects the rights of "Denominational Schools." Since religious orders provided much of the educational services in the nineteenth and well into the twentieth centuries in Canada, denominational schools were not just institutions for preserving religion, but language and culture as well. These are in indeed "considerable provincial powers."

> As this Court [has] observed . . . the protection of minority religious education rights was a central consideration in the negotiations leading to Confederation. In the absence of such protection, it was felt that the minorities in what was then Canada East and Canada West would be submerged and assimilated.[4]

However, New Brunswick was not covered by this provision.[5] The key wording here, found in section 93(1), is: "Nothing in any such Law shall prejudicially affect any Right or Privilege with respect to Denominational Schools *which any Class of Persons have by Law in the Province at the Union*" (emphasis added). New Brunswick had "Denominational Schools" — almost all of which were Roman Catholic, although some were Anglican — and had such schools in 1867. But they were only tolerated; they were not protected by legislation. They did not exist in law at the time of union. Therefore, this section of the BNA 1867 did not apply.

The lack of explicit protection for francophone rights in New Brunswick in the BNA 1867 became an issue almost immediately after Confederation and continued to be an issue until the *Constitution Amendment, 1993* (New Brunswick) added section 16.1 to the CA 1982. It is not an exaggeration to say that had the BNA 1867 contained explicit protection for (and promotion of) francophone language and culture in New Brunswick, it is unlikely that the province's initial failure to ratify the Meech Lake Accord would have occurred.

New Brunswick's Linguistic Communities

The first European settlements in what is now the Maritime provinces were French-speaking, a people we collectively call the Acadians. Despite their expulsion by the British in the 1750s, the Acadians began returning shortly after in the 1760s, forced to do so surreptitiously. Not all were successful, and imprisonment followed by deportations continued. With the Treaty of Paris in 1763, such practices ended, but this did not mean the Acadians were able to return to their former homesteads: much of their valuable farmland — particularly in Nova Scotia's Annapolis Valley — was now occupied by New England Planters. Léon Thériault writes: "In general, Acadians who returned to the Maritimes avoided resettling their former land because it was now occupied by English colonists and because the British authorities preferred to have them scattered in small groups. . . . [I]n New Brunswick, they settled in the north, the east and the St. John River Valley."[6] So the Acadian returnees settled in the far peripheries of the three Maritime provinces as far from the centres of British power (Halifax, Saint John, and Charlottetown) as possible. By the end of the eighteenth century, the Acadian population in the Maritimes numbered more than 8,000.[7]

Acadian rights, specifically language and education, came about only after a protracted struggle. Although Nova Scotia boasts the first elected Legislative Assembly in what would become Canada, Acadians were not allowed to vote, the franchise being limited to non-Catholic Christian British males over the age of 21 years who owned property.[8] Over the years, Acadians did win their right to vote and stand for office,[9] but language rights were a more difficult achievement. As the Supreme Court said, the preservation and promotion of a people's language is inextricably connected to education and until the latter half of the twentieth century education in the Maritimes was in turn directly connected to religion; that is, education was a secular activity. Even with the advent of public schools, ostensibly non-secular but usually Protestant, education for Catholics in the Maritimes was through schools run by orders of the Roman Catholic Church. Catholics in the Maritimes were primarily descendants of Irish, Scottish and Acadian settlers, and so schools offering a French curriculum were also run by the Catholic Church.

On 17 May 1871, the New Brunswick government passed the *Common School Act*.[10] Ostensibly, the Act was designed to create a comprehensive public school system that would provide free education to all children, regardless of their "sex, religion, language or colour."[11] But the Act (section 60) also prohibited religious instruction in publicly-funded schools, meaning that Catholic schools could no longer function as such.[12] Under the older New Brunswick *Parish Schools Act* (1858),[13] Catholic schools had been accommodated but, as mentioned above, not established in law.

The advent of the *Common Schools Act* (1871)[14] divided the population of New Brunswick and violence ensued on the North Shore in protest against the Act.[15] John Costigan, the Member of Parliament for Victoria, and Timothy Anglin, the Member of Parliament for Gloucester — both Irish-Catholics — were successful in convincing fellow parliamentarians to pass a resolution requesting the Governor General exercise his powers of disallowance to veto the New Brunswick bill, although in fact the resolution was really designed to bring the Judicial Committee of the Privy Council (JCPC) into the picture: it was assumed, correctly, that the Governor General would immediately seek a ruling from the UK court. However, the JCPC declined to hear the case, pointing out that the BNA 1867, section 93 provided exclusive jurisdiction of education to the provinces and only protected "Denominational Schools which were established by 'Law in the Province at the Union' (95.1)." Incidentally, while John A. Macdonald said he was sympathetic to the Acadian cause, he did not consider the use of disallowance appropriate in this instance. The power, he said, should be used only for disallowing unconstitutional laws, not laws of which the government disapproves.[16]

New Brunswick did quickly figure out a new accommodation, what Hugh Thorburn calls an agreed-upon *modus vivendi*. Although the School Acts over the years consistently stated that "All schools to be non-sectarian,"[17] Catholic schools were allowed to operate as such (that is, receive funding) and to provide religious instruction (catechism classes) as long as such instruction was offered outside regular school hours. Those whose teaching qualifications came through a Catholic normal school could sit for the teaching licence examination.[18] This system would be in place until the 1970s when the major reforms brought in by the Equal Opportunities Program and the *Official Languages Act* were instituted.[19] Beginning in 1971 and continuing to 1985, schools and school boards were revised so that the province's education system was formally divided by language, not religion.

With the patriation of the Constitution in 1982, New Brunswick's status as an officially bilingual province was entrenched in CA 1982, section 16(2), which reads:

> English and French are the official languages of New Brunswick and have equality of status and equal rights and privileges as to their use in all institutions of the legislature and government of New Brunswick.[20]

The origin of this section was the legislation known popularly as Bill 88, passed by the New Brunswick government in 1981.[21] The PCs, under Richard Hatfield, were in power in 1981 and had been since 1970 but their electoral success was almost exclusively due to anglophone support. Without suggesting that Hatfield's motives were entirely political, he did understand that he needed support beyond his anglophone base in order to continue to be successful. Meanwhile, while overtures to the province's francophone population were paying off, his party had only modest gains to show for the efforts. In 1978, PC candidates did win five seats out of sixteen in northern New Brunswick,[22] but that election was very close: the PCs won thirty seats to the Liberals' twenty-eight. Soon after, the PCs introduced legislation extending rights to the "two official *linguistic communities* within New Brunswick whose values and heritages emanate from and are expressed through the two official languages of New Brunswick."[23] The Act also tasked the government of New Brunswick with ensuring that these two linguistic communities were treated equally:

> (2) The Government of New Brunswick shall ensure protection of the equality of status and the equal rights and privileges of the official linguistic communities and in particular their right to distinct institutions within which cultural, educational and social activities may be carried on.
>
> (3) The Government of New Brunswick shall, in its proposed laws, in the allocation of public resources and in its policies and programs, take positive actions to promote the cultural, economic, educational and social development of the official linguistic communities.

The importance of this Act to the Acadian community was that it established a right to services such as French schools that could not be mitigated by criteria such as declining population (such as "where numbers warrant"). This would help — or was meant to — protect the Acadian population from the assimilation cycle whereby as more francophones become assimilated, fewer services such as French schools were made available and so more francophones were assimilated. The Act gave power to the government to take action on behalf of "linguistic communities." These communities are not defined geographically; rather, they are defined by the language its members speak. Who, precisely, would have standing in order to force a government to fulfill its prescribed role of taking "positive actions to promote the cultural, economic, educational and social development" of the linguistic communities is not specified. However, at least one subsequent court case accepted the claim of the Société des Acadie du Nouveau-Brunswick's (SANB) to do so.[24]

The assumption was that, when the Constitution was patriated and the *Charter of Rights and Freedoms*[25] entrenched, Bill 88 would form a part of the language rights section (section 16). However, this did not happen, and instead (and frankly, more appropriately for a *Charter of Rights and Freedoms*), rights of individuals — not linguistic communities — to have their language protected by guaranteeing them the right to interact with their government in either French or English were entrenched (CA 1982, section 16.1).[26] While this was still seen by the francophone community as an advancement of individual language rights, many argued that it did not go far enough to protect culture.[27] Premier Hatfield responded to these concerns by establishing the *New Brunswick Task Force on Official Languages*, the results of which were presented in March 1982 and known as the Poirier-Bastarache Report.[28] Highly charged but in the end peaceful public hearings on that report followed.[29] Bernard Poirier was the Language Commissioner for New Brunswick. Michel Bastarache was at the time dean of the Université de Moncton law school but would go on to become a justice of the Supreme Court of Canada in 1997.[30] The Poirier-Bastarache Report called for the expansion of language rights in the province but also pointed out a structural problem with the New Brunswick education system. So-called bilingual schools — schools which accommodated both English and French language classes — were "assimilation factories." A typical "bilingual" school — which this author attended — would have grades from one to nine in English, paralleled with separate grades one to nine in French. There would be little interaction between the two streams except in the schoolyard or on sports teams. But during such interaction, English would dominate. Further, over time many French students would migrate over to the English side. There was little to no effort to encourage English students to speak French.

The Meech Lake negotiations might have provided an opportunity to include Bill 88 into a revised *Charter*, but Premier Hatfield refrained or failed to do so.[31] In the leadup to the 1987 election campaign, Liberal leader Frank McKenna promised to insist that Bill 88 be included in the revisions, or else he would not ratify the Accord if his party was elected (I discuss McKenna's strategy and fallout over Meech Lake, below). Although eventually agreeing to support the Accord, the McKenna government proposed a "Companion Resolution," which included recognition of the province's two linguistic communities. When that initiative failed, New Brunswick was successful in convincing the framers of the Charlottetown Accord to include such a provision.[32] When the Charlottetown Accord failed, New Brunswick then proceeded with a resolution to amend the CA 1982 under the bilateral formula, so CA 1982, section 43. This amendment initiative did succeed, with the final proclamation made 12 March 1993. With *Constitution Amendment, 1993 (New Brunswick)*,[33] section 16.1 was added to the CA 1982:[34]

English and French linguistic communities in New Brunswick

16.1 (1) The English linguistic community and the French linguistic community in New Brunswick have equality of status and equal rights and privileges, including the right to distinct educational institutions and such distinct cultural institutions as are necessary for the preservation and promotion of those communities.

(2) The role of the legislature and government of New Brunswick to preserve and promote the status, rights and privileges referred to in subsection (1) is affirmed.

Language rights are important in all three Maritime provinces and all three provide a measure of protecting those rights. However, language issues dominate the politics of New Brunswick.[35] Only New Brunswick has entrenched the rights, not just of citizens to access government services in either French or English, but through the CA 1982, section 16.1(1), the New Brunswick government is tasked with and empowered to preserve and protect the rights of the province's two linguistic communities, French and English. Any attempt to unify the three Maritime provinces would have to confront New Brunswick's unique set of constitutional guarantees for its francophone population. Given the long road New Brunswick's Acadians travelled to achieve the rights they have now, there is little chance they would be willing to see any of these rights diminished. On the other hand, the governments of Prince Edward Island and Nova Scotia, while both quite amenable to protecting francophone language and culture, might not be so willing to see language rights as extensive as those enjoyed by New Brunswick's francophones. Such guarantees as independent and separate school boards, French medical services[36] — controversial even in New Brunswick — and other services required may well be seen as too much a price to pay by the other two provinces.

However, if these political obstacles were overcome, then amending CA 1982, section 16.1 would require the use of the bilateral formula, with each province agreeing to change the name of the province referred to from New Brunswick to whatever new name the united province adopted. Or, Prince Edward Island and Nova Scotia could work to amend the CA 1982 to add their names to section 16.1. The likelihood of that happening is, of course, remote. But not impossible.

To recap, a unified Maritime province would have to amend CA 1982, sections 16–19 to remove references to New Brunswick. It would then have to decide whether these references would be replaced with the name of the new united province, and whether all of the subsections of sections 16 to 19 would be so retained or just some of them. Would, for example, the references to "linguistic communities" remain? Hypothetically, all references that identify New Brunswick could be removed, but for reasons explained above, this would not work politically. Regardless, once agreement was reached (if that was possible), the amendments could be made through the use of the bilateral formula, so CA 1982, section 43.[37]

CHAPTER ELEVEN

Other Amendments

I may say here that our case was always six and nothing but six; and any press reports that you may have that we were making claim or giving consideration to anything less are absolutely wrong.

Prince Edward Island premier J.A. Mathieson (1914)[1]

There are several other sections of the Constitution that would have to be seriously examined if the Maritime provinces were united. These are not sections of the Constitution that would require amendment, although that is a possibility (and for some, a very remote possibility). But these sections would be affected by Maritime Union, or Maritime Union would be affected by them. Some of these, particularly the two described next, would likely be deal breakers.

Constitution Act 1867, Section 51A: Provincial Guarantee of Seats

The *Constitution Act, 1867* (CA 1867), section 22 originally assigned seats in the Senate of Canada by region. When Nova Scotia, New Brunswick, and the Province of Canada joined in 1867, the Senate held seventy-two seats (*British North America Act, 1867* (BNA 1867, section 21),[2] with twenty-four allocated to each of the new provinces of Ontario and Quebec and twenty-four divided between Nova Scotia and New Brunswick. Section 147 stipulated that, upon Prince Edward Island's (obviously anticipated) entry into the union, it would receive four Senate seats but not in addition to the region's twenty-four. Rather, Prince Edward Island would receive its seats by attrition, so that in time New Brunswick and Nova Scotia would have ten Senate seats apiece, and Prince Edward Island four, so maintain the Maritime allotment of Senate seats at 24.[3]

When Prince Edward Island did join in 1873, the Terms of Union provided the province with six House of Commons seats, two for each of the Island's three counties: Kings, Queens, and Prince. The Terms of Union also pointed out that the population of Prince Edward Island had been increasing "by fifteen thousand or upwards since the year 1861," and so the representation of the province in the House of Commons would be adjusted as necessary under the provisions provided by the BNA 1867, section 51; that is, reapportionment based on the decennial census. Likely, the Island anticipated an increase in its Parliamentary representation as it grew. However, despite Prince Edward Island's steady increase in population, the overall population of the nation — particularly in the West — outpaced that of the Island. As a result, its portion of the Canadian population became smaller. Prince Edward Island's six House of Commons seats were reduced to five following the 1891 census, and then to four after the 1901 census. After the 1911 census, that number was reduced to just three. Different administrations did what they could to fix the number of seats on the Island, even taking their case to the Judicial Committee of the Privy Council (JCPC).[4] However, the courts ruled that the terms of Union and the BNA 1867 made it quite clear that representation in the House of Commons was to be based on "proportionate representation."

In 1914, Premier J.A. Mathieson met with Sir Robert Borden asking that Prince Edward Island's original allocation of six seats be restored. Borden offered a compromise: four seats, but with that number now fixed to the number of Senate seats.[5] That led to the 1915 amendment and the addition of section 51A:

> Notwithstanding anything in this Act a province shall always be entitled to a number of members in the House of Commons not less than the number of senators representing such province.[6]

The resulting amendment to the *British North America Act, 1915* (BNA 1915) was important for several reasons. Paul Gérin-Lajoie considered the BNA 1915 as "a landmark in the history of the process of requesting and securing amendments to the Constitution" as it provided the Parliament of the United Kingdom[7] with the full draft of the proposed legislation in the Address to the King, assuming that it would be passed without change, as it was.[8] The Act not only provided what is now known as the "Senate floor," or the minimum number of Members of Parliament (MPs) a province can have; it also increased the number of senators from seventy-two to ninety-six, provided the four "Western Provinces" with six senators apiece, and increased the number of Senate seats that could be added under BNA 1867, section 26 from three or six to four or eight. Finally, and significantly for our purposes, the BNA 1915 assigned senate seats specifically to provinces, not just the region, so that New Brunswick and Nova Scotia now each have ten and Prince Edward Island has four (the four Western provinces were allocated six seats apiece).

CA 1867, section 147 (see above) is now spent as it was meant to deal with an anticipated union, so no changes there would be required were the three Maritime provinces to unite. However, *Constitution Act, 1915* (CA 1915) might require revision since it allocates Senate seats by province and establishes a minimum number of House of Commons seats based on that allocation. If the three provinces no longer had a particular claim for Senate seats — that is, if the result of union was a return to the regional (now provincial) allocation, then the Senate floor would no longer apply to the old provinces. One way around this would be to define the old provincial territories as senatorial districts something like the district allocation of Senate seats in Quebec.[9] Possibly, however, the broader reading of both CA 1915 and CA 1867, section 51A would allow for an allocation of Senate seats (twenty-four) to the new province, and thereby create a new Senate floor of twenty-four House of Commons seats. Although ostensibly assigning senate seats to specific provinces, it is not clear that the purpose of the BNA 1915 was to fix such representation. In fact, David Smith points out that the 1915 Act instead "reiterated the constitutional logic of the Fathers of Confederation," by recognizing the importance of "senatorial regions"[10] (note that the Maritime region is now represented by twenty-five MPs: Nova Scotia has eleven, or one more than its Senate allocation of ten).

CA 1867, section 51A, then, might not require amendment as the principle would remain the same. Neither would there be any necessity of invoking an amendment under section 42(1)(c): "the number of members by which a province is entitled to be represented in the Senate." The new province would also still be guaranteed a minimum of twenty-four seats in the House of Commons.

Still, there would be practical considerations. With Prince Edward Island no longer a province, it could not claim the right to four House of Commons seats nor for that matter four specifically assigned Senate seats (unless the district model described above was used).

Seat allocation under the current reapportionment formula is outlined in Figure 11.1:[11] The allocation of seats according to the formula used by Elections Canada through the redistribution process is designed to ensure that regions of the country where the population is increasing will be able to gain new seats. While the total population of the three Maritime provinces is also increasing, the region has benefited from overrepresentation for many years, and so it will be a long time before it is regarded as a region requiring more seats.

If the rules that prevent provinces from losing seats were not in place and the allocation of seats by population was the only criteria, then the Maritime provinces would be allocated sixteen seats. This

FIGURE 11.1. THE REPRESENTATION FORMULA

Provincial population ÷ electoral quotient = initial provincial seat allocation
Applying the Senatorial Clause and Grandfather Clause
Applying the Representation Rule
Total provincial seats + One seat per territory = Total number of seats

Source: Elections Canada, "The Representation Formula," online: www.elections.ca/content.aspx?section=res&dir=cir/red/form&document=index&lang=e.

can be determined by dividing the estimate of the total population as of October 2021 (1,945,598)[12] by the electoral quotient (121,891) for the latest redistribution process. However, there is another provision regarding representation that would affect this allocation. This is CA 1867, section 51(1)(2), as amended by the *Representation Act, 1985*.[13] This latter amendment guarantees that no province's representation would drop below the number it had when this Act came into force (1986).[14] If the new Maritime province was then seen as inheriting the total number of seats guaranteed by this section to the three constituent provinces, then the number of seats to be allocated after union would be twenty-five. If, on the other hand, the fact that the united Maritime province is not able to claim the previous representation numbers, then the province would have twenty-four seats, as per the Senate floor rule.

Regardless, as a single province, the next redistribution process would have to adjust boundaries to provide for a minimum variance. Using twenty-four as the number (twenty-five does not make a huge difference in the calculation: it adds one seat to the Nova Scotia totals). If the seats in the Maritime province were to be redrawn to a minimum variance, then the population of each riding should be 81,067.[15] That would give Prince Edward Island two seats with a population each of 72,159 and a variance of +1 percent of the Maritime average. Under this formula, Nova Scotia would gain a seat (from eleven to twelve) and New Brunswick would remain at ten, on the assumption that the border between Nova Scotia and New Brunswick would be considered as a boundary separating "communities of interest"[16] (Prince Edward Island would obviously constitute its own community of interest). Even if the boundary between New Brunswick and Nova Scotia was ignored, then the remainder of the Maritime province (so excluding Prince Edward Island) would be allocated twenty-two seats. New Brunswick's seat allocation would remain the same and Nova Scotia would gain one, so those two provinces would likely be happy with the new arrangement. But reducing Prince Edward Island's seats from four to two would not sell well.

Nor would Prince Edward Island's four seats in the House of Commons be protected by CA 1982, section 41(b). To repeat, this is the section that stipulates that "the right of a province to a number of members in the House of Commons not less than the number of Senators by which the province is entitled to be represented at the time this Part comes into force," and it can only be changed through the unanimous formula. But by itself, this would not protect Prince Edward Island's four seats as Prince Edward Island would no longer be a province and hence would have no constitutional rights of its own. There is nothing in the current legislation or Constitution that would privilege Prince Edward Island — or any other sub-provincial a region within a united Maritime province — so that its seat allocation would remain the same. If it did, then Prince Edward Island's four seats, with a population of just under 40,000, would have a variance of almost -50 percent compared to the Maritimes as a whole (and -66 percent variance of the national average). It is difficult to imagine a scenario where this would be acceptable.

Neither is it conceivable that the principle of proportionate representation guaranteed by the CA 1867, section 52 would be amended in Prince Edward Island's favour. CA 1982, section 42(1) provides that any change to "the principle of proportionate representation of the provinces in the House of Commons prescribed by the Constitution of Canada" can only be made in accordance with the General Formula. However, it is not clear what precisely this principle as "prescribed by the Constitution of Canada" is and as Peter Hogg points out it "has never been applied rigidly." Hogg goes on to say that "in Campbell v Canada (1988), it was held that a provision to protect the representation of a declining province should not be regarded as offending 'the principle' of proportionate representation, and did not require a seven-fifty amendment under s. 42(1) (a)."[17] As such, even without the current guarantees of representation, a province like Prince Edward Island can still justify retaining its four seats under the current system, but as a region within a province like the united Maritimes, it would have no such claim.

Constitution Act 1982, Section 38: General Amendment Formula

The unification of the Maritime provinces would have a serious impact on the General Amendment procedure for amending the Constitution of Canada. That procedure is based on a mathematical formula and so the number of provinces matters. The formula is as follows:

38 (1) An amendment to the Constitution of Canada may be made by proclamation issued by the Governor General under the Great Seal of Canada where so authorized by

(a) resolutions of the Senate and House of Commons;

and

(b) resolutions of the legislative assemblies of at least two-thirds of the provinces that have, in the aggregate, according to the then latest general census, at least fifty per cent of the population of all the provinces.

The General Amendment formula is designed to ensure that no region of the country is without a veto for those amendments not covered by more specific formulae, such as the bilateral (section 43) or unanimity (section 41) formulae. In addition to resolutions from both houses of Parliament, resolutions from the legislative assemblies of "at least two-thirds of the provinces" whose aggregate population constitutes "at least fifty percent of the population of all the provinces."

Although this formula is popularly known as the 7/50 rule, the formula does not use a specific number (that is, seven) of provinces. Rather, it uses a fraction: two-thirds. Clearly there was anticipation that in the future Canada might not have ten provinces. This was likely because it was anticipated that someday one or all of the territories might achieve provincial status. Possibly, and given the time the CA 1982 was first developed, the framers also considered the possibility that Canada might someday consist of just nine provinces, were Quebec to separate.

The formula does two things. With ten provinces, two-thirds means seven provinces (6.66, etc.) are required for amendments covered by this section (which is most amendments), and given that the Atlantic region comprises four provinces, while the West broadly defined also comprises four provinces, it would be impossible to amend the Constitution with this formula unless at least one province in either region was on board. Obviously, only one in each region would not be sufficient, but if all provinces but the four Western provinces were in agreement, then there would only be six on side; the same is true of the Atlantic provinces.

All four Western and all four Atlantic provinces would total eight, which is more than enough to satisfy the two-thirds or seven provinces requirement. But the second requirement then comes into play, which is the population requirement: provinces representing 50 percent of the aggregate population of all ten provinces are required for agreement. For now, anyway, that means either Ontario or Quebec must agree as their combined population is more than 50 percent of the aggregate population of all ten provinces. There are other provisions that protect a province from an amendment that "derogates from the legislative powers, the proprietary rights or any other

rights or privileges of the legislature or government of a province"
(CA 1982, section 38(2)–(3)).

Back to the two-thirds, fifty-percent rule: as explained,
two-thirds of ten is six and two-thirds, which is rounded up to
seven as there is no such thing as two-thirds of a province (ignoring the inevitable jokes about Prince Edward Island). But a single
Maritime province would reduce the number of Canadian provinces by two, so there would now be eight provinces. Two-thirds
of eight is five and one third. Rounding up five and one-third to
six might seem less intuitive but the same principle applies: there's
no such thing as one-third of a province. Hence, with a single
Maritime province the seven/ten plus fifty percent (7/10 + 50%)
rule becomes six/eight plus fifty percent (6/8 + 50%) rule. Six provinces out of eight would mean that having at least one province
from Atlantic Canada would no longer be required for the General Formula: the four Western provinces plus Ontario and Quebec
would be capable of amending the Constitution without needing
the support of Newfoundland and Labrador or the new Maritime
province. Thus, the purpose of the regional veto formula would
be lost. The regional veto formula is not there by accident; it is an
essential feature of the Constitution, a protection of the federal
principle. The General amending formula could be itself amended,
but amending the amending formulae, that is any part of Part V,
falls under the unanimity formula, so section 41(e). Or the new
Maritime province could simply accept that Atlantic Canada no
longer enjoyed a veto. But that would be an astonishing concession
and would be proof that Maritime Union meant that the region
was giving up more than it was gaining.

Even if there was agreement to amend this formula, how would
it be amended? Is there even a way to amend the formula to restore
the Atlantic Canada veto? Could the amending formula, as is the
case under *An Act Respecting Constitutional Amendments*,[18] specify provinces rather than numbers of provinces? *An Act Respecting Constitutional Amendments*, which is still ordinary legislation despite its title,
pretends to prohibit "ministers of the Crown" (oddly, not identified

as specifically federal ministers)[19] from proposing amendments under CA 1982, section 38(1),

> unless the amendment has first been consented to by a majority of the provinces that includes (a) Ontario; (b) Quebec; (c) British Columbia; (d) two or more of the Atlantic provinces that have, according to the then latest general census, combined populations of at least fifty per cent of the population of all the Atlantic provinces; and (e) two or more of the Prairie provinces that have, according to the then latest general census, combined populations of at least fifty per cent of the population of all the Prairie provinces.[20]

The CA 1982, section 38(1)(b), then, might be amended to read,

> resolutions of the legislative assemblies of a majority of the provinces that includes (a) Ontario; (b) Quebec; (c) British Columbia; (d) one Atlantic province; and (e) one Prairie province.

Whether this would be palatable to the rest of the country is highly questionable. However, surely there are other configurations that would work. If the Maritimes had united prior to Confederation, then the negotiations that eventually led to the patriation of the Constitution would still have succeeded, and the amendment formulae the framers figured out would reflect this different provincial configuration. It cannot be the case that it is impossible to work out something. However, it would be very difficult, given how entrenched the regional veto model is in Canada's constitutional culture.

For and Against

Not in Our Lifetime

I have long argued for Maritime Union though I have come to accept that full political union will not become a reality, at least not in my lifetime.

Donald Savoie (2006)[1]

The arguments in favour of Maritime Union are compelling, at least to those who live outside the region. And Maritime Union has had passionate defenders from within the Maritimes. Why, then, with such seemingly compelling reasons has Maritime Union not been embraced? The constitutional barriers and difficulties that I have outlined would be obvious reasons; however, these have not been discussed or analyzed in any comprehensive way prior to this book, so fear of constitutional difficulties is not the reason why a concerted effort to unite the Maritimes has not occurred. Nor have there been Maritime Union initiatives ultimately thwarted by the difficulties of amending the Constitution, because there have been no Maritime Union initiatives in recent times, certainly none since the patriation of the Constitution.

Why not? One argument, which we have already seen, is that every advantage in policy harmonization or political influence that would occur with union — and critics maintain that these advantages would be small if they even exist — are offset by the perceived losses to provincial autonomy and identity. Maritime Union would mean giving up a lot for a little. To repeat Beck's point, "it is essential to demonstrate that substantial positive good is likely to result from Maritime Union before incurring the wastage through ill will and conflict that will inevitably follow any attempt to effect it."[2] This is a counterargument to Maritime Union that predates Confederation. P.B. Waite quotes the correspondent of the *"Toronto Leader"* who upon visiting the Maritimes in 1864, reported that "The people here are rather content to suffer the evils they bear than fly to others they know not of."[3] There is no guarantee that the Maritimes would actually be better off united and the fact that those outside the region consider three separate Maritime provinces as illogical is by itself not an argument.

Finally, critics maintain that efforts to ensure regional cooperation have been successful; they merely have yet to realize their full potential. This, of course, raises an important question: what are the impediments that have kept the potential for regional cooperation and indeed integration from being fully realized? Could it not be the simple fact that, regardless of good intentions, three provincial governments will invariably advance their own interests and that those interests rarely coincide with the interests of the other provinces?

There are basically three interlocking arguments used to support Maritime Union: increased political clout, improved economic performance, and more efficient services and institutions. I begin with political clout.

CHAPTER THIRTEEN

Political "Clout"

Is that gonna make us a "have" province? Nope. Is it gonna lessen our clout in Confederation? Yeah. If the Atlantic provinces merge, there's still gonna be oil in Alberta.

Prince Edward Island Premier Robert Ghiz (2012)[1]

The mere possession of political resources does not ensure success, for they must be exploited in various strategies and tactics.

Richard Simeon (1972)[2]

An oft-repeated argument in favour of Maritime Union is that a united Maritimes would have more "clout"; that is, the new province would be now of a significant size and economic importance that its leaders would have more influence in national affairs. This is an argument that has been made many times, even going back to Confederation and before. It was the dominant argument for union in the years leading up to the Maritime Rights Movement in the early years of the twentieth century. As the columnist who wrote under the pen name "Bluenose" claimed in 1908, "the three provinces of Nova Scotia, New Brunswick and Prince Edward Island would be today a far greater force in federal politics . . . were they united and fighting shoulder to shoulder for what they are justly entitled to as partners in the confederation."[3]

Interestingly, the same argument in reverse is often used to dismiss Maritime Union as a useful project. Even if a united Maritime province had more influence nationally, such national influence would be at the expense of whatever influence its constituent parts now hold on their own. With union, these former provinces would be nothing more than regions within the new larger province, and the leaders of the united Maritimes would not necessarily concern themselves with, for example, the "region" of Prince Edward Island. The Island would no longer have its own premier and so no longer have its own seat at the table at a First Ministers' conference. The Halifax powerbrokers would have little interest in advancing Prince Edward Island's issues, a problem that residents of Cape Breton would no doubt appreciate. Having a premier matters.[4] In the words of Prince Edward Island Member of Parliament (MP) Wayne Easter (1996):

> We do better as three separate political entities than one region, even if there is some overlap and duplication. When we compete with each other, in areas like tourism, that's healthy, and benefits us all. A unified province won't have all these projected efficiencies just because it's combined. You'll still have bureaucracy, with all its shortcomings. Also, you'd get more have-not areas: if the province were administered from Halifax, which would be the most likely capital, you'd see outlying areas with opportunities lessened, because they would lack influence with the bureaucracy or representation at the cabinet table.[5]

This, then, is one of the great dilemmas of Maritime Union. To argue that the new province would have more clout assumes that whatever largesse came from such improved influence would be evenly distributed. It's an argument Maritimers have heard before: Confederation promised to benefit all citizens and all regions. The Maritimes have since questioned that promise and have wondered what precisely "benefit" means.

A second and related concern is that even if a united Maritime province did have more clout, this new influence would likely be marginal. As Premier Ghiz said, Alberta would still have the oil. But the cost to identity and autonomy for Prince Edward Island or for that matter New Brunswick and maybe even Nova Scotia would be significant. Maritime Union would mean giving up a lot for a little.

What Is Political Clout?

Political clout is, in essence, a type of political power and defining political power is complicated as the concept delves into both political theory and human psychology. Joseph Nye, who has written extensively about political power, writes that "Power is a contested concept, and no one definition suits all purposes."[6] For example, some theorists see power in terms of coercion, so that power involves forcing someone to comply to your will, against theirs.[7] But power also includes influence and persuasion, such that those who comply may have been convinced that to do so is indeed in their interests. Sometimes this means that those who comply are deceived. But that is not the same as being forced to do something against your will. It is not, then, the case that power is always exercised in a hostile manner.

The multifaceted aspects of power are well explained by Nye, who distinguishes between hard, soft, and smart power. Initially, Nye used these concepts in his analysis of American foreign policy and how it would need to adapt to a rapidly changing world. He then applied them to power in general, whether that be the authority of a university president or the CEO of a corporation.[8] Hard power involves the use of the "carrot" or the "stick," usually in some combination. The carrot is the ability to influence behaviour (policies) through inducements such as foreign aid or favoured-nation status. The stick is the use of force, or the threat of such use, such as military action or a blockade or a trade embargo. For the CEO of a corporation, an example of hard power would be the ability to fire an employee or to give a promotion and a raise, or to threaten the first or promise the second. Soft power, however, is "the ability to obtain preferred outcomes through attraction."[9] Soft power might involve moral or charismatic leadership, or personal friendships and compatibility between leaders.[10] Smaller states (and smaller provinces) are more likely to rely on soft power. Finally, smart power is simply knowing which power to use and when; in other words, using power — either hard or soft — wisely.

When applied to intergovernmental relations, political clout is a type of "soft" power and is connected to the art and practice of diplomacy.[11] In international relations, clout refers to the ability of nation-states to influence the behaviour of others without the need for the use of force, while diplomacy is a tool that is used to so influence. The connection between clout and diplomacy is that the effectiveness of diplomacy depends upon the clout of the diplomat: clout is primarily reputational. Diplomacy is very effective when it is well understood that if the diplomatic endeavours of a nation fail, that nation will resort to force to get its way. As Carl Von Clausewitz famously wrote, "War is a mere continuation of policy [*politik*] by another means." He could very well have used the word "diplomacy" rather than "policy."[12]

When force is not an option then nations rely on a different form of diplomacy, one in which there is no underlying threat. This is something that Canadian leaders and diplomats have understood very well, or once did.[13] One Canadian leader who understood this better than most was Prime Minister Lester Pearson who spoke about the importance of not just having a voice that is heard, but one that impresses as well. Pearson meant to impress, not with a show of force, but with solid reasoning and a reputation for moral leadership. This is akin to what Joseph Nye calls smart power.

As long as we recognize some crucial differences when applied to intergovernmental relations in Canada, Nye's concepts can give us some insights into how provinces, with their wildly differing sizes and economic strengths, deal with each other and with the federal government.[14] Obviously, some of the tools available to nations — military force, for example — do not figure in interprovincial or federal-provincial relations.[15] But neither do such options figure in most if not all of Canada's international relations, particularly not with its allies.[16] In many ways, the Maritime provinces' ability to influence the federal government or other provinces is much like Canada's ability to influence the United States or other partners in the North Atlantic Treaty Organization (NATO) or the North American Free Trade Agreement (NAFTA), or other similar international organizations. Canada relies on a complex network of diplomatic and foreign policy endeavours. Depending on what party is in power, Canada positions itself as a nation that the world should want to do business with and does so with varying degrees of success and perseverance.[17] The same could be said about provincial diplomacy, particularly that practised by smaller provinces.

In Canada, political clout comes from the perceptions other provinces have of each other's economic and political positions in the federation. Some provinces are able to exercise hard power; others are not. An example of a province that is capable of exercising hard power in a Canadian intergovernmental context is Quebec. That province's periodic threat to separate from the rest of Canada is always taken seriously. Although Richard Simeon is quoting a federal minister in the 1960s, what was said then could easily be attributed to a minister today:

> Certainly Quebec has more weapons than the other provinces. The biggest weapon in Quebec is that it is the only province that could wreck Confederation. This is their main weapon. They can make the threat and be taken seriously. It is not possible for the other provinces to do that.[18]

What is interesting about this statement is that it is not true. Quebec is not the only province "that could wreck Confederation." The separation of other provinces such as Alberta would have an equally profound impact on Canada and is now just as realistic a possibility as Quebec separation is. In fact, I would go so far as to say that the loss of *any* province in Canada would be devastating to the federation. But this does not matter. What matters is that it has long been accepted that Quebec could and would separate from Canada if the situation demanded it, and that this would be disastrous for the rest of the country, perhaps for Quebec as well.[19]

Now, perhaps the federal minister misspoke or was misquoted. Perhaps what the minister meant to say was not that Quebec was the only province that could wreck Confederation but rather *would* go so far as to wreck Confederation.[20] Again, it doesn't matter whether Quebec would or could. What does matter is that Quebec has, by chance or design, convinced much of Canada — and in particular, the Canadian political leadership[21] — that it would separate if it did not receive the accommodations it demanded and this same leadership seems to believe the country could not survive were that to happen. As Simeon writes, referencing Robert Dahl, political influence is primarily subjective and depends "on the beliefs and perceptions of the participants."[22] It is that belief and perception of the real possibility of Quebec separation that gives Quebec such power.

Quebec, then, has hard power. And now, so does Alberta. In the case of Alberta, the power is not just in the threat of separation, but the economic power of the province and the resources that it possesses. Alberta still has the oil, and while oil might be a natural resource whose time of value is coming to an end, that end is not any time soon. Another arrow in Alberta's quiver, newly arrived, is its threat to withdraw from the Canada Pension Plan. While analysts are quick to point out that Alberta would be the loser in the end, none deny the fact that such a move — legally permissible under the *Canada Pension Plan Act*[23] — would harm the fund and thus hurt the rest of Canada.[24]

Now consider the possibility of Maritime separation. As we have seen, this was also a real, if somewhat remote, possibility in the years following Confederation.[25] However, it is inconceivable that the Maritimes would leave Canada. The economic harm to the region would be immense while the economic harm to the rest of Canada would be uncertain — perhaps greater than people realize, but the fact that they do not realize this is precisely the point. Maritime separation is not a credible threat because credible threats are those that are believed. The Maritimes, then, do not have hard power. Without hard power, the Maritimes must rely on soft power. Soft power for Maritime premiers almost always means cooperating and finding ways to get along with other provinces and the federal government, what is usually referred to as "collaborative federalism,"[26] although that covers only a part of the overall cooperative strategies.[27]

Can the Maritime premiers also use smart power? If, according to Nye, smart power is knowing how to balance hard with soft power, how can the Maritimes maximize their influence — their clout — when hard power is not an option? Or to put it another way, in the absence of hard power can the Maritimes use soft power smartly?

The first problem the Maritime provinces have in exercising any sort of political influence is that they are "have-not" provinces; that is, they receive significant transfer payments from the federal government. Equalization payments make up the lion's share of these payments and the three provinces receive the most per capita in the country. Overall, equalization grants account for 20% of the Maritime provinces' operating budgets, which is the highest percentage in the country.[28] The Maritime provinces, then, depend on equalization grants to operate. Indeed, that is the point of the payments. Without them, the Maritime provinces would have great difficulty providing the services their citizens require. As the Department of Finance web page explains:

> The purpose of Equalization is to ensure that provincial governments have sufficient revenues to provide reasonably comparable levels of public services at reasonably comparable levels of taxation. Total Equalization funding grows in line with a three-year moving average of nominal gross domestic product, and is allocated amongst provinces based on a formula set out in legislation. In 2023-24, the program will provide support to Manitoba, New Brunswick, Nova Scotia, Ontario, Prince Edward Island, and Quebec.[29]

Note that Ontario and Quebec, two provinces with considerable clout, also receive equalization payments and although the

Maritimes receive the most per capita, in actual dollars Ontario and Quebec receive almost two-and-a-half times the amount that the Maritimes do.[30] However, the population of these two provinces is twelve times that of the Maritimes, so this number hardly seems comparable. Neither Ontario or Quebec is regarded as being dependent on equalization grants, and while this might not be entirely true for Quebec, again it is the perception, not the reality that matters.

Why exactly such dependency affects clout is a complicated question. It is not because the federal government, let alone other provinces, is in a position to cut off these payments; that is, to use hard power to intimidate the Maritimes. Nor do the Maritime premiers spend time worrying that one day the federal government will turn off the tap. Instead, what equalization payments do is provide a perception of servility. The assumption is then made that Maritime strategy of cooperation is the product of their dependency. As Robert Finbow writes:

> Many analysts argue that Atlantic governments have adopted a docile attitude because of fiscal dependence on Ottawa. Their position as "supplicants" has allegedly affected the mentality and outlook of Atlantic politicians and citizens. For these analysts, the provinces have become "mere satrapies of the federal government insofar as federal-provincial relations are concerned."[31]

One of those analysts who sees the Maritimes as servile dependents is Richard Simeon, who Finbow quotes. Simeon argues that Maritime docility has contributed to their economic plight, and that the region lacks "the activist political orientations of British Columbians." Were Maritimers more politically confrontational, then "conflict between the Maritime provinces and Central Canada or the federal government would be much more intense, since Maritimers would be much less willing to accept their deprived lot."[32]

That Simeon believes the region's economic disparity stems from Maritimers being "willing to accept their deprived lot" is problematic, to say the least. It does carry an odour of blaming the victim. This is akin Stephen Harper's "culture of defeat" argument, voiced twenty-five years before Harper's famous "slight" of Atlantic Canada.[33] Commenting on Harper's remarks, Donald Savoie writes:

> Stephen Harper may well have hit a nerve in the Maritime provinces when he said that the region suffered from a "culture of defeat." But the observation may have resonated in other parts of the country as well, because such thinking absolves them of any responsibility for circumstances in the Maritimes. The implication is that the "have" regions gained their superior status by picking themselves up by their own bootstraps — so why can't the Maritime provinces do the same?[34]

There is another angle to Simeon's statement concerning Atlantic Canada's accepting their "deprived lot," and that is the assumption that the Maritimes (or Atlantic Canada) would have political influence, of a sort anyway, were they only to assert themselves more. In other words, political influence is there; it is just not being utilized.

What influence do the Maritime provinces have and how could they use it more effectively? Finbow explains that there is strong evidence that the Atlantic provinces are quite capable of asserting their own interests when necessary. During the protracted years of constitutional negotiations, the Atlantic provinces consistently supported policies that balanced provincial autonomy with the needs for a robust federal system.

> Despite differing views on how to achieve their own goals, the four provinces have been successful in resisting harmful reforms proposed by other provinces, balancing concessions on the division of powers exceptions for regional preferences, equalization and cost sharing.[35]

We need to first deconstruct the argument that the Maritime provinces — that is, their premiers — are docile when it comes to dealing with the federal government and that this is because they are dependent on federal largesse. Does this argument stand up to scrutiny? Is it reasonable to believe that they fear a federal government would cut off such transfers? Aside from the obvious, which is that equalization grants are guaranteed by the Constitution,[36] would a federal government ever be so vindictive? Do Maritime premiers really believe that their federal counterparts are vengeful?

Simeon's earlier work, *Federal-Provincial Diplomacy* (1972), painted a different picture than that depicted in his 1975 article, albeit one no less problematic. In fact, in *Federal-Provincial Diplomacy*, Simeon presents the Maritime provinces as wielding considerable influence over the federal government, simply because the federal government — regardless of which party is in power — genuinely cares about the welfare of the region:

> For the Maritimes the need is obvious, and, as we have seen, Ottawa is strongly committed to help alleviate the need. This gives the province a resource, as an Ontario official pointed out: "Who has most influence? For hot political reasons Quebec must be number one. Then come the Maritimes. Their position is so dire they just cannot be ignored."[37]

This argument, which would appear to contradict the "satrapies" characterization, is also problematic. It paints a picture of a region getting what it wants by brazenly appealing to sympathy. That is not a docile role; one can hardly be fearful and brazen at the same time. If true, it may be a form of influence, but it is hardly clout. There is nothing to use as a threat; there is nothing to withdraw.

Simeon's 1972 example is now quite dated, but so is the quotation from Winter above concerning "satrapies."[38] Both, in fact, were written around the same time, just when an initiative to unite the Maritimes came closest to succeeding (and, of course, well before equalization grants were entrenched in the Constitution). Both analyses of Maritime influence and dependency miss the mark. Returning to Simeon's point about the lack of "activist political orientations" in the Maritimes, why is it assumed that a conflictual relationship between the Maritimes and Central Canada or the federal government would be a good thing? If we stop trying to think of intergovernmental relations in Canada as competitions, and think instead of such relations as cooperative, then the historic strategy of the Maritime premiers makes sense. Canada may be a federation, but it is nonetheless a nation for that, and it is pure sophistry to try to pretend that individual provinces must always behave like separate nations, notwithstanding their own sometimes rhetoric. As Statistics Canada has shown over the years, every province except Quebec expresses a stronger sense of belonging to Canada than to their own province.[39]

Indeed, even the argument — perhaps especially — that Quebec or Alberta have hard power because their threats to separate are taken seriously needs deconstruction. It assumes that the Canadian federation is held hostage by those provinces that threaten to leave. This is not true. While the referenda on separation in Quebec, and in particular the 1995 election with its razor-thin defeat of the Yes side, did cause considerable concern across the country that Quebec might very well separate, it is not the case that separation dominates discussions of Quebec's position in Canada. Quebec's argument is essentially one of justice; it is a moral argument that says that in a federation a province like Quebec has particular needs and concerns that must be addressed, or else the moral foundation of the federation is undermined. This does not mean that every demand Quebec makes must be accommodated, any more than Alberta's attacks on federal environmental programs or its threat to withdraw from the Canada Pension Plan must be accepted at face value. But there is an obligation to consider the demands and to negotiate some sort of settlement. That's what federalism is: a compromise between what Samuel LaSelva calls universalism and particularism.[40] So why would accommodation of Maritime needs be seen as anything else than a just distribution of resources in a federal system? And why would efforts of Maritime premiers to work with rather than against the federal government be anything less than virtuous federal citizenship?

For the most part, the strategy of Maritime premiers has been this: work well with others so that they will work well with you.[41] In political philosophy, this would be considered an example of *prudentia*, and is precisely how Prime Minister Lester Pearson conducted

Canada's foreign policy: "Patience, strength, prudence, and vision are, then, four qualities which should guide our policies and our diplomacy," Pearson said in a 1954 speech.[42] In political philosophy, *prudentia* or prudence refers to pragmatism and balance. It means looking to the future and assessing the long-term consequences of one's actions. Smart power is certainly an example of *prudentia*, but any use of power and in particular soft power, which is tempered by an understanding that relationships will continue, and favours will be both required and requested, can be seen as *prudentia*. Maintaining good relations with the federal government is always a priority for the Maritime provinces. Perhaps nowhere is this more obvious than on Prince Edward Island. Canada's smallest province is profoundly aware of its precarity. As University of Prince Edward Island's Godfrey Baldacchino wrote in 2005, "An island is a nervous duality."[43] Prudence and pragmatism, not bluster or confrontation, have always been its strategy. Note that Prince Edward Island's motto is *parva sub ingenti*: the small under the protection of the great.

In a conversation I had with Premier Dennis King, he explained that his government spends a lot of time "surveying the political landscape," because it was very important that the province know what direction the federal government was going with regards to policies that affected Prince Edward Island. The province's ability to influence federal policy was limited. Worse, too often federal politicians would renege on promises made, not being worried that a backlash in a province with just four seats would be of concern. However, King said that the Island did have some methods that it could use to convince the federal government to accommodate Prince Edward Island. One way was to convince the federal government that Prince Edward Island, as a very small province, could implement federal-provincial programs much more easily and quickly. The Island can act as a test ground for new programs and, if successful, provide the federal government with a quick turnaround on its investment and a "win" it could point to.[44]

As far as inter-provincial relations were concerned, Premier King uses what Nye identified as a key element of "soft power": moral leadership. Prince Edward Island can act as a mediator between other provinces, as Premier King did in 2022 in a dispute between Nova Scotia and New Brunswick when protests blocked the highway connecting the two provinces at the Chignecto Peninsula. Another example was when the Island delivered personal protection equipment (PPE) to Ontario in the early days of the COVID-19 pandemic. "Kindness can be repaid," said King. "We're easy to deal with," said Premier King, "That gives us influence."

Finally, as far as the clout of the region as a whole, Premier King acknowledged that when the four Atlantic premiers or the three Maritime premiers, spoke in concert — for example, at a First Ministers' Conference — the region did have influence. However, this was difficult to do. Regardless of goodwill, each province had its own interests. In any case, even a united voice afforded the region far less influence than exercised by Quebec or Ontario or British Columbia or Alberta.

The McKenna Miracle and the Meech Lake Debacle

There are some circumstances in which every province, no matter how small, can exercise considerable influence and that is during constitutional negotiations, especially those times when unanimity or near-unanimity is required. Since the patriation of the Constitution in 1982, it has only happened once and that was during the Meech Lake Accord initiative.[45] Unanimous consent was required to implement the comprehensive reforms the Accord called for, and so every province needed to be onside. In the end, the initiative failed to receive such consent with Manitoba and Newfoundland and Labrador not on board. Manitoba and Newfoundland and Labrador each had their own reasons and circumstances for why their legislatures did not ratify or repeal the ratification of the Accord, but an argument has been made that neither province would have even been in a position to withdraw support had it not been for the actions of New Brunswick's premier, Frank McKenna. Andrew

Cohen wrote, "In a sense, Frank McKenna made Gary Filmon and Clyde Wells possible."[46]

McKenna's time as premier of New Brunswick provides a good example of the perils of a small province overreaching. McKenna was the Liberal premier of New Brunswick from 1987 to 1997. He became an excellent example of a premier using soft power smartly. His economic reforms became the talk of the country and his aggressive "open for business" strategy was seen as a model for have-not provinces to break the cycle of dependency on federal transfers. New Brunswick's economic turnaround under McKenna became known as the "McKenna Miracle," even though critics now debate whether in the end there was much to show for the policies.[47] Nevertheless, given that New Brunswick was not an economic powerhouse like Ontario or Alberta, what allowed McKenna to be so influential on the national stage was his own personality, his work ethic, and his determination. People – business and political leaders – wanted to work with McKenna. As such, he had clout.

But McKenna's premiership did not start out that way. In 1987, the Liberal party under McKenna's leadership won all fifty-eight seats in the New Brunswick provincial election. This took place on 13 October 1987. The Meech Lake Accord agreement, pending ratification by the provincial legislatures, was reached on 30 April 1987 while Richard Hatfield was still PC premier of the province. At this point, the PCs had been in power in New Brunswick for an unprecedented seventeen years.[48] In the previous election, held 12 October 1982, Hatfield's PCs won thirty-nine seats to the Liberals' eighteen (the NDP won one seat); at the time, this was a record landslide win in the province.[49] By April 1987 the Hatfield government was now looking at four years and six months since its election win in 1982 and so an election call was both imminent and constitutionally necessary. However, the PCs were struggling in the polls and a series of scandals had undermined the public's confidence.

Hatfield did not think that ratifying the Accord with the current Assembly was appropriate and stated that a matter of such constitutional magnitude should be left to the new legislature, regardless of which party won. Meanwhile, the new leader of the Liberals, Frank McKenna, had voiced his opposition to the Accord.[50] McKenna's main concerns were the lack of protection for linguistic minorities, specifically francophones in New Brunswick, as well as the reduction of the powers of the federal government. Speaking during the debate on sending the Accord to the Law Amendments Committee (23 June 1987), McKenna explained: "The fundamental character of Quebec is recognized in the accord. The fundamental character of New Brunswick should also be recognized." He also said, "Throughout our history, a strong national government had been in the best interests of all Canadians. It has certainly been in the best interests of the less wealthy provinces of this country. The government of Canada must not be hamstrung in continuing to deliver quality programs of benefit to all Canadians."[51] The debate concluded but the motion to ratify the Accord was not brought forward.

With McKenna's stunning victory, all eyes turned on the new premier to see what he would do. But more than eyes were turned. Screws were turned as well, and McKenna experienced first-hand the carrot and stick of hard power. A frigate program for Saint John and infrastructure money to rebuild the Trans-Canada Highway were offered, but would be withdrawn if New Brunswick didn't come on side.[52] Meanwhile, public hearings took place across the province throughout 1989[53] and on 21 March 1990 McKenna proposed a "companion resolution" addressing several concerns that had been voiced during the public hearings.[54] In particular, the parallel accord dealt with the problem of minority francophone rights in New Brunswick, as well as protecting the rights of women (from being overridden by the distinct society clause) and deleting the unanimous approval required for the creation of new provinces (which would have virtually put an end to the ambitions of Yukon and the Northwest Territories to become full provinces). It also gave a place of some prominence to native rights and issues, and gave the federal government power to promote (not just preserve) linguistic duality.[55] The parallel accord, as its name suggests, was not to replace the Meech Lake Accord, but to revise it subsequently: the deal was that New Brunswick would ratify the Meech Lake Accord if the other provinces agreed to then ratify New Brunswick's parallel amendments. However, "the day after McKenna introduced his plan, [Premier Clyde Wells of Newfoundland] started the process of rescinding his province's approval of the accord," completing the process 6 April 1990.[56]

That one premier could be held responsible for such a failure is manifestly unfair. McKenna's initial opposition to the Accord was because of its failure to protect minority francophone rights in New Brunswick. New Brunswick would eventually be able to do so with the addition of section 16.1 to the CA 1982 (see above). But that protecting minority language rights in his province was regarded as obstinate perfidy speaks volumes about how the Maritimes are regarded by the rest of Canada. The whole point of Meech Lake's constitutional amendments was to protect a minority francophone population: les québécois. Les québécois are a minority in Canada, and legitimately demand protection. Why is it different for francophones in New Brunswick, who are a minority in that province?

Yet even championing that cause did not garner McKenna much respect among some of his francophone critics, who dismissed his support for their linguistic communities as political opportunism. Pierre Fournier writes: "Leaders of the francophone minorities hesitated between lukewarm approval of Meech and outright opposition to it. Such reluctance served Premier McKenna and his counterpart Gary Filmon wonderfully well, as they were then able to evoke a 'noble cause' to explain part of their opposition."[57]

Constitutional amendments give provinces — or more precisely, provincial legislatures — clout. Depending on the amendment, each province can have considerable power to derail the initiative. This is particularly true when it comes to amendments that require unanimity, as the Meech Lake Accord provisions did. Any province, whether it be Ontario or Prince Edward Island, has the ability to derail a proposed amendment by simply refusing to ratify it. That gives the province considerable power. But this power is a two-edged sword, as McKenna would find out. Although New Brunswick had every constitutional right to refuse to ratify the Accord, its initial failure to do so came with a significant political and personal price.[58]

There are moments in history when a premier from the Maritimes, or the Maritimes in general can exercise influence beyond their position in the political hierarchy. But for the most part, the premiers must rely on their ability to exercise soft power: to persuade through reasoned arguments, show they are willing to collaborate, and present themselves as premiers doing their best to improve the lot of their provinces. Whether doing so as a unified province would improve the success of this policy is questionable. Regardless, the essence of the strategy will need to remain the same. Therefore, unified or not, the best way for Maritime premiers to advance the interests of the region is still to be prudent and collaborative. But just as Canadian soft power works best when Canada's international reputation is strong, Maritime premiers must show they are eager and willing to work together to advance the interests of the region. What Prime Minister St-Laurent called for in 1956 remains true today:

> The initiative and the ideas, the energies and determination to accomplish this redevelopment cannot originate in other parts of Canada, they must come from the Atlantic Area itself. It will then be up to us elsewhere to co-operate and help to make such ideas and efforts fruitful in providing better opportunities for workers in those areas.[59]

When this happens, the premiers have clout. Whether the premiers are up to this challenge remains to be seen.

CHAPTER FOURTEEN

Federalism as a Social Contract: Union and Secession

In the broadest sense, federalism involves the linkage of individuals, groups, and polities in lasting but limited union in such a way as to provide for the energetic pursuit of common ends while maintaining the respective integrities of all parties. It does so by pact and constitution grounded in some shared set of commandments that ultimately rest on some moral principles and suffi-cient mutual trust. Federal principles are concerned with the combination of self-rule and shared rule.

Daniel Elazar, *Covenant and Civil Society*[1]

The *Quebec Secession Reference* case[2] has contributed considerably to con-stitutional jurisprudence around the world.[3] The Canadian decision was broad in scope and implications. However, critics have challenged this very broadness. Specifically, critics have argued that the Supreme Court went too far in looking beyond the confines of the written text of the Canadian Constitution in its decision. The Court acknowledged that the Constitution provided no means for a province to secede uni-laterally: few constitutions do.[4] However, the Court also ruled that the Constitution encompassed more than what was contained in the written text. That should not have surprised anyone, but the scope of the principles outlined generated concerns that this decision was grounded more in political expediency than solid jurisprudence.[5]

That may well be. Yet I would argue that the Court was less concerned with political expediency then it was with what Samuel LaSelva has called the moral foundation of federalism.[6] Federalism, as Montesquieu, Mill, Tocqueville, and others have shown, is a social contract. Furthermore, it is a contract based on a moral agreement, a "covenant" in Daniel Elazar's words. The Court's reasonings in the *Quebec Secession Reference* therefore provide valuable insights into the nature of the Canadian Constitution, as well as providing guidelines on just what would be required were a province, or in our example, three provinces, to effect constitutional changes that profoundly altered the nature of the federation. The Supreme Court of Canada decision did not anticipate Maritime Union, although interestingly enough it did mention the issue.

In the *Quebec Secession Reference*, the Supreme Court was asked three questions:

1. Under the Constitution of Canada, can the National Assembly, legislature or government of Quebec effect the secession of Quebec from Canada unilaterally?

2. Does international law give the National Assembly, legislature or government of Quebec the right to effect the secession of Quebec from Canada unilaterally? In this regard, is there a right to self-determination under international law that would give the National Assembly, legislature or government of Quebec the right to effect the secession of Quebec from Canada unilaterally?

3. In the event of a conflict between domestic and international law on the right of the National Assembly, legislature or government of Quebec to effect the secession of Quebec from Canada unilaterally, which would take precedence in Canada?[7]

Questions two and three, which involve international law and Quebec's international status were it to secede unilaterally, do not apply to the question of Maritime Union: the new province would still be in Canada. Question one deals with the power of a province — specifically Quebec but not only Quebec — to "effect the secession of Quebec from Canada unilaterally." On the surface, this also does not appear to apply to Maritime Union as the constitutional question being asked is not whether the Maritimes could unite unilaterally but how they could unite under the Constitution. Nevertheless, it is the Court's answer to the first question that provides us with insights into what would be necessary for union of provinces under the Canadian Constitution. The Court explained that

> [t]he Constitution is more than a written text. It embraces the entire global system of rules and principles which govern the exercise of constitutional authority . . . It is necessary to make a more profound investigation of the underlying principles animating the whole of the Constitution, including the *principles of federalism, democracy, constitutionalism and the rule of law, and respect for minorities.* Those principles must inform our overall appreciation of the constitutional rights and obligations that would come into play in the event that a clear majority of Quebecers votes on a clear question in favour of secession.[8]

Furthermore, "The Constitution vouchsafes order and stability."[9] These principles, then, must be preserved under any scheme to unite the Maritime provinces.

Confederation in 1867 (and for Prince Edward Island in 1873) was a contract: a social contract whereupon each province gave up certain rights and powers to a central authority with the understanding that they would preserve other rights and powers and that in the end, being a part of a federal system was better than being independent. The same logic applies to unifying the three provinces: would the united province afford greater benefits to the three provinces — and all the rights and benefits minorities within those provinces enjoy — than remaining as separate provinces would? Confederation was an acceptable alternative to full unification of the three provinces. As the Court stated:

> Federalism was also welcomed by Nova Scotia and New Brunswick, both of which also affirmed their will to protect their individual cultures and their autonomy over local matters. All new provinces

joining the federation sought to achieve similar objectives, which are no less vigorously pursued by the provinces and territories as we approach the new millennium.[10]

Although Premier Tupper preferred a full union — basically recreating the old Nova Scotia — many New Brunswick and Prince Edward Island leaders were relieved that they could retain a degree of autonomy. Yet the concerns of the Maritime provinces over the years have been that Confederation still came at too great a cost. That cost was not just the autonomy of the Maritimes, but the autonomy of each province. Prince Edward Island joined Confederation reluctantly but did so with assurances that it would still be Prince Edward Island after joining. As Prince Edward Island Premier Pat Binns said in 1996, "We entered Confederation in 1873 on the basis of being an equal partner."[11] The same can be said of the other two provinces. The constitutions of the three provinces were to remain intact with Confederation. Recall that the *British North America Act, 1867* (BNA 1867), section 7 guaranteed that the provinces of Nova Scotia and New Brunswick would "have the same limits as at the passing of this Act." If Maritime Union meant that the autonomy of these provinces was now erased together with their borders, then the original contract would be broken.

This appears to be an argument against the forced unification of the Maritimes and no one is arguing for that. Surely, if the Maritimes wanted to unite then these arguments would be irrelevant. A contract in which all partners agree to change can be changed. However, this argument raises a question: what competent authority would there be to agree to such an alteration of the original contract? Who is competent to decide whether the Maritimes really did want to unite? What process would be necessary to uphold the principle of democracy? What process would be necessary to protect minority rights? It is significant that the Supreme Court did not consider the provincial government of Quebec to be, by itself, competent to effect Quebec secession (so not unilaterally) but nor did it rule that the Quebec government and the federal government were together competent. Much more was required, and that involved robust consultation and hard evidence of the will of the Quebec people to separate.

In the *Quebec Secession Reference* case, the Supreme Court of Canada also ruled that a clear question with a clear majority would obligate the federal government to negotiate with Quebec regarding separation. The Court clearly believed that a referendum successfully conducted under such conditions would carry weight. Whether that weight was legal or moral or political is not entirely clear. But certainly, no move to unite the Maritime provinces could take place without a plebiscite of some sort. However, a vote on uniting the Maritime provinces would need to go beyond clarity. An important and difficult decision would have to be made with regard to what a "clear majority" is when dealing with three separate provinces.

All three Maritime provinces have experience with plebiscites and two have specific acts governing plebiscites and referenda.[12] In New Brunswick and Prince Edward Island, plebiscites on video gambling were held in 2001. Sunday shopping was the issue in a plebiscite held in Nova Scotia in 2004. Prince Edward Island has held plebiscites on whether the Island should be connected to the mainland with a fixed link (1988), and (as described above) has had three such votes on electoral reform (2005, 2016, and 2019). In neither province are plebiscites binding, nor can they be under our Constitution (there is no provision for referenda in the Constitution overruling Parliament or a provincial legislature). However, whether the results of a plebiscite are binding is a different question from whether a plebiscite of some sort would be required before Maritime Union would be effected. With the *Quebec Secession Reference* case, it appears that major constitutional change requires some sort of vote; that is, it cannot be left entirely to the legislators. Interestingly enough, the issue of whether the "people's representatives" had the authority to join their provinces to the new Dominion or whether the people themselves needed to be consulted was raised — and rejected — during the Confederation negotiations. "This is clearly a conspiracy to defraud and cheat the people out of the right to determine for themselves whether this Union shall now take place," wrote New Brunswick's Timothy Anglin in his newspaper, *Freeman*.[13] In Nova Scotia, Joseph Howe claimed that by failing to consult the people, the Tupper government had no constitutional authority to agree to Confederation.[14]

We must also assume that there would be opposition to any attempt to unify the three provinces and that such opposition would eventually land in court and probably the Supreme Court. If so, it is safe to assume that the Court would rely on its opinion in the *Quebec Secession Reference* case. We can begin, then, with the assumption that a plebiscite on Maritime Union would be necessary: if not constitutionally necessary, certainly politically and morally necessary. The rules for such a plebiscite would be complicated, but not impossible.

The several Prince Edward Island votes on electoral reform attempted to ensure comprehensive support or rejection of the reform initiative so that no sub-region of the province could argue that its views were not represented.[15] The 2019 vote was the most comprehensive (the lessons learned from the 2005 and 2016 votes were in place for the 2019 vote). First, the question allowed for a simple yes or no response (as opposed to a preferential ballot comprising several choices).[16] Second, a threshold was set: an absolute majority of all votes cast, plus a majority in 60% of the province's twenty-seven ridings.[17]

A similar formula would likely be demanded, so that a majority in each province was required and likely a majority in some sort of intra-provincial breakdown, such as was proposed by the New Brunswick Commission on Legislative Democracy with regard to regional multi-member districts. The commission, in conjunction with a recommendation for the adoption of a mixed-member proportional system, proposed that the province be divided into four regional districts, each containing nine single-member constituencies. The "four regions provide an appropriate reflection of the cultural and linguistic communities comprising the province."[18] Such an arrangement would need to be made for a plebiscite. Within each province, decisions would also have to be made regarding First

Nations communities and Nova Scotia's special status for Acadian and African-Canadian communities. In all these cases, the question of whether such districts individually or in some combination had a veto would have to be determined.

The wording of the question would also need to be carefully considered. The reason the Supreme Court of Canada declared that a clearly worded question was necessary is a result of the referenda questions used in the 1980 and 1995 referenda. The 1980 referendum question was particularly convoluted, asking for a mandate to negotiate some sort of sovereign status.[19]

One criticism of plebiscites is that the voter may not have a clear understanding of what is at stake. Just as various opinion polls on Maritime Union have been criticized for providing insufficient information on what was being asked, a plebiscite on Maritime Union would have to ensure that the full consequences of union — positive and negative — were well understood.

None of this is impossible and designing an appropriate referendum process would be easier, I believe, than figuring out a new representation model for a united legislature. But a considerable amount of care and planning would need to go into the Maritime Union plebiscite nevertheless.

CHAPTER FIFTEEN

Maritime Union or a Maritime Common Market?

It's time to get off the dole and stand on our own two feet. I firmly believe that we must become more self-sufficient if we are ever to become have provinces in a have region. . . . It is my conclusion that the Maritime provinces must begin to operate as a single economic unit. The time has come to create a single integrated market of over 1.5 million people, and coordinate our strategic objectives so that we speak with a single voice at national and international levels.

Premier of New Brunswick, Frank McKenna (1990)[1]

Not everyone who champions a union of the Maritimes or of the Atlantic provinces wants full political union or even thinks that such a union would be a good idea. Many believe that economic union— a Maritime Common Market — would be a better option. A Common Market would be a far easier sell: each province would still keep its identity and the premiers their jobs. This is a debate that has gone on as long as Maritime Union was considered. Even when the initial meetings for Maritime Union were being planned for Charlottetown in 1864, some like New Brunswick's Samuel Tilley advocated for a customs union rather than full political union.[2]

The former Liberal premier of New Brunswick (1987–97), Frank McKenna, is one of many leaders in the Maritimes who has also advocated, not for full political union, but rather economic union: "a single integrated market of over 1.5 million people."[3] The argument is that every advantage that would be gained through a union could be realized without one: the Maritime provinces just need (more) programs and policies that integrate the region's economies, or do so more effectively. Further, efforts to ensure regional cooperation have been successful; they merely have yet to realize their full potential. This, of course, raises an important question: what are the impediments that have kept, after all these years, regional cooperation and indeed integration from being fully realized? Could it not be the simple fact that, regardless of good intentions, three provincial governments will always advance their own interests?

Certainly, more cooperation and collaboration among the Maritimes would be beneficial; I do not believe anyone argues the contrary. Donald Savoie, long a proponent of full political union, still maintains that in the absence of full political union increased Maritime cooperation could nevertheless do the job:

> It is hardly possible to point to a single policy field where the Maritime region would not benefit from a multiprovince perspective: regulatory policies; tax policy; trade and investment promotion; attracting new Canadians; research and development; securing more risk capital to move the region's industrial structure up the value chain; increasing value-added to its natural resources; Internet commerce; and using knowledge.[4]

From a constitutional standpoint, such cooperation should not be difficult. The *Constitution Act, 1867* (CA 1867)[5] provides a number of protections for free trade among the provinces. In fact, one of the most important motivations for Confederation in 1867, at least for New Brunswick, Nova Scotia, and what would become Ontario, was free trade among the provinces.[6] The *British North America Act, 1867* (BNA 1867)[7] made this clear. Section 121 reads: "All Articles of the Growth, Produce, or Manufacture of any one of the Provinces shall, from and after the Union, be admitted free into each of the other Provinces."

Furthermore, the Parliament of Canada was authorized to pass legislation on customs and excise duties for the nation as a whole (section 122) and section 91(2) placed the regulation of "trade and commerce" under the heads of power assigned to the Parliament of Canada. Other pertinent heads of power include section 92(10), which established the authority of Parliament to regulate interprovincial transport and to declare local works "although wholly situated within the Province," to be of national importance and therefore beyond the authority of a province.[8] Banking section 91(15), weights and measures section 91(17), bills of exchange and promissory notes section 91(18), interest section 91(19), and bankruptcy and insolvency section 91(21) are all included under the powers of Parliament. Finally, BNA 1867, section 94 empowers the Parliament of Canada to unify provincial laws dealing with property and civil rights in Ontario, Nova Scotia, and New Brunswick. In these provinces such laws regulating commerce, such as real estate transactions, are a part of the common law of the provinces. Quebec's *Civil Code* covers such laws, and so was not included.[9]

But even with a federal government constitutionally empowered to ensure interprovincial free trade, barriers persist. These include "prohibitive barriers" such as those regulating the "movement of alcohol or tobacco between provinces," technical and regulatory barriers, such as "provincial differences in requirements within specific sectors [such as] licensing" or "trucking regulations or the different regulations with regard to agriculture and agri-food industries."[10] One study estimated that the elimination of all barriers to interprovincial trade in Canada would increase the country's GDP between one and four percent (in 2021 numbers, $92 billion).[11]

Over the years, there has been a plethora of attempts to reduce and eliminate such barriers, and now all Canadian provinces are engaged in a number of programs and agreements that have as a goal the freer movement of goods and services. But these agreements are often sector specific and bilateral or regional rather than national. Some agreements have actually made things worse.[12]

Why such barriers persist is in no small part due to the fact that Canada is not a unitary state but a federation and that invariably means that no constitutional power is absolute. For example, in the case of *Citizens Insurance Company of Canada v Parsons*, the Judicial Committee of the Privy Council (JCPC) ruled that very precision of how classes of subject relating to trade and commerce were included under section 91 was proof that section 121 was not meant to be "unlimited"; if it were, then these other subjects listed under 91 would be redundant.[13]

More recently, in *R v Comeau*, the Court explained that section 121 was never meant to erase all provincial powers over trade:

> Reading s. 121 to require full economic integration would significantly undermine the shape of Canadian federalism, which is built upon regional diversity within a single nation. The need to maintain balance embodied in the federalism principle supports an interpretation of s. 121 that prohibits laws directed at curtailing the passage of goods over interprovincial borders, but allows legislatures to pass laws to achieve other goals within their powers, even though the laws may have the incidental effect of impeding the passage of goods over interprovincial borders.[14]

The Supreme Court of Canada justices are, of course, quite right. But this acknowledgement of the need to preserve regional diversity is precisely why regional agreements will never reach the full potential of a common market. Only a unitary state, or in the case of the Maritime provinces, only a unified province, will be able to avoid having some — perhaps many — local restrictions on trade and commerce, and so the great advantages of a Maritime Common Market will likely never be realized, at least not fully or at least not in perpetuity. To borrow a line from a premier of a different province: "borders matter."

The question, then, is this: if we accept the fact that full political union of the Maritime provinces is not an option, could the Maritimes create a Maritime Common Market instead? How exactly would a free-trade Maritime bubble work?

A notable scholar and policy expert who advocates for a Maritime Common Market is Charles McMillan, Professor of Strategy at the Schulich School of Business, York University. McMillan has been a consultant to Atlantic Canadian governments for many years concerning how the Maritimes, and later how Atlantic Canada, can maximize efficiencies through regional cooperation. His ground-breaking 1989 consultant's report, *Standing Up to the Future: The Maritimes in the 1990s*[15] set the tone for much of the discussion and policies regarding regional cooperation for the next three decades. The McMillan thesis is compelling and straightforward: the existence of systemic obstacles to economic cooperation are responsible for the underdevelopment of the region. Remove the barriers, allow for the free movement of goods and services and economic prosperity will follow.

The McMillan report identified twelve main trade barriers that were hindering economic development in the Maritimes: government procurement contracts; wine, beer, liquor boards; highway construction tenders; product labelling, protection, safety programs; supply management boards; Crown corporation policies; professional credentials; direct grants and subsidies to companies; provincial advertising contracts; provincially funded loan boards; provincial trucking regulations; and provincial incentive programs for industrial development.[16]

However, Memorial University economist James P. Feehan criticized the McMillan report in a 1993 article titled "Atlantic Provinces Economic Union." Feehan acknowledged that McMillan was far from alone in maintaining that systemic obstacles have hindered economic development in the region. The Rowell-Sirois report (1940) said as much, as did the Royal Commission on the Economic Union and Development Prospects for Canada (MacDonald Commission). In 1991, both the Council for Maritime Premiers and the Atlantic Provinces Economic Council called for a rationalization and integration of the region's economies.

The problem, according to Feehan, was that these calls for Maritime free trade and economic integration are based on intuition, not empirical evidence. Feehan provided a detailed analysis of the effects that removing trade barriers and such would have on the region's economy. In a nutshell, the three or four economies of Atlantic Canada are just too small for these reforms to have anything but a modest, and perhaps imperceptibly modest, effect. Further, the more likely result would not be overall economic gain, but a redistribution within the region; that is, certain parts of the Maritimes (perhaps the larger metropolitan areas) would benefit but others would lose.

McMillan, however, remains unconvinced. In 2001, McMillan was asked again to report on regional cooperation, and this resulted in his *Focusing on the Future: The New Atlantic Revolution*[17] which makes similar arguments to those he made in 1989. Then in June 2023, the Brian Mulroney Institute of Government at St. Francis Xavier University held the "first-ever" Atlantic Economic Forum. McMillan reported on the forum in a piece he wrote for *Policy: Canadian Politics and Public Policy*, which he titled "The New Disparity: Atlantic Canada is Booming."[18] Although this was not his intention, the article pinpoints the precise problem with Maritime or for that matter, Atlantic Common Market. McMillan points to the progress the region has made regarding cooperation and the benefits that have resulted. There was, wrote McMillan,

> a new vocabulary among the speakers [at the conference]; discussions and informative Q & As — startup, scaling, collaboration, competition, digital tools, regional cooperation, private sector funding, community involvement, self-reliance, deregulation, speed of government approvals, dynamic ecosystems, silo mentality and a recurring theme of far less dependence on transfer payments and government support.[19]

Yet the provinces in the region are still the poorest in the country. With all this cooperation, why have the Maritimes yet to reach their full potential? Consider energy policy. Although McMillan considered the region's "shift to green energy sources — wind, solar, hydrogen, tidewater, hydro" as "another example of a leadership role for the region," energy policy remains "a contentious political issue":

> The four provinces have applied different systems: nuclear in New Brunswick, coal in Nova Scotia, hydro in Newfoundland, and a mix in PEI, with an emphasis on wind farms. The thought that Atlantic Canada could be an [*sic*] clean energy powerhouse, to use the prime minister's phrase, has potential, but requires a measure of collaboration in the region, and close alliances with other provinces, especially Quebec, with its deep expertise in hydro development, transmission, and venture funding.[20]

This is the crux of the Maritime Union debate, and now the Maritime Common Market debate. Is regional cooperation enough? If it is, then is the problem that the current cooperative activities are not at the level that is required? Are they not enough? If cooperation is all that is standing in the way of prosperity, can the requisite levels of cooperation take place without political union? The Maritime economic union argument boils down to this. A Maritime or Atlantic Common Market would produce only minimal benefits for the region and would likely also increase regional disparities within the Maritimes. For an economic union to be truly beneficial for the region, the entire country would need to eliminate interprovincial barriers. This is something that has been called for repeatedly over the years, but constitutional obstacles have prevented this from happening. Nevertheless, were Canada to figure out how to be an inter-provincial common market, then a Maritime economic union would be of no value and would likely be counterproductive.[21]

The Atlantic Canada Opportunities Agency (ACOA)

While browsing in the bookstore on the Saint John campus of the University of New Brunswick back in the mid-1990s, I came across a book in the humour section. It was hardbound, thick, and its title was "ACOA Success Stories." Intrigued that such a book existed, and not yet picking up on the clue that the book was in the humour section, I opened its cover and leafed through the text. All the pages were blank. It was a notebook, with what someone obviously thought was a funny title and cover.

ACOA is another agency that has worked to foster Atlantic cooperation, although specifically its job is to support entrepreneurial activity. Since its creation in 1985, the agency has borne its share of criticism and damaging headlines. "New Atlantic agency prompts skepticism: development scheme is progress of another political pork barrel?" read the headline to the June 1987 article in *The Globe and Mail*.[22] The Canadian Taxpayers Federation's 2000 report on ACOA titled it "ACOA: The Lost Decade."[23] "ACOA mistaken money mounts," was the headline of a 2002 CBC story, which went on to say that ACOA "has paid out at least $12 million in error in the past four years."[24] Writing specifically about Newfoundland and Labrador, Barb Sweet of *SaltWire News* reported in 2010 that ACOA wrote off just under $40 million in the past decade.[25] "People currently only seem to hear about ACOA's mistakes," reported a study commissioned by ACOA in 1991.[26] Not much has changed since then.

ACOA was created in 1985 by the PC government under Prime Minister Brian Mulroney. Charles McMillan sketches the history of the precursors to ACOA in his book *The Age of Consequence*.[27] McMillan begins with the Rowell-Sirois Report of 1940, which laid the foundation for the need for an equalization payment program. The 1957 Royal Commission on Canada's Economic Prospects recommended that Atlantic Canada adopt a "bold comprehensive and coordinated approach . . . to make the best possible use of the underlying problems of the area and to improve transportation and other basic services."[28] Other initiatives which followed include the 1961 *Agriculture Rehabilitation and Development Act* (ARDA) followed by the Atlantic Development Board in 1963. An alphabet soup of agencies and ministries (some new, some renamed) sprung up in the years following: FRED, DREE, DRIE, ERDAS, MSERD and finally ACOA.[29]

The PC Government's Speech from the Throne in 1986 promised to tackle regional disparity. This included "diversifying the economic base of Western Canada," and creating "an Atlantic Canada Opportunities Agency":

> As a first step in achieving improved results from this sustained national approach, an Atlantic Canada Opportunities Agency will be constituted to facilitate and coordinate all federal development initiatives in the area. This agency will make fuller use of the expertise available in the Atlantic region and invite the maximum participation of other governments and organizations in the area.[30]

According to McMillan, the idea for ACOA came from a conversation between McMillan, Dalton Camp, and Prime Minister Mulroney while on a flight to Ottawa in September 1985. After a few false starts, Mulroney met with the premiers of the four Atlantic provinces: John Buchanan of Nova Scotia, Richard Hatfield of New Brunswick, Jim Lee of Prince Edward Island, and Brian Peckford of Newfoundland.[31] All four were PC premiers. Hatfield provided Mulroney with a brief "calling for the establishment of a new economic development agency for Atlantic Canada" prepared by Donald Savoie.[32] This corresponded with the conversation Mulroney had had with McMillan and Camp, and so McMillan was tasked with creating the new agency, which would be called the Atlantic Canada Opportunities Agency, or ACOA. The word "opportunity" was chosen to brand the agency as encouraging entrepreneurial activities, rather than government-supported "development" projects. Savoie was then asked to write a report "on the machinery and mandate."[33]

Savoie's report echoed the words of Louis St-Laurent back in 1956. In his book on regional economic development, Savoie quotes from this report, writing, "It is Atlantic Canadians themselves who 'will have to provide the energy, the skills and the imagination to conceive and organize economic activity if the region is to prosper.'"

> No longer can hopes for economic development be tied solely to the ability of governments (particularly the federal government) to lure to the region major investors in the manufacturing sector with cash grants and other schemes. This approach failed in the

best of economic times; there is little reason to believe that it could work now or in the foreseeable future. It has become very difficult to argue that economic activity should be diverted from one region to another on the grounds of economic or national efficiency.[34]

After adjustments and reconsiderations of the agency's reporting structure, ACOA began operations in 1987. "We begin with new money, a new mission and a new opportunity. [ACOA] will succeed where others have failed," proclaimed Prime Minister Brian Mulroney upon announcing the establishment of agency on 6 June 1987 in St. John's.[35]

ACOA would be different. All the other development agencies and departments were Ottawa-centric. ACOA's headquarters would be in Moncton and not come under DRIE (Department of Regional Industrial Expansion), which would soon be phased out. ACOA would have a broad mandate, open to any and all "good ideas." It would begin with a $1.05 billion budget over its first five years (announced coincidentally with the admission by industry minister Michel Coates that DRIE had already overspent its own budget).[36] Senator Lowell Murray, fresh off the success of the Meech Lake Accord,[37] would be the minister in charge.[38] Maritimer Donald McPhail, a career civil servant with extensive experience in regional economic development, not to mention the former ambassador to West Germany, would be the first president. Nova Scotia's premier John Buchanan shared in the optimism. "This program will work," he said, "because it will be our program."[39]

Has it? Over the years, analysts have questioned ACOA's role. In 1994, Jim Bickerton questioned the folly of "channelling large amounts of public money to roving entrepreneurs."[40]

In 2006, Savoie summed up the problems with the agency he helped create. Not only has the agency has been hobbled by underfunding, but its role as an advocate for Atlantic Canada has been undermined by one of the very features that originally was supposed to make it a success: its headquarters in Atlantic Canada (Moncton). By operating out of Moncton, ACOA does not have direct access to federal ministers and their staff. "The fact that the federal government and Parliament would delegate the 'advocacy function' to a small government agency with its head office in Moncton speaks volumes," writes Savoie.

But Savoie is not arguing that ACOA should be headquartered in Ottawa; rather that the agency itself should not be expected to assume all roles in economic development:

> It would be unthinkable for the federal government to delegate such responsibility for Ontario to a single agency. Again, one can only underline that the regional interests of Ontario are considered central to the national policy, while those of the Atlantic provinces might as well be delegated to a small agency on the periphery of the Ottawa machinery of government. At the same time, federal departments have virtually no policy specialists in the Maritime region.[41]

On the surface, this looks like yet another paradox: Maritime development requires federal support but also expects regional independence. However, the core issue here is a call for the federal government to take Maritime economic development seriously and not assume that there are single and simple solutions. In a review of Savoie's *Looking for Bootstraps* (2017), the reviewer wrote: "It is likely that many who pick up this book will be sympathetic to the topic, but it is less clear, perhaps, to a general reader of Canadian politics, or (maybe less likely) an international reader, why the region's development is important from a broader point of view."[42] *Why the region's development is important?* That such an argument needs to be made also speaks volumes.

CHAPTER SIXTEEN

Representation and Other Issues

A comparison with other provinces suggests perhaps 65–70 [MLAs] would be sufficient if the Maritime provinces joined forces. Combining the three provinces would mean at least two premiers and half of the MLAs would be out of a job, so we should not be surprised at their lack of enthusiasm.

New Start Nova Scotia[1]

Representation

All Canadian provinces use single-member ridings in which representatives are elected by a simple plurality. This is known as the Single-Member Plurality System (SMP), and commonly called First-Past-The Post (FPTP). Otherwise, each province has a representation model based on its own regional considerations, histories, and populations. In New Brunswick, the rough division of North East (Acadian) and South West (anglophone), together with the steady migration from north to south in the province, has convinced various Electoral Boundary Commissions (EBCs) to decrease the number of ridings overall by expanding northern ridings rather than increasing the number in the more populated south.[2] In Nova Scotia, formally since 1991 and informally before that, EBCs have tried to ensure certain populations — particularly Acadian and

African-Canadian[3] — have ridings where they constitute a majority. In Prince Edward Island, the old two-member ridings which served to accommodate the 1893 combination of the Legislative Council and Assembly into one body, became a *de facto* means of accommodating the Catholic and Protestant division in the province.[4]

Two court challenges, one in Nova Scotia and one in Prince Edward Island, have established rules regarding variance exceptions. In 2012, the attorney general of Nova Scotia overruled the province's EBC and that commission's decision to maintain ridings that were meant to "encourage more effective representation for the Acadian and Black communities." The attorney general had insisted instead that the ECB ensure that the population of all ridings complied the legislated variance margin of plus or minus 25%. Subsequently, a reference case was submitted to the Nova Scotia Court of Appeals. The Court ruled that the attorney general's intervention was unconstitutional.[5] In Prince Edward Island, a challenge to the old two-member (councillor and assemblyman), county-based riding system resulted in a judicial ruling that the Prince Edward Island electoral system was unconstitutional as the variances this produced were so great as to undermine the one-person, one-vote principal.[6]

Both cases referenced the 1991 decision in *Reference re Provincial Electoral Boundaries (Sask)*,[7] also known as the *Carter* decision. This established that, while a province has a right to amend its own constitution, nevertheless, "the provincial exercise of its legislative authority is subject to the Charter." Therefore, while "[t]he province is empowered by convention to establish its electoral boundaries . . . that convention is subject to s. 3 of the Charter":

> The right to vote therefore comprises many factors, of which equity is but one. The section does not guarantee equality of voting power. Relative parity of voting power is a prime condition of effective representation. Deviations from absolute voter parity, however, may be justified on the grounds of practical impossibility or the provision of more effective representation. Factors like geography, community history, community interests and minority representation may

need to be taken into account to ensure that our legislative assemblies effectively represent the diversity of our social mosaic. Beyond this, dilution of one citizen's vote as compared with another's should not be countenanced.[8]

In the words of the Nova Scotia Court of Appeal, "After Carter, it was clear that electoral boundaries were no longer the exclusive domain of the legislatures or the playground of majority governments. Boundaries that offended the constitutional principles of s. 3 could be declared as having no force and effect under s. 52(1) of the Constitution Act, 1982."[9] To date, no decision of New Brunswick's provincial EBC has resulted in a judicial ruling. A challenge was made in 1997 by the Société des Acadiens et Acadiennes du Nouveau-Brunswick (SAANB) concerning reapportionment of federal ridings following the report of the federal EBC for New Brunswick.[10] However, the motion was dismissed. Nevertheless, the New Brunswick EBCs have consistently been mandated to "consider the effective representation of the English and French linguistic communities in compliance with section 3 of the Canadian Charter of Rights and Freedoms."[11] New Brunswick's acceptable variance is plus or minus 15 percent.

In a united Maritime province, these decisions and policies would have to be incorporated in whatever model of representation the new province adopted. On the assumption that in the first stage of union the current electoral system (SMP) would be maintained, the most important question would then be: "how many seats would the new province need or want?" The second would be "how would these seats be distributed?"

How Many MLAs Would the Maritime Province Need or Want?

There is no specific number of MLAs that would be required. The new province would be able to decide for itself how many seats in its Legislative Assembly it thought necessary, just as the constituent provinces once did, albeit within the considerations described above. The citizens of each province would no doubt be concerned that the model they were now accustomed to was changing. A fulsome consultation process would be required, likely using criteria set out in the Supreme Court's decision regarding Quebec secession (I discuss this in Chapter 15.)

Let us begin by rejecting the idea that each province could simply keep the seats they now have, and so then the Legislative Assembly of the new province would have 131 seats, of which twenty-seven would come from Prince Edward Island, forty-nine from New Brunswick, and fifty-five from Nova Scotia. Prince Edward Island's *Electoral Boundaries Act* allows for a variance of plus or minus 25%; New Brunswick's *Electoral Boundaries and Representation Act* allows for 15% variance; Nova Scotia uses an "exceptional ridings" provision, but otherwise has a variance policy of 25%.[12] Using Nova Scotia and Prince Edward Island's variance, a combined Legislative Assembly that simply retained the existing seats would mean that Prince Edward Island's twenty-seven seats would have an unacceptable variance of minus 59%. Regardless, this would be a bizarre configuration,[13] and undermine one of the main arguments in favour of Maritime Union: the reduction in the total number of elected representatives.

For simplicity's sake, let's assume a number of different scenarios in which we do not calculate specific variance exceptions (they would be nuances added after the fact anyway and would mostly affect riding sizes, not the overall number). We can begin with adopting the Prince Edward Island model, in which each riding has just over 4,000 voters.[14] Such a model would mean that Nova Scotia, with 767,618 registered voters, would receive 189 seats. New Brunswick, with 579,514 registered voters, would be allocated 143 seats. Prince Edward Island, with 109,587 registered voters, would keep its twenty-seven seats. The total number of seats in the assembly would be 359. No province in Canada has this many seats (Quebec, the largest, has 125 seats). As a result of the latest redistribution process, the Canadian House of Commons will have 343, but still fewer than this fictional Maritime assembly. So, this scenario is just as odd as simply allowing each province to keep its current number of representatives.

New Brunswick has an average of 12,000 voters per riding. If we adopted the New Brunswick model, then New Brunswick would keep its forty-nine seats, Nova Scotia would go up to sixty-five and Prince Edward Island would drop to nine, for a total of 123. Only Quebec (125) and Ontario (124) would have more provincial representatives, so also an excessive number for new province still considerably smaller than either of those two. If we followed the Nova Scotia model, with 14,000 voters per riding, then Nova Scotia would keep its fifty-five seats, New Brunswick would be reduced to forty-two and Prince Edward Island would drop to eight. The Assembly would then have 105 seats: again, still very large for a province this size. This, then, is barely an improvement over the New Brunswick model. Obviously, no current provincial Maritime model would serve the new province.

The other way of calculating the numbers of seats is simpler, but also not without its own drawbacks. That method involves choosing a number of total seats for the united province and then working back to see how many each former province would receive. If, say, that number was sixty — so just five more than what Nova Scotia has now — then the number of voters per riding would be 24,279. Under such a model, Nova Scotia would have thirty-two seats, New Brunswick twenty-four, and Prince Edward Island five. Would Prince Edward Island accept such a drastic reduction in its representation? I can confidently predict the answer would be "no." As Liberal Member of the Legislative Assembly (MLA) Peter Doucette said back in 1991, Islanders "like to deal directly with their governments."[15] Any attempt, then, to unite the three provinces will have to confront the issue of representation. Although the provinces would have every legal right to determine the number of seats that the new province would have in its Legislative Assembly, those advocating Maritime Union would have some formidable obstacles to overcome in convincing the citizens of each province, and particularly those in Prince Edward Island, that a reduction in the number of representatives was beneficial. While it is true that complaints are sometimes raised that Prince Edward Island has too many MLAs, these complaints do not envision a reduction of MLAs in a united legislature in which Prince Edward Island is reduced to a mere rump. Still, this is the most reasonable model in my mind.

Another solution to this problem might be to abandon the FPTP system altogether and adopt a hybrid model such as the mixed-member proportional system almost adopted by Prince Edward Island in 2016,[16] or the hybrid proportional representation system (in which the province used both single-member constituencies as well as four proportional-representation districts) recommended by the New Brunswick Commission on Legislative Democracy in 2004.[17] Under the latter system, in addition to the four districts in New Brunswick, Prince Edward Island could comprise a district of its own while Nova Scotia could be divided into four or five districts, based on local communities of interest. Whether such a model would placate those who feared their former provinces were now marginalized under Maritime Union is doubtful, but it might provide opportunities to argue for an enhanced and more robust representation model that would better reflect local concerns. Given the lack of success of either New Brunswick or Prince Edward Island in moving forward with electoral reform despite several commissions and, in the case of Prince Edward Island, three plebiscites, such an outcome also remains highly unlikely.

I am not arguing that it is impossible to come up with a representation model that is just. Had the Maritime provinces united prior to Confederation, they would have figured out something. With time, the number of MLAs would become accepted as the norm, even a drastically reduced number for Prince Edward Island. But this would take time. Constitutionally speaking, adopting a new system of representation would not be very difficult. Politically, however, it might well be insurmountable. If not, it would require considerable discussion and reassurance that Prince Edward Island would be fairly represented.

CHAPTER SEVENTEEN

Why Hasn't Maritime Union Occurred: Identity or Parochialism?

[T]hese recommendations envisage the adoption of a program of formal co-operation and joint action which moves progressively to full political union, which should be accepted as a definite objective from the outset. The intervening steps would in themselves constitute important progress in advancing common regional interests, and in solving urgent regional problems.... At the end of, say five years it would be desirable to make a realistic assessment of the results achieved, and of the progress made toward full political union.

Maritime Union Study, 1970[1]

The Maritime Union Study called for an incremental approach to union. By creating regional agencies and agreements, harmonizing regulations and so forth, Maritimers would get used to the idea of a single Maritime authority and would see the benefits of Maritime Union. In five years, a review of the process would take place.

Surely the authors of that study did not envision that almost fifty-five years later, little would have been accomplished. Why, despite the careful blueprint for union laid out by the Maritime Union Study, has full integration not occurred? One place to look is at the efforts to unify the nations of Western Europe in the years following the Second World War. We can learn from the failure to create the United States of Europe.

It is not a coincidence that in 1969, at the same time that Maritime Union discussions were at their most enthusiastic level, the concept of regional integration was also hotly debated and a much-studied phenomenon in political science.[2] Such prominent scholars as Raymond Aron, Ernst Haas, Karl Deutsch, Joseph Nye, Amitai Etzioni, James Rosenau, and Stanley Hoffmann — to name just a few — were trying to understand how "how and why states cease to be wholly sovereign, how and why they voluntarily mingle, merge, and mix with their neighbours so as to lose the factual attributes of sovereignty while acquiring new techniques for resolving conflict between themselves."[3]

The answer proposed was neofunctionalism, a theory that postulated that as economic integration (common market) and mutual defence structures such as the North Atlantic Treaty Organization (NATO) took over key functions of the nation-state, the *raison d'être* of domestic governments would wither and be replaced by supranational state structures complete with new identities and citizenship loyalties. In other words, as long as the European Common Market was responsible for a citizen's material well-being and NATO for their security, then the citizens' allegiances would cease to be French or German but would become instead European. This did not happen and now well into the twenty-first century, the question of whether any sort of common European identity exists is still being debated.[4]

There was an agenda attached to regional integration theory: regional integration was not simply a passive observation of a phenomenon that social scientists hope to better understand. It was assumed by many academics and diplomats that the full integration of the Western European countries into, at the very least, a European federation was essential for global peace and economic prosperity.[5] Although the concept of a pan-European identity can be traced back to the Holy Roman Empire,[6] the theory of how such an identity could and should emerge in the time of post-Napoleonic nation-states[7] — that is, states whose legitimacy is based on a definition of what constitutes a nation (rather than, say, a kingdom) — emerged in the years after the Second World War and at the beginning of the Cold War. A united Europe was understood to be necessary to combat Soviet expansionism and to ensure that Europe could play a role in a world now dominated by two superpowers. This was more than an economic concern: the Cold War standoff between the NATO bloc (dominated by the United States) and the Warsaw bloc (dominated by the Soviet Union) represented a tangible threat. Only a united Europe could find a balance to offset this bipolar power struggle. Regional integration theory was supposed to provide both an explanation for and a means by which Europe would and could develop a common identity.

By 1969, almost twenty-five years after the end of the Second World War and a dozen years after the creation of the European Economic Community with the Treaty of Rome in 1957, Europe was certainly more "integrated" than it had been prior to the war. Still, it was far from functioning as a cohesive federation. The idea of a United States of Europe had yet to catch on. The French were still French; the Germans were still German. Why? Regional integration theorists concluded that "Regional cooperation, organization, systems, and subsystems may help describe steps on the way; but they should not be confused with the resulting condition."[8] In other words, these regional measures by themselves had not resulted in a full union. Something else was going on and something else was needed before full integration could take place. These European organizations and agreements were either the result of, or worked in tandem with, regional integration but by themselves could not bring about integration.

A few salient reasons emerged. First, identity, both national and subnational, was a powerful counterforce to full integration. Not only did national identities remain strong, but subnational identities were now also proliferating.[9] Second, state actors were not willing to take the steps that full integration required and instead challenged the view that such integration was always necessary or beneficial. The second reason is somewhat of a truism for it does not explain why state actors resisted integration. But the bottom line was this: state actors deferred to regional agreements and institutions when they saw such a move as to their advantage and did not when they did not; further, they were not particularly perceptive as to what was or was not to their advantage, particularly when choosing between short-term and long-term gains.[10]

The parallels to the failure of the Maritime provinces to unite are striking. The Maritimes also embarked on an ambitious integration program, all laid out in careful detail in the Maritime Union Study. Provincial agreements and agencies like the Maritime Provinces Higher Education Commission (MPHEC) would be vanguards and as more regulatory activities became Maritime wide, other pan-Maritime functions would follow. Economic integration, already promised by the *British North America Act, 1867* (BNA 1867), would be enhanced. Integrated transportation policies including common licensing would be implemented, professional qualifications would now be Maritime-wide rather than provincially specific, and so on. This incremental approach, much loved by regional integration theorists, would gradually and inexorably unite the Maritimes into one province.

But this did not happen. A Council of Maritime Premiers still exists, although interestingly it has been upstaged now by the Council of Atlantic Premiers, formally established in 2000. The agency meant to rationalize post-secondary education and prevent inefficient duplication, the MPHEC, has long dropped such a mandate and focuses its attention on report writing, "Quality Assurance," and bulk purchases.[11] There is a considerable amount of regional cooperation, as a quick scan of the Council of Atlantic Premiers website attests: the Atlantic Provinces Education Foundation; the Atlantic Apprenticeship Harmonization Project; the Atlantic Growth Strategy (under which can be found the Atlantic Immigration Program, the Regional Electricity Cooperation and Strategic Infrastructure Initiative, the Clean Power Roadmap, Atlantic Trade and Investment Growth Strategy, Enhancing Broadband, and the Atlantic Trade and Procurement Partnership Memorandum of Understanding); the Office of Regulatory Affairs and Service Effectiveness and the Atlantic Workforce Partnership.[12] Yet, despite this and despite close to seventy years of regional institutions, programs, and agreements, calls are still being made for more cooperation and less competition. If these institutional arrangements were effective, surely the integration would have already taken place.

One of the highlights of The Atlantic Economic Forum (see Chapter 15) was discussion about the Atlantic Loop, an ambitious project that would unite the power grids of Quebec and Newfoundland and Labrador to the Maritime grids, forming a power loop. The project could be completed by 2030 but is now "bogged down in cost negotiations."[13] Indeed. On 11 October 2023, Nova Scotia announced it was abandoning the project as costs had grown out of reach. Prince Edward Island responded by saying that it would now have to "look after itself."[14] Once again, regional cooperation collapses. Once again, the priorities of a specific province outweighed the advantages to the region as a whole.

While persistent national identities have been seen as the reason why the full integration of Europe has not occurred, proponents of Maritime Union — both political and economic —speak instead of parochialism as the problem. In 1977, Prince Edward Island's premier Alex Campbell complained that parochialism was undermining Atlantic Canada's economic development:

> We are four separate, competitive, jealous and parochial provinces. We fight each other for industrial development. We fight each other for subsidiaries and we bicker about energy and transportation. And too often, the lines of battle are drawn on purely political grounds or selfish local considerations.[15]

In 1995, Stephen Tomblin published a study of regional integration in Canada titled *Ottawa and the Outer Provinces*. In a chapter titled "The Atlantic Region of Canada," Tomblin wrote:

> Imagine the advantages of a united Atlantic region with . . . the determination to deal with mutual problems arising from external challenges, according to the needs of local people. However, we live

in a federation with multiple contradictions where there is ample opportunity for mischief making. Atlantic Canadians share problems but each province is also the product of distinct institutional and cultural experiences. In the final analysis, our institutional structure, which placates parochialism, also reinforces a style of competitive statecraft that displays internal divisions and ambiguities in the worst way.[16]

The essence of Tomblin's analysis is correct, although I would question the assumption that "internal divisions" are being displayed "in the worst way" or that our institutional structure "placates parochialism." These are value judgments and if applied to, say, Quebec within Canada, they would be seen as disrespectful to the legitimate aspirations that Quebecers express for their self-determination and determination to preserve their unique culture and identity. Surely Prince Edward Island has the same right. Recall that Richard Simeon believes that standing up for your province in confrontation with Ottawa shows that you are not willing to accept your deprived lot.

Nevertheless, Tomblin has identified the core issue. In the end, provincial leaders have not and will not give up their autonomy and so "territorial considerations have remained a central concern for all stakeholders."[17] This is an argument that has been made many times before, what Richard Hatfield of New Brunswick called "the policy of cutthroat competition."[18]

Yet Campbell was not advocating Maritime, let alone Atlantic Union. For such a union to take place, according to Campbell, there needed to be a unifying identity, a common loyalty to a supra-provincial entity. That did not exist. Atlantic Canada did not constitute a region and so there was no legitimate or practical basis for a political union: "The only people who consider Atlantic Canada as a region are those who live outside of Atlantic Canada, the planners and the bureaucrats in Ottawa, the newscasters in Toronto and the airline executives in Montreal."[19]

This is where the debate over Maritime Union becomes muddy. Is a pan-Maritime identity a necessary precondition to union, or the desired outcome of union? J. Murray Beck's contribution to the 1978 *Joint Atlantic Canada/Western Canada Studies Conference* demonstrates how intertwined these arguments are. Also dismissing the argument that the Maritimes constituted a region, Beck claimed that

> unless the criteria of a region are taken simply as geographical propinquity, likeness in historical and population background, and similarity of economic problems, the Maritime provinces . . . do not constitute a region in any meaningful way.[20]

On first reading my former political science professor's remarks, I assumed Professor Beck was being ironic. Surely "geographical propinquity, likeness in historical and population background, and similarity of economic problems" are more than enough to constitute a region. But Beck was not being ironic. The provinces do not meet

> the requirements of the political scientist that the adjacent parts of a region should not only differ in character from other entities in the political organism but also be capable of being treated as though they were a political actor; nor those of the sociologist who sees a region "as part of a national domain . . . sufficiently unified to have a consciousness of its customs and ideals and thus [possessing] a sense of identity distinct from the rest of the country"; nor those of the planner who defines a region in terms of a set of problems and then estimates the degree of regionalism by the capacity to respond jointly to them.[21]

Frankly, I would argue that the Maritimes, anyway, fulfill all these criteria. However, Beck, like other political scientists such as Donald Smiley, believed that provinces were the only sub-national units that warranted attention. Smiley called on political scientists "to banish the term region from our vocabulary and speak instead of provinces." Provinces have a "concrete and unambiguous existence," while regions were ambiguous demarcations at best.[22] Smiley was correct that regions are ambiguous. "Region," writes Lachlan MacKinnon, "is a slippery idea."[23] Regions are clear and specific to observers living outside the region, and the farther away they live, the clearer the regional identity becomes. But those living in the region know well how complicated local identities are.

However, Beck added another layer to his rejection of the Maritimes as a coherent region. As befits a political scientist, Beck argues that the reason why the Maritimes do not constitute a region is precisely because they have been separate provinces for so long. Their separate provincial status has prevented the creation of a unified identity. State structure matters:

> [I]t took no little time for the provincial capitals to establish their hegemony over the scattered out-settlements, [but] once it was established the provinces' residents turned to their provincial governments as the source of benefits, in the beginning for expenditures on roads and bridges, later for a growing multitude of other services. More and more they rated their premier by his [sic] competence in safeguarding their interests. Hence arises the difficulty of his making concessions to his fellow premiers even if it is simply a question of arranging "trade-offs," and the more political he is the less he is likely to engage in genuine co-operation. The outcome is inevitable: to New Brunswickers and their premier, for example, Halifax, Charlottetown, and St John's are almost as much foreign capitals as are London and Washington.[24]

This is a classic neofunctionalist argument. Citizens identify with the authority that provides for their well-being. But there is an irony here. First, if the state structure — that is, the fact that the Maritimes comprise three provinces with their own governments and capitals — has created three separate provincial identities, then why would a single provincial government of a unified Maritime province not do the same? If the source of identity is government services, then such services provided by a united Maritimes should have the same effect. It might well take "no little time" but it would still occur. No one argued that the scattered communities with their own identities at the time of the creation of New Brunswick, Nova Scotia, or Prince Edward Island required their own provinces. The assumption was that they would now be united as New Brunswickers or Nova Scotians or Islanders.

The corollary question is this: is Beck's premise even true? Is it even the case that provincial identities in the Maritimes are strong and coherent? Were strong provincial identities indeed created through state hegemony over the "the scattered out-settlements"? If so, how do we explain the persistence of the also strong sub-provincial cultural identities held by Acadians, Cape Bretoners, and the Brayon of Madawaska, and so on?[25]

We have, then, a bit of a paradox. One argument is that provincial identities are too entrenched for Maritime Union to be acceptable. Yet these provincial identities are themselves problematic. The question that now emerges is this: Just how important is it that the three Maritime provinces share an identity sufficient to allow for their union? On the surface, this question seems straightforward. There is certainly a cultural affinity shared by the three provinces, one which makes this region unique in Canada, and certainly separates it from its neighbour, Quebec. The Maritimes have more in common than any one of those provinces would have with, say, Ontario or Manitoba or British Columbia.

However, the question becomes even more complicated when we challenge the assumptions built into the query. What identity are we speaking of? Just what is a regional identity? Why must an identity be shared to warrant union? Other questions emerge from this question. Do regions integrate (on the path to unification) without intervention, and if so, how? If not, what intervention is required from state actors to facilitate integration and ultimately union?

The fear of loss of provincial identities is real, but it is not a persuasive argument against Maritime Union. Other arguments against union are stronger, such as the sheer enormity of the task from a constitutional standpoint and the legitimate concern that a unified Maritime province would be dominated by a single centre whose interests would always prevail. On the other hand, the argument that the Maritimes have a single identity and therefore should unite is also false. There is such a thing as a Maritime identity, but it is one of many, and not necessarily the strongest one. Yet a province, or for that matter, a nation-state, does not require a homogenous national identity to succeed. Few nation-states have such a single identity. Anthony Smith, writing about European unity, argues that "however dominant the nation and its national identification, human beings retain a multiplicity of allegiances in the contemporary world. They have multiple identities. These identifications may reinforce national identities."[26] If we substitute "province" for "nation" and "provincial" for "national," we have a fair assessment of the Maritimes.

Conclusion

If the Provinces of Nova Scotia and New Brunswick were to be annexed to Prince Edward Island, great benefits might result to our people; but if this Colony were to be annexed to these Provinces, the opposite might be the effect. . . . We are here to maintain our rights, and we shall never enter a Union which will deprive us of this birthright.

John Hamilton Gray, 1864[1]

Both the proponents and opponents of Maritime Union struggle with difficult arguments that I suspect each side, deep down, knows are fundamentally flawed. Proponents realize that the project is constitutionally difficult — very difficult — so much so that the efforts required outweigh the benefits they promise. Those opposing Maritime Union are aware that their position that all the region needs is more cooperative programs and policies cannot be wholly true: such cooperation has been going on for a century and the region still struggles.

Those who oppose union on the grounds that they would lose their provincial identities must conveniently ignore the many sub-provincial identities that already exist. Yes, identity is linked to state structures: provinces matter. But identity is a relative concept; we all enjoy many identities, and a united Maritimes would encourage yet another and not necessarily at the expense of those we already hold. For that matter, there already is a pan-Maritime identity and strengthening this identity will not necessarily erase those already held. Just because a larger state structure can destroy sub-regional identities, it does not follow that they must do so in order to prosper, or that such destruction is inevitable, or that sub-regional identities cannot thrive within a larger province.

But Maritime Union will certainly have an effect on identity, and it is also true that we cannot simply assume that in a united Maritimes the region's many identities will survive on their own. Care must be taken. Recall that in the past identities were targeted for erasure by state structures. Our First Nations peoples know this all too well. Today, Cape Bretoners are Cape Bretoners without having their own province (although many wish they did). The same could be said about the region's Acadians. Yet this did not happen without a struggle. Constitutional guarantees are essential.

Those that believe one Maritime government will ensure efficiencies put much too much faith in governments' abilities to solve problems and naively believe such a government would be equitable in how the sub-regions within a united province would be treated. The argument that there are economic advantages of union is strong, but this assumes that collaboration necessarily produces greater prosperity. This is unproven and runs counter to another common argument for economic growth, which is that competition is the basis for efficiency. But even if it is true that collaboration will allow the region to prosper, this is a false promise unless it is firmly established that such prosperity will accrue to the region equitably. The old saw that a rising tide lifts all boats is a cynical cliché that conveniently ignores the fact that an improved economy is not an ocean; it is not a uniform body of water. Some boats will rise. Others will sink. Metaphors are not arguments.

On the other hand, the problem facing the Maritimes in terms of economic cooperation is less about competition and more about overregulation: too much bureaucracy, too many jurisdictions policing the same industries. Transaction costs, bureaucratic delays, lack of central planning, the right hand not knowing what the left hand is doing: these are all complaints one hears constantly abut doing business in the Maritimes. Add to these calls for improved economies of scale, the pooling of talent and expertise, and avoiding costly duplication and triplication. Surely there are advantages to finding better means for the Maritimes to work together.

Finally, there has to be a better understanding of just what the role the federal government has in dealing with the Maritimes. The Maritimes must take the lead on this question. The federal government hears contradictory messages: "stop interfering and let us manage our own affairs," followed by "why aren't you providing us with the assistance we need?"

The one-time premier of Nova Scotia, James Johnston, supported the idea of a British North American federation, but thought the Maritime provinces should nevertheless unite into one province first. He worried about the ability of the Maritime province to broker a good deal if they were still three separate provinces. Perhaps, he mused, it would be better if the Maritimes fulfilled their quest to unite before negotiating with Canada. Speaking in the Nova Scotia Legislative Assembly in 1864, Johnston said: "What we want is to produce a real unity — make the parts that are now separate a homogeneous whole — give them a oneness of existence and purpose." Charles Tupper agreed, adding "this union when required will be . . . more easy of accomplishment when these Maritime provinces are united."[2]

What if Johnston and Tupper had had their way? What if the new Dominion began as a federation comprising Ontario, Quebec, and the Maritimes? How would this have changed our constitutional history? Would this mean that French language rights would never have been entrenched? That the patriation effort would have failed because there was no means by which an amending formula could accommodate a Canada with eight rather than ten provinces? That does not seem to make sense. The current 7/50 formula is based on the happy coincidence that there are four "Western" provinces and four "Atlantic" provinces. But if that were not the case, surely another solution would have been found. As well, questions concerning representation in the Maritime Legislative Assembly would have already been settled; indeed, what did the Maritime delegates have in mind in the first place regarding Maritime Union? They must have given it some thought. It cannot be an impossibility to determine an equitable distribution of seats in a united province.

The constitutional and other structural problems associated with Maritime Union may appear to be insurmountable. They would indeed be difficult, yet they are not impossible. Certain questions would have to be answered: would the union of the provinces mean their abolishment and then re-creation, or simply the merger of three existing constitutions? What effect would union have on the office of the Lieutenant Governor? What would be the collateral impact on other parts of the Constitution?

The political consequences of union would be, frankly, more difficult to overcome. Whether provincial and sub-provincial identities should matter is not the same question as whether they do matter. They do and would. As much as I believe the long-term benefits outweigh the short-term concerns, no Maritime premier is likely to risk such a project.

Maritimers and Maritime leaders tend to be pragmatic and prudent, so what we are left with is the need to keep advocating for more cooperation and more innovative collaborative programs. Despite the criticism referred to in this text, the Maritime Union Study had it right: incremental change through cooperative efforts such that Maritimers became more and more accustomed to working together is the only route that will eventually lead to some sort of economic union and some sort of political rapprochement. But, to borrow once again from Donald Savoie, I do not expect to see this happen in my lifetime.

Notes

Opening Epigraph

1   Quoted in Frank MacKinnon, *Government of Prince Edward Island* (Toronto: University of Toronto Press, 1951) at 288 [Laurier to A.E. Burke, 30 November 1906, *Public Archives of Canada, Laurier Papers*, no 3581].

Preface

1   Canadian Press, "Buchanan Raises Spectre of Joining United States" *The Globe and Mail* (19 April 1990) at A1. Buchanan, who would be appointed to the Senate just a few months later, was asked what would happen if the Meech Lake Accord failed and this resulted in Quebec separating. His remarks echoed comments made by some Nova Scotia politicians many years before, just after Confederation in 1867. See Donald F. Warner, "The Post-Confederation Annexation Movement in Nova Scotia" (1947) 28 *The Canadian Historical Review* 156–65.

2   This is a question that continues to emerge. See, for example, David Milne, "Consequences of Quebec Independence on Atlantic Provinces" (2002) 51 *University of New Brunswick Law Journal* 289–96. This book is about Maritime, not Atlantic Union. Many arguments for and against Atlantic Union apply to Maritime Union and vice versa. But some do not, particularly when the geographic and cultural differences between Newfoundland and Labrador and the Maritime provinces are taken into account. When those differences matter, I will make it explicit whether I mean Maritime or Atlantic Union.

3 With a 93.52 percent turnout, 49.42 percent of registered voters in Quebec voted in favour of the referendum question: "Do you agree that Quebec should become sovereign after having made a formal offer to Canada for a new economic and political partnership within the scope of the bill respecting the future of Quebec and of the agreement signed on June 12, 1995?" [*Acceptez-vous que le Québec devienne souverain, après avoir offert formellement au Canada un nouveau partenariat économique et politique, dans le cadre du projet de loi sur l'avenir du Québec et de l'entente signée le 12 juin 1995?*], online: www.electionsquebec.qc.ca/resultats-et-statistiques/referendum-sur-laccession-du-quebec-a-la-souverainete-de-1995/.

4 David Milne, "Consequences of Quebec Independence on Atlantic Provinces," above note 3 at 5.

5 For example, see by Andrew Parkin, Justin Savoie & Charles Breton, "Is One Region Favoured by Ottawa?" *Policy Options* (23 May 2023), online: https://policyoptions.irpp.org/magazines/may-2023/one-region-favoured-ottawa/. Atlantic Canadians were least likely to agree with the statement that the federal government "treats all regions equally." When asked which province gets the most preferential treatment, the choices were British Columbia, Alberta, Quebec, and Ontario. Atlantic Canada did not factor. The survey referenced in this article was Environics "Confederation of Tomorrow" survey, online: www.environicsinstitute.org/projects/listing/-in-tags/type/confederation-of-tomorrow.

6 Robert Finbow, "Atlantic Canada: Forgotten Periphery in an Endangered Confederation" in K. McRoberts, ed, *Beyond Quebec: Taking Stock of Canada* (Montreal: McGill-Queen's University Press, 1995) at 61–80.

7 Donald J. Savoie, *Visiting Grandchildren: Economic Development in the Maritimes* (Toronto: University of Toronto Press, 2006) at 213.

8 *Reference re Secession of Quebec*, [1998] 2 SCR 217.

9 I discuss this at greater length in Chapter 14 in this book.

10 J. Murray Beck, *The History of Maritime Union: A Study in Frustration* (Fredericton: Maritime Union Study, 1969) at 46.

Introduction

1 [1998] 2 SCR 217 [emphasis added].

2 The Atlantica Party, founded in 2010, did call for a union of some sort of the four Atlantic provinces (so the Maritimes plus Newfoundland and Labrador), but the party received only 0.4 percent of the vote (running fifteen candidates) in the 2017 Nova Scotia provincial election. Its current website does not list union in its platform (online: www.atlanticaparty.ca/Platform) and is focused entirely on Nova Scotia.

3   The Canadian Press, "Revived Maritime Merger Proposal Gets No Political
     Support" CBC News (2 December 2012), online: https://www.cbc.ca/news
     /politics/revived-maritime-merger-proposal-gets-no-political-support-1.1173955.

4   The three were senators John Wallace of New Brunswick, Michael Duffy
     of Prince Edward Island, and Stephen Greene of Nova Scotia. See Stephen
     Greene, "Time for Maritime Union" *Policy Options* (1 December 2012), online:
     https://policyoptions.irpp.org/fr/authors/stephen-greene.

5   Innovative Research Group, "Maritime Union Not Likely Any Time
     Soon" (6 February 2016), online: https://innovativeresearch.ca/
     maritime-union-not-likely-any-time-soon/. (Survey conducted 22–26
     January 2013, sample size 553, MoE +/- 4.2%.) On the other hand, as the
     IRG pollster Greg Lyle pointed out, "the fact that more than a third of Nova
     Scotians support Maritime union without much of a case being made says
     the idea is not dead on arrival."

6   The Maritime Union Study commissioned a comprehensive poll in 1970:
     Market Facts of Canada, *The Maritimes and Maritime Union: An Opinion Study*
     (Fredericton: Maritime Union Study, 1970). Gallup also polled in 1970 on
     this question, concluding that while those opposed to union measured only
     38%, those supporting union were just 44%. In the mid-1980s, Ian Stewart
     also polled residents of New Brunswick and Nova Scotia with regard to
     Maritime Union in a study of the differences in political culture on either
     side of the New Brunswick-Nova Scotia border. Stewart's results break out
     the three border counties, so Westmorland (NB) and Cumberland/Colches-
     ter (NS) but his results are similar. Ian Stewart, "More than Just a Line on
     the Map: The Political Culture of the Nova Scotia-New Brunswick Bound-
     ary" (1990) 20 *Publius* 99–111.

7   Donald J. Savoie, *Visiting Grandchildren: Economic Development in the Maritimes*
     (Toronto: University of Toronto Press, 2006) at ix.

8   According to the 2021 census, the populations of the three provinces are:
     Prince Edward Island: 154,331; New Brunswick: 775,610; and Nova Sco-
     tia: 969,383 for a total of 1,899,324. Manitoba's population is 1,342,153,
     Saskatchewan's is 1,132,505, and Newfoundland and Labrador's is 510,550
     (online: www12.statcan.gc.ca/census-recensement/2021/dp-pd/prof/index
     .cfm). The projected populations are slightly higher.

9   Donald J. Savoie, *Canada: Beyond Grudges, Grievances, and Disunity* (Montreal:
     McGill-Queen's University Press, 2023), deals with the relationship between
     provincial size and political clout in federal-provincial relations. See particu-
     larly ch 3.

10   *The Constitution Act, 1982, Schedule B to the Canada Act 1982 (UK)*, 1982, c 11.

11   Peter H. Russell, *Constitutional Odyssey: Can Canadians Become A Sovereign People?*
     (Toronto: University of Toronto Press, 1993).

12 *Re: Resolution to Amend the Constitution*, [1981] 1 SCR 753 [Patriation Reference]. For an analysis of Quebec's dissatisfaction, see Kenneth McRoberts "Canada's Constitutional Crisis" (1991) 90 *Current History* 411–16.

13 Michael Lusztig, "Constitutional Paralysis: Why Canadian Constitutional Initiatives are Doomed to Fail" (1994) 27 *Canadian Journal of Political Science* 747–71. For a contrary view, see Warren J. Newman, "Living with the Amending Procedures: Prospects for Future Constitutional Reform in Canada," in Graeme Mitchell et al, eds, *A Living Tree: The Legacy of 1982 in Canada's Political Evolution* (Markham: LexisNexis Canada, 2007) at 747–80.

14 Adam Dodek, "Uncovering the Wall Surrounding the Castle of the Constitution: Judicial Interpretation of Part V of the Constitution Act, 1982" in Emmett Macfarlane, ed, *Constitutional Amendment in Canada* (Toronto: University of Toronto Press, 2016) at 42–64 (42).

15 Erin Crandall, "Amendment by Stealth of Provincial Constitutions in Canada" (2022) 45 *Manitoba Law Journal* 172–96 at 173.

16 *Ibid.* at 174.

17 See also Mark D. Walters, "Common Law Constitution in Canada: Return of Lex Non Scripta as Fundamental Law" (2001) 51 *University of Toronto Law Journal* 91–142.

18 When I began writing this book, I wrote: "The prospect of Maritime Union, even if only hypothetical, provides us with an opportunity to *clarify precisely what a provincial constitution is. . . .*" After much study, I now realize that this was an overly ambitious claim to make!

19 Consider the experience in Prince Edward Island regarding electoral reform and the three referenda that it has held. Newfoundland's experience with the referendum on whether to join Canada is also a useful case. I address the obligation for consultation in Chapter 14 below. See the references cited there.

20 *R v Hills*, [2023] SCC 2 at para 68(a). Of course, in general Supreme Court reference cases dealing with constitutional questions are, by definition, hypothetical, viz. *Reference re Secession of Quebec*. See also Kim Lane Scheppele: "Constitution builders *guess* about the future and what will most successfully guide them through it. They know about the past and the present and what they want to avoid." "Aspirational and Aversive Constitutionalism: The Case for Studying Cross-Constitutional Influence Through Negative Models" (2003) 1 *International Journal of Constitutional Law* 296–324 at 298 (original emphasis).

21 Christopher Cochrane & Andrea Perrella, "Regions, Regionalism and Regional Differences in Canada" (2012) 45 *Canadian Journal of Political Science* 829–53 at 830.

22 Lachlan MacKinnon, "A Region in Retrospective" (2019) 48 *Acadiensis* 230–40 at 230.

23   Richard Simeon, "Regional and Canadian Political Institutions" (1975) *Queen's Quarterly* 82 at 499–511 (499).

24   Ron MacDonald, "Maritime Union — We Rise Again" (1995–96 Winter) *Canadian Parliamentary Review* 2–5 at 5.

25   See Chapter 17 in this book.

26   J. Murray Beck, *The History of Maritime Union: A Study in Frustration* (Fredericton: Maritime Union Study, 1969) at 1.

27   Prince Edward Island has an area of 5,660 km² and has a population of 162,866 (2021 census). British Columbia's Vancouver Island's area is 32,100 km² and has a population of 864,000. Note that in 1849, Vancouver Island was its own colony. The Vancouver Island Party called for the secession of the island from British Columbia. It was deregistered as a party in 2020.

28   Cf. *Constitution Act, 1982*, Schedule B to the *Canada Act 1982* (UK), 1982, c 11, s 35.

29   For example, *R v Paul*, 1993 CanLII 4705 (NB CA).

30   [1999] 3 SCR 456, 177 DLR (4th) 513.

31   James [Sákéj] Youngblood Henderson, "Constitutional Powers and Treaty Rights" (2000) 63 *Saskatchewan Law Review* 719–50.

32   A good place to start is John R.H. Matchim, "A Bibliography on Indigenous Peoples and the History of the Atlantic Region" (2020) 49 *Acadiensis* 223–64. See also Andrew Costa, "Interrelated Treaty Orders Across the Generations: Autonomy, Obligation and Confederacy in the Wabanaki Compact (1725–26)" (2018) 35 *Windsor Yearbook of Access to Justice* 463–85; Robert Hamilton, "After Tsilhqot'in Nation: The Aboriginal Title Question in Canada's Maritime Provinces" (2016) 67 *University of New Brunswick Law Journal* 58–108; John Reid, "Empire, the Maritime Colonies, and the Supplanting of Mi'kma'ki/Wulstukwik, 1780–1820" (2009) 38 *Acadiensis* 78–97; Jaime Battiste, "Understanding the Progression of Mi'kmaw Law" (2008) 31 *Dalhousie Law Journal* 311–50; Willard Walker, "The Wabanaki Confederacy" (1998) 37 *Maine History* 110–39. More generally, see John Borrows, "Indigenous Legal Traditions in Canada" (2005) 19 *Washington University Journal of Law & Policy* 167–224; William C. Wicken, *Mi'kmaq Treaties on Trial: History, Land, and Donald Marshall Junior* (Toronto: University of Toronto Press, 2002); Thomas Isaac, *Aboriginal and Treaty Rights in the Maritimes: The Marshall Decision and Beyond* (Saskatoon: Purich Publishing Ltd, 2001).

33   John Ralston Saul, *A Fair Country: Telling Truths about Canada* (Toronto: Viking Canada, 2008) at 71–72.

34   B.V. LeBlanc & R. LeBlanc, "Traditional Material Culture in Acadia" in Jean Daigle, ed, James Crombie, trans, *Acadia of the Maritimes* (Moncton: Université de Moncton, 1995) at 62–95. See also Laura Ewen Blokker & Heather A. Knight, "Louisiana Bousillage, The Migration and Evolution of a French

Building Technique in North America" (2013) 28 *Construction History* 27–48 and Hilary Doda, "Scissors, Embellishment, and Womanhood: The Material Culture of Acadian Sewing to 1755" (2021) 50 *Acadiensis* 62–95.

35 A.J.B. Johnston, "The Call of the Archetype and the Challenge of Acadian History" (2004) 5 *French Colonial History* 63–92; J. Brian Bird, "Settlement Patterns in Maritime Canada: 1687–1786" (1955) 45 *Geographical Review* 385–404; Jacques Vanderlinden, "French Jurisdictional Complexity on the Fringe, Acadia 1667–1710" (2019) 12 *Journal of Civil Law Studies* 33–52. See also Jacques Vanderlinden, "Acadie: A la rencontre de l'histoire du droit avant le dérangement" (1995) 23 *Manitoba Law Journal* 79–102; Naomi Griffiths, *From Migrant to Acadian: A North American Border People, 1604–1755* (Montreal: McGill University Press, 2005); David Bell, "Maritime Legal institutions under the *Ancien Regime*, 1710–1850" (1995) 23 *Manitoba Law Journal* 103–31; Jean Daigle, "Acadia, 1604–1763. An Historical Synthesis" in Jean Daigle, ed, *The Acadians of the Maritimes* (Moncton: Université de Moncton, 1982) 17–46 at 21. In the same volume just cited, Philippe Doucet provides a detailed explanation of the Acadian position on oaths in "Politics and the Acadians" in Jean Daigle, ed, *The Acadians of the Maritimes* (Moncton: Université de Moncton, 1982) at 219–69, particularly 222ff.).

36 Cape Breton: 1763, 1765, 1820; Prince Edward Island: 1769; New Brunswick: 1784.

37 David Bell, "A Note on the Reception of English Statutes in New Brunswick" (1979) 28 *University of New Brunswick Law Journal* 195–201; David Bell, *Early Loyalist Saint John: The Origin of New Brunswick Politics, 1783–1786* (Saint John: New Ireland Press, 1983); David Bell, "Sedition among the Loyalists: The Case of Saint John, 1784–1786" (1995) 44 *University of New Brunswick Law Journal* 163–78; Barry Cahill, "How Far English Laws Are in Force Here: Nova Scotia's First Century of Reception Law Jurisprudence" (1993) 42 *University of New Brunswick Law Journal* 113–56; Shirley B. Elliott, "An Historical Review of Nova Scotia Legal Literature: A Select Bibliography" (1984) 8 *Dalhousie Law Journal* 197–212; Elizabeth Gaspar Brown, "British Statutes in the Emergent Nations of North America: 1606–1949" (1963) 7 *American Journal of Legal History* 95–136; Peter Hogg, "Reception," *Constitutional Law of Canada: 2020 Student Edition* (Toronto: Carswell/Thomas Reuters, 2020) ch 2 at 2-1–2-10; Philip Girard, "Themes and Variations in Early Canadian Legal Culture: Beamish Murdoch and His Epitome of the Laws of Nova-Scotia" (1993) 11 *Law and History Review* 101–44; Philip Girard, "The Supreme Court of Nova Scotia, Responsible Government, and the Quest for Legitimacy, 1850–1920" (1994) 17 *Dalhousie Law Journal* 430–57; Philip Girard, *Lawyers and Legal Culture in British North America: Beamish Murdoch of Halifax* (Toronto: University of Toronto Press, 2011); Elizabeth Mancke, "Early Modern

Imperial Governance and the Origins of Canadian Political Culture" (1999) 32 *Canadian Journal of Political Science* 3–20; Elizabeth Mancke, "Idiosyncratic Localism, Provincial Moderation, and Imperial Loyalty: Planter Studies and the History of 18th-Century Nova Scotia" (2013) 42 *Acadiensis* 169–81; J. E. Read, "The Early Provincial Constitutions" (1948) 26 *Canadian Bar Review* 621–37.

38 Michael Lienesch, "Founding: Audacity, Ambition, Adaptability" in *New Order of the Ages: Time, the Constitution, and the Making of Modern American Political Thought* (New Jersey: Princeton University Press, 1988) at 139–140, 141 & 142.

39 Gad Horowitz, "Conservatism, Liberalism, and Socialism in Canada: An Interpretation" (1966) 32 *Canadian Journal of Economics and Political Science* 143–71.

40 Kenneth McRae, "The Structure of Canadian History" in Louis Hartz, ed, *The Founding of New Societies* (New York: Harcourt, Brace & World, 1964) at 219–74.

CHAPTER ONE | **A Vision of Union**

1 To Rt Hon William Windham, Secretary of State for War and the Colonies. Quoted in D.C. Harvey, "Uniacke's Memorandum to Windham, 1806" (1936) 17 *The Canadian Historical Review* 41–58 at 53 (second "sic" is in Harvey's text).

2 A recent plea for Maritime Union claimed that "Maritimers have more in common with each other than with people in Quebec, Ontario, Saskatchewan or any other province you could name. We in fact have more in common with people in Maine than with people in any other Canadian province. We are a distinct people and we have a distinct culture" (Stephen Greene, "Time for Maritime Union," *Policy Options*, 1 December 2012). However, Greene's arguments are entirely based on the economic precarity of the region, not the need to protect this common identity. (I would also question his claim about commonality with the people of Maine.)

3 Uniacke (together with Michael Francklin) was immortalized in Thomas Raddall's work of fiction *His Majesty's Yankees* as a key figure in Nova Scotia during the American Revolution: Thomas H. Raddall, *His Majesty's Yankees* (Garden City: Doubleday, Doran and Co, 1942). See also David Creelman, "Conservative Solutions: The Early Historical Fiction of Thomas Raddall" (1995) 20 *Studies in Canadian Literature* 127–49.

4 Richard Uniacke, *The Statutes at Large Passed in the Several General Assemblies Held in His Majesty's Province of Nova-Scotia: From the First Assembly Which Met at Halifax the Second Day of October, in the Thirty-Second Year of His Late Majesty*

Geo. II. A.D. 1758, to the Forty-Fourth Year of His Present Majesty Geo. III A.D. 1804, Inclusive; with a Complete Index and Abridgement of the Whole (Halifax: John Howe and Son, Printers to the King's Most Excellent Majesty, 1805).

5   In general, see R. Douglas Francis et al, *Origins: Canadian History to Confederation* (Toronto: Holt, Rinehart and Winston of Canada, 1988); J.M. Bumsted, *The Peoples of Canada: A Pre-Confederation History* (Toronto: Oxford University Press, 1992); and Margaret Conrad, *At the Ocean's Edge: A History of Nova Scotia to Confederation* (Toronto: University of Toronto Press, 2020). See references in Introduction at note 32 above for the Wabanaki Confederacy and Acadia.

6   Indeed, even the understanding of what constituted a boundary differed under First Nations' law. See James Youngblood Henderson, "First Nations Legal Inheritances in Canada: The Mikmaq Model" (1995) 23 *Manitoba Law Journal* 1–31.

7   See J. Murray Beck, *The Government of Nova Scotia* (Toronto: University of Toronto Press, 1957) at 9.

8   It was re-annexed in 1820. For Cape Breton's in-and-out status vis-à-vis Nova Scotia, see Robert Morgan, "Separatism in Cape Breton 1820–1884" in Kenneth Donovan, ed, *Cape Breton at 200: Historical Essays in Honour of the Island's Bicentennial, 1785–1985* (Sidney: University College of Cape Breton Press, 1985) 41–51 and Christopher Mark Macneill, "Canada's Post-Colonial Orphan Province: Cape Breton Island's Quest for Autonomy" (2021) 4 *International Journal of Law Management & Humanities* 52–68.

9   [John Allan] "To George Washington from a Citizen of Nova Scotia, 8 February 1776," Founders National Archives, online: https://founders.archives.gov/documents/Washington/03-03-02-0192. [Original source: Philander D. Chase, ed, *The Papers of George Washington, Revolutionary War Series*, vol 3, 1 January 1776–31 March 1776 (Charlottesville: University Press of Virginia, 1988) at 259–65.]

10 B.C. Cuthbertson, "Uniacke and the Struggle for Patronage in Nova Scotia" (1986) 12 *The Canadian Journal of Irish Studies* 148–65 at 148.

11 See Ernest A. Clarke, "Cumberland Planters and the Aftermath of the Attack on Fort Cumberland" in Margaret Conrad, ed, *They Planted Well: New England Planters in Maritime Canada* (Fredericton: Acadiensis Press, 1988) at 42–60.

12 B.C. Cuthbertson, "Uniacke and the Struggle for Patronage in Nova Scotia" above note 10 at 148–49 and 165.

13 Mind you, while Uniacke was quite capable of moderating his political views he was anything but a moderate in other parts of his life. Beck writes that having "a temperament unwilling to tolerate anything detracting him from his dignity, meant that no one would challenge him with impunity." J. Murray Beck, "Rise and Fall of Nova Scotia's Attorney General: 1749–1983"

(1984) 8 *Dalhousie Law Journal* 125–42 at 127. Beck also labels Uniacke as one of the "extremists" on the question of the role of the Church of England in Nova Scotia state affairs, demonstrating little toleration for other sects and creeds, even within Anglo-Protestantism: J. Murray Beck, "Actors on the Governmental Stage" in *The Government of Nova Scotia*, above note 7 at 23.

14 I discuss the question of neutrality and moderation in eighteenth century Nova Scotia in Donald A. Desserud, "An Outpost's Response: The Language and Politics of Moderation in Eighteenth-Century Nova Scotia" (1999) 29 *American Review of Canadian Studies* 379–406, and Donald A. Desserud, "Nova Scotia and the American Revolution" in Margaret Conrad, ed, *Making Adjustments: Change and Continuity in Planter Nova Scotia, 1759–1800* (Fredericton: Acadiensis Press, 1991) at 89–112. See also J.B. Brebner, *The Neutral Yankees of Nova Scotia: A Marginal Colony during the Revolutionary Years* (New York: Columbia University Press, 1937) and J.B. Brebner, *New England's Outpost: Acadia Before the Conquest of Canada* (Hamden, CT: Archon Books, 1965).

15 On the importance of Montesquieu to Canadian constitutionalism, see Philip Resnick, "Montesquieu Revisited, or the Mixed Constitution and the Separation of Powers in Canada" (1987) 20 *Canadian Journal of Political Science* 97–115, and more recently, Samuel V. LaSelva, *Canada and the Ethics of Constitutionalism: Identity, Destiny, and Constitutional Faith* (Montreal: McGill-Queen's University Press, 2018).

16 The colony of Quebec was divided into Upper and Lower Canada in 1791 to accommodate the influx of United Empire Loyalists, refugees of the American Revolution.

17 *The Union Act*, 1840 3-4 Vict, c 35 (UK).

18 Harvey, "Uniacke's Memorandum to Windham" above note 1 at 52 and 43.

19 Reginald Trotter, commenting on the 1826 memorandum, wrote that Uniacke "thinks that the intention of obtaining possession of British America, which was 'the great object of the war of 1812', 'as a step towards overthrowing the power of England', has not been abandoned, but only awaits a favourable opportunity for a renewal of the attempt." Reginald G. Trotter, "An Early Proposal for the Federation of British North America" (1925) 6 *The Canadian Historical Review* 142–54 at 148.

20 "Observations on the British Colonies in North America with a Proposal for the Confederation of the whole under one Government By Richard John Uniacke Esq'r His Majesty's Attorney General and a Member of the Council in the province of Nova Scotia," *Canadian Archives*, C. O. 217, vol 146 at 334–70. My discussion here is based entirely on Trotter's account of the memorandum, above note 19, and not on the original document.

21 For the history of Responsible Government, see among others Phillip Buckner, *The Transition to Responsible Government: British Policy in British North America,*

1815–1850 (Westport: Greenwood Press, 1985). For the principle of Responsible Government, an excellent and concise explanation can be found in Peter Aucoin et al, *Responsible Government: Clarifying Essentials, Dispelling Myths and Exploring Change* (Ottawa: Canadian Centre for Management Development, 2004), online: https://publications.gc.ca/collections/Collection/SC94-107-2004E.pdf. On the confidence convention see Andrew Heard, *Canadian Constitutional Conventions: The Marriage of Law and Politics* (Toronto: Oxford University Press Canada, 1991) and Donald A. Desserud, *The Confidence Convention under the Canadian Parliamentary System* (Ottawa: Canadian Study of Parliament Occasional Paper Series No 7, 2006).

22   "[W]e wrested it, step by step, against the prejudices and apprehensions of various Secretaries from 1837 to 1847." Joseph Howe, quoted in Jennifer Smith & Lori Turnbull, *The Nova Scotia House of Assembly: On the Cusp of Change?* (Ottawa: Canadian Study of Parliament Group, 2008), online: http://cspg-gcep.ca/pdf/NS_Paper_Formatted-e.pdf at 4.

23   Beck considers Howe to have been an idealist, rejecting the label of opportunism but not embracing the label of pragmatism. See J. Murray Beck, "Joseph Howe: Opportunist or Empire-builder?" (1950) XLI *Canadian Historical Review* 185–202. Beck is responding to James Roy's *Joseph Howe: A Study in Achievement and Frustration* (Toronto: The Macmillan Company of Canada Limited, 1935). See also J. Murray Beck, *Joseph Howe: Vol. 1: Conservative Reformer, 1804–1848; Vol. 2: The Briton Becomes Canadian, 1848–1873* (Montreal: McGill-Queen's University Press, 1983). As well, see George Rawlyk, ed, *Joseph Howe: Opportunist? Man of Vision? Frustrated Politician?* (Toronto: Copp Clark, 1967).

24   Frank MacKinnon, *Government of Prince Edward Island* (Toronto: University of Toronto Press, 1951) at 247.

CHAPTER TWO | **Confederation and the Great Compromise**

1   Quoted in D.C. Harvey, "Confederation in Prince Edward Island" (1933) 14 *The Canadian Historical Review* 143–60 at 149. At the time, Frederick Brecken was a member of Prince Edward Island's House of Assembly. Harvey describes this statement by Brecken as having "unconsciously enunciated the policy of the future."

2   Francis William Pius Bolger, "Prince Edward Island and Confederation; 1863-1873" (1961) 28 *Canadian Catholic Historical Association (CCHA) Report* 25–30 at 25. See also Francis William Pius Bolger, "Long Courted, Won at Last" in *Canada's Smallest Province: A History of P.E.I.* (Charlottetown: Prince Edward Island 1973 Centennial Commission, 1973) ch 9.

3   As reported by the *Islander* newspaper, 2 September 1864.

4 Phillip Buckner summarizes (and then refutes) what he calls the "conspira-
torial theories" to explain why the Maritime leadership agreed to Confederation: "Maritimers are treated as if they lived on a different continent from
the more enlightened inhabitants of the United Province of Canada; they
had to be bribed, coerced, deceived and railroaded into union." Phillip Buckner, "Beware the Canadian Wolf: The Maritimes and Confederation" (2017)
XLVI *Acadiensis* 177–95 at 180.

5 P.B. Waite, The Life and Times of Confederation: Politics, Newspapers, and
the Union of British North America (Toronto: University of Toronto Press,
1962) at 73.

6 Mind you, when the Governor General of Canada Charles Monck wrote to
the Lt Governor of Prince Edward Island, George Dundas (8 August 1864)
concerning the Charlottetown Conference, he wrote: "Sir — I have the honor
to acknowledge the receipt of your Despatch of the 28th July, informing
me of the Delegates from the Governments of the Provinces of Nova Scotia,
New Brunswick, and Prince Edward Island, to consider the propriety of a
Union of these Provinces, had been fixed to take place in Charlottetown on
September 1st. I have the honor to inform you, the Honorable Messrs. Macdonald, Cartier, Brown and Galt, have been appointed as a Deputation from
the Government of Canada to attend the Conference, *with a view to ascertain
whether Canada might not be included in the proposed union*" [emphasis added].

7 D.C. Harvey, "Confederation in Prince Edward Island" (1933) 14 *The Canadian
Historical Review* 143–60 at 145.

8 Desmond Morton, *A Short History of Canada* (Edmonton: Hurtig Publishers,
1983) at 60.

9 The standard references for the Maritimes and Confederation are: Harvey,
"Confederation in Prince Edward Island" (1933) 14 *The Canadian Historical
Review* 143–60; Frank MacKinnon, *The Government of Prince Edward Island*
(Toronto: University of Toronto Press, 1951) at 86–104; Beck, *The Government
of Nova Scotia* (Toronto: University of Toronto Press, 1957) at 143–53; Peter
B. Waite, *The Life and Times of Confederation, 1864–1867* (Toronto: University
of Toronto Press, 1962); W.S. MacNutt, *New Brunswick, A History: 1784–1867*
(Toronto: Macmillan of Canada, 1963; Donald G. Creighton, *The Road to
Confederation: The Emergence of Canada, 1863–1867* (Toronto: Macmillan of
Canada, 1964); Kenneth G. Pryke, *Nova Scotia and Confederation 1864–1874*
(Toronto: University of Toronto Press, 1979); George Rawlyk, *The Atlantic
Provinces and the Problems of Confederation* (St. John's: Breakwater, 1979); R.
Douglas Francis et al, *Origins: Canadian History to Confederation* (Toronto:
Holt, Rinehart and Winston of Canada, 1988); J.M. Bumsted, *The Peoples of
Canada: A Pre-Confederation History* (Toronto: Oxford University Press, 1992);
Phillip A. Buckner & John G. Reid, eds, *The Atlantic Region to Confederation: A*

History (Toronto: University of Toronto Press, 1994); Buckner, "Beware the Canadian Wolf: The Maritimes and Confederation," above note 4; Christopher Moore, *1867: How the Fathers Made a Deal* (Toronto: McClelland and Stewart, 1998); Margaret Conrad, *At the Ocean's Edge: A History of Nova Scotia to Confederation* (Toronto: University of Toronto Press, 2020).

10 Buckner writes: "it was becoming apparent by the 1860s that wooden shipbuilding was an industry with a limited future and that wooden ships represented a risky enterprise both for the capitalists who owned them and for the seamen who sailed on them." "The 1860s: An End and a Beginning" in Buckner & Reid, *The Atlantic Region to Confederation: A History*, above note 9 at 361.

11 W.O. Raymond, "New Brunswick: Political History, 1867–1912," in Adam Shortt & Arthur G. Doughty, eds, *Canada and its Provinces: A History of the Canadian People and Their Institutions by One Hundred Associates* (Toronto: Publishers' Association of Canada Limited, 1914) 403–31 at 429.

12 The standard references are: S.A. Saunders, *The Economic History of the Maritime Provinces* (Fredericton: Acadiensis Press, 1984) and Harold Innis, "An Introduction to the Economic History of the Maritimes, Including Newfoundland and New England" in Harold Innis, *Essays in Canadian Economic History* (Toronto: University of Toronto Press, 1956) at 27–42. Counter arguments can be found in Forbes, Buckner and Acheson cited elsewhere.

13 Whether the dependency of the Maritime economy on outdated shipbuilding technology was responsible for the region's economic decline, and indeed whether the region was in fact so dependent, remains a much-debated topic. At the crux of the debate is why a transition to newer technologies occurred in other shipyards in New England and in Britain, but not those in the Maritimes (at least not until much later). Given the abundance of coal, it seems odd that the Maritimes did not see the advantages of steel manufacturing.

14 In general, see A.A. Den Otter, *The Philosophy of Railways: The Transcontinental Railway Idea in British North America* (Toronto: University of Toronto Press, 1997). Not everyone shared the enthusiasm for the railway project.

15 Garth Stevenson, *Ex Uno Plures: Federal-Provincial Relations in Canada, 1867–1896* (McGill-Queen's University Press, 1993) at 108. Today, Toronto is more than forty times the size of Greater Saint John, and twelve times the size of the Halifax Regional Municipality.

16 Lachlan MacKinnon, "A Region in Retrospective" (2019) 48 *Acadiensis* 230–40 at 235. MacKinnon references Alex Chernoff, "1871 Productivity Differentials and the Decline of the Maritime Manufacturing Sector" (2014) 43 *Acadiensis* 65–88.

17 [Unsigned], "Canada," *The Examiner* (22 August 1864) at 2.

18 Buckner, "The 1860s: An End and a Beginning," above note 9 at 363.

19 This was a bit of an exaggeration. The population estimate for Canada in 1867 was 3,463,000 (Statistics Canada, "Estimated population of Canada, 1605 to present," online: www150.statcan.gc.ca/n1/pub/98-187-x/4151287 -eng.htm#50.

20 Quoted by Moore, *1867: How the Fathers Made a Deal*, above note 9 at 188. McDonald was the Financial Secretary of Nova Scotia in the Tupper administration. Nova Scotia Legislative Assembly, 17 April 1866, Nova Scotia Confederation with Canada, online: https://hcmc.uvic.ca/confederation/en/lgNSLA_1866-04-17.html.

21 Reginald C. Stuart, *United States Expansionism and British North America, 1775–1871* (Chapel Hill: University of North Carolina Press, 1988).

22 Edward MacDonald, "Who's Afraid of the Fenians? The Fenian Scare on Prince Edward Island, 1865–1867" (2009) 38 *Acadiensis* 33–51. See MacDonald's references for further information on the Fenians and their impact on the Maritimes.

23 "Canada To Be Invaded by 50,000 Fenians" *The Globe* (20 December 1864) at 1.

24 "Old Canada" was the term used for some years after Confederation to refer to the former Province of Canada.

25 Harold A. Davis, "The Fenian Raid on New Brunswick" (1955) 36 *The Canadian Historical Review* 316–34.

26 See Margaret Conrad, "Confederation and its Discontents" in *At the Ocean's Edge*, above note 9 at 295–333 (315 ff).

27 For example, the Colonial Secretary Edward Cardwell wrote to the lieutenant governors of the three Maritime provinces 24 June 1865 concerning the responsibility the provinces had for "their own defence." "[T]he Provinces of British North America are incapable, when separated and divided from each other, of making those just and sufficient preparations for national defence, which would be easily [sic] undertaken by a Province uniting in itself all the population and all the resources of the whole." *Sessional Papers (no 63)*, 31 Vict 1868, c 18–19 (UK).

28 F.R. Scott, "Political Nationalism and Confederation" in *Essays on the Constitution: Aspects of Canadian Law and Politics* (Toronto: University of Toronto Press, 1977) 3–34 at 5.

29 Quote in Buckner, "Beware the Canadian Wolf," above note 4 at 179. Buckner references G.P. Browne, ed, *Documents on the Confederation of British North America* (Montreal: McGill-Queen's University Press, 2009) at 129.

30 J. Murray Beck, *The History of Maritime Union: A Study in Frustration* (Fredericton: Maritime Union Study, 1969) at 16–18.

31 Johnston, a Conservative, was premier of Nova Scotia from 1857–1860 and again from 1863–1864.

32   Janet Ajzenstat, ed, *Canada's Founding Debates* (Toronto: University of Toronto Press, 2003) at 262.

33   Johnston and Tupper, Nova Scotia House of Assembly, 28 March 1864, in Ajzenstat, *Canada's Founding Debates*, above note 32 at 262 and 328. Tupper would succeed Johnston as premier 11 May 1864.

34   Beck, *The History of Maritime Union*, above note 30 at 17.

35   Coles was premier of Prince Edward Island on three occasions — 1851–54, 1854–59, and 1867–68 — all prior to the Island joining Confederation in 1873.

36   *The Examiner* (24 August 1864) at 2.

37   This complicated issue is well explained by J.M. Bumsted, *Land, Settlement, and Politics on Eighteenth-Century Prince Edward Island* (Kingston: McGill-Queen's University Press, 1987).

38   Ben Guilding, "The Silent Framers of British North American Union: The Colonial Office and Canadian Confederation, 1851–67" (2018) 99 *The Canadian Historical Review* 349–93.

39   MacNutt, *New Brunswick, A History: 1784–1867*, above note 9 at 430.

CHAPTER THREE | **Maritime Rights and Buyers' Remorse**

1   Fielding to James A. Fraser, 25 August 1886, cited in C.D. Howell, "W.S. Fielding and the Repeal Elections of 1886 and 1887 in Nova Scotia" (1979) 8 *Acadiensis* 28–46 at 42 [Fielding Papers, nos. 505–7, PANS].

2   Donald F. Warner, "The Post-Confederation Annexation Movement in Nova Scotia" (1947) 28 *The Canadian Historical Review* 156–65.

3   Robert C. Vipond, "Constitutional Politics and the Legacy of the Provincial Rights Movement in Canada" (1985) 18 *Canadian Journal of Political Science* 267–94 at 273. Vipond, referencing Christopher Armstrong, *Politics of Federalism: Ontario's Relations with the Federal Government* (Toronto: University of Toronto Press, 1981) writes at 268: "the paradox is that the very Ontarians who became Macdonald's most refractory opponents after Confederation were, at the time of Confederation, among his staunchest allies." See also Vipond's thorough references on the provincial rights movement. See also Christopher Armstrong, "Ceremonial Politics: Federal-Provincial Meetings Before the Second World War" in Kenneth Carty & W. Peter Ward, *National Politics and Community in Canada* (Vancouver: University of British Columbia Press, 1986) at 112–50.

4   Manitoba's premier at the time was John Norquay, a supporter of Macdonald and a Conservative.

5   Joseph Pope, *Correspondence of Sir John Macdonald* (Toronto: Oxford University Press, 1921) at 398.

6 "[I]n March [1887] Mercier had written to Mowat of Ontario, arguing strongly that 'there should be an understanding between the provincial governments with a view to the organization of a system of common defence.'" Donald Creighton, *The Old Chieftain* (Toronto: Houghton Mifflin, 1955) at 472. (Creighton's reference: Province of Ontario, Sessional Papers, 1887, No 51, Mercier to Mowat, 8 March 1887.)

7 Phyllis Blakeley, "The Repeal Election of 1886 in Nova Scotia" (1945) 26 *Nova Scotia Historical Society Collections* 131–53; Howell, "W.S. Fielding and the Repeal Elections of 1886 and 1887 in Nova Scotia," above note 1.

8 P.B. Waite quotes a letter from a Lachlan Cameron who wrote to Sir John Thompson, that "in reality [Fielding's] success was neither Grit nor Tory. It was the embers of the great fire of '67 that still smouldered and blazed anew with the Repeal cry" (21 June 1886). P.B. Waite, *The Man from Halifax: Sir John Thompson, Prime Minister* (Toronto: University of Toronto Press, 1985) at 169.

9 Howell, "W.S. Fielding and the Repeal Elections of 1886 and 1887 in Nova Scotia," above note 1 at 35. Howell is quoting the Halifax *Morning Chronicle*, 10, 12, 15 June 1886. See also T.W. Acheson, "The National Policy and the Industrialization of the Maritimes, 1880–1910" *Acadiensis* (1972) 3–28.

10 Howell, "W.S. Fielding and the Repeal Elections of 1886 and 1887 in Nova Scotia," above note 1 at 28–29.

11 Quoted in D.C. Harvey, "Fielding's Call to Ottawa" (1949) 28 *The Dalhousie Review* 369–85 at 371.

12 Ten Conservatives and four Liberal-Conservatives.

13 The definitive work is Ernest R. Forbes, *The Maritime Rights Movement, 1919–1927* (Montreal: McGill-Queen's University Press, 1979).

14 Donald Savoie, "History Matters" in *Visiting Grandchildren: Economic Development in the Maritimes* (Toronto: University of Toronto Press, 2006) ch 2.

15 Reginald V. Harris, "The Union of the Maritime Provinces" (1906) 5 *Canadian Law Review* 475–80 at 475.

16 [unsigned] "Maritime Union" *The Evening Mail* (Halifax) (13 November 1919) at 9 [emphasis in the original].

17 For example, [unsigned], "Maritime Union a Measure Alike of Economy and Patriotism" *The Evening Mail* (Halifax) (15 March 1918) at 15; [unsigned], "Maritime Union Must Come; And Cannot Come Too Soon," *The Evening Mail* (Halifax) (29 May 1926) at 4.

18 T.W. Acheson, "The National Policy and the Industrialization of the Maritimes, 1880–1910" above note 9 at 3. Harold Innis is normally credited with expounding the staple thesis. For an overview, see Robin Neill, *A New Theory of Value: The Canadian Economics of H.A. Innis* (Toronto: University of Toronto Press, 1972).

19 Acheson, "The National Policy and the Industrialization of the Maritimes, 1880–1910," above note 9 at 3.

20 Stephen Tomblin, *Ottawa and the Outer Provinces: The Challenge of Regional Integration in Canada* (Toronto: James Lorimer, 1995) at 27. Among others, Tomblin quotes from Vernon Fowke, *The National Policy and the Wheat Economy* (Toronto: University of Toronto Press, 1957).

21 Unfortunately, geography was not in either Maritime port's favour, at least for exports going east. The distance by train from Montreal to Halifax along the Canadian route was [is] about 1,346 kilometres (836 miles); Montreal to Portland was about 480 kilometres (300 miles).

22 Ernest Forbes, "The Origins of the Maritime Rights Movement" (1975) 5 *Acadiensis* 54–66 at 57. See also Ken Cruikshank, "The Intercolonial Railway, Freight Rates and the Maritime Economy" (1992) 22 *Acadiensis* 87–110; E.R. Forbes, "Misguided Symmetry: The Destruction of Regional Transportation Policy for the Maritimes" in David Jay Bercuson, ed, *Canada and the Burden of Unity* (Toronto: University of Toronto Press, 1977) at 60–86.

23 Acheson, "The National Policy and the Industrialization of the Maritimes, 1880–1910," above note 9 at 14. Rolling mills produce structural steel by rolling the metal into sheets.

24 Three of the sugar refineries merged to form the Acadia Sugar Refining Company. In 1912, that company renamed itself as the Atlantic Sugar Refineries and built a refinery in Saint John. Atlantic Sugar was renamed Lantic Sugar. The Saint John refinery was the last holdout and was shut down in 2000, with operations moving to Montreal.

25 Quoted in James D. Frost, "The Union Bank of Halifax, 1856–1910" (2012) 15 *Journal of the Royal Nova Scotia Historical Society* 82–102 at 89–90.

26 Alexander Paterson, *The True Story of Confederation* (Saint John: Government of New Brunswick, 1926), quoted in Phillip A. Buckner, "The 1860s: an End and a Beginning," Phillip A. Buckner & John G. Reid, eds, *The Atlantic Region to Confederation: A History* (Toronto: University of Toronto Press, 1994) at 360.

27 Steven Henderson, "'A New Federal Vision': Nova Scotia and the Rowell-Sirois Report, 1938–1948," in Dimitry Anastakis & P.E. Bryden, eds, *Framing Canadian Federalism* (Toronto: University of Toronto Press, 2009) 51–74 at 69, n 21.

28 Robin Neill, *A New Theory of Value: The Canadian Economics of H.A. Innis*, above note 18 at 31.

29 Forbes, "The Origins of the Maritime Rights Movement," above note 22 at 55.

30 Forbes explains that classes here referred to "broad occupational interest groups." Today, we might say commercial or industrial interests. This is not to say that the movement was devoid of class struggle. See Ian McKay & Suzanne Morton, "The Maritimes: Expanding the Circle of Resistance" in

Craig Heron, ed, *The Workers' Revolt in Canada, 1917-1925* (Toronto: University of Toronto Press, 1998); David Frank & L.D. McCann, "The 1920s: Class and Region, Resistance and Accommodation" in E.R. Forbes, D.A. Muise & Bill Parenteau, eds, *The Atlantic Provinces in Confederation* (Toronto: University of Toronto Press, 1993) at 233-71.

31 Forbes, "The Origins of the Maritime Rights Movement," above note 22 at 55. (Forbes cites P.J. Veniot to W.L.M. King, 27 February 1923, W.L.M. King Papers, Public Archives of Canada.)

32 J. Murray Beck, "An Atlantic region political culture: a chimera" in David Jay Bercuson & Phillip A. Buckner, eds, *Eastern & Western Perspectives: Papers from the Joint Atlantic Canada/Western Canadian Studies Conference* (Toronto: University of Toronto Press, 1981) 147-68 at 168, note 66.

33 Forbes, *The Maritime Rights Movement*, 1919-1927, above note 13 at 158ff.

34 Andrew Rae Duncan, *Report of the Royal Commission on Maritime Claims* (Ottawa: F. A. Acland, Printer to the King, 1926) at 10, 15, 34 and 44. See also Savoie, *Visiting Grandchildren*, above note 14 at 36-40.

35 Forbes, The Maritime Rights Movement, 1919-1927, above note 13 at 158.

36 Quoted by Tomblin, *Ottawa and the Outer Provinces*, above note 20 at 32; Anthony Careless, *Initiative and Response: The Adaptation of Canadian Federalism to Regional Economic Development*, Canadian Public Administration Series (Montreal: McGill-Queen's University Press, 1977) at 19.

37 Edward MacDonald, *If You're Stronghearted: Prince Edward Island in the Twentieth Century* (Charlottetown: Prince Edward Island Museum and Heritage Foundation, 2000) at 170.

38 E.R. Forbes & L.D. McCann, "The 1930s: Depression and Retrenchment" in E.R. Forbes et al, *The Atlantic Provinces in Confederation*, cartography by L.D. McCann (Toronto: University of Toronto Press, 1993) 272-305 at 272.

39 For example, in May 1931, the CCF member for Winnipeg North Centre J.S. Woodsworth proposed the motion that "in the opinion of this house, it is desirable that Canada should have the right to amend her own constitution, but that in proceeding to make amendments, scrupulous care should be taken to safeguard the rights of minorities." *House of Commons Debates* 11 May 1931 at 1466.

40 *Statute of Westminster 1931*, 22 & 23 Geo V, c 4 (UK) [An Act to give effect to certain resolutions passed by Imperial Conferences held in the years 1926 and 1930].

41 "Nothing in this Act shall be deemed to apply to the repeal, amendment or alteration of the British North America Acts, 1867 to 1930, or any order, rule or regulation made thereunder" (s7). See, among others, Peter W. Hogg, "Formal Amendment of the Constitution of Canada" (1992) 55 *Law and Contemporary Problems* 253-60.

42 J. Murray Beck, *Pendulum of Power* (Scarborough: Prentice-Hall, 1968) at 207.

43 Quoted in Armstrong, "Federal-Provincial Meetings Before the Second World War," above note 3 at 131.

44 Larry A. Glassford, "The 1935 Election: Going Down with the Ship" in *Reaction and Reform: The Politics of the Conservative Party Under R.B. Bennett* (Toronto: University of Toronto Press, 1992) at 175–204.

45 The 1993 collapse will now always be the worst showing for the federal PCs, with the party winning just two seats. The federal party was formally dissolved 7 December 2003 when it united with the Canadian Alliance Party to form the Conservative Party of Canada.

46 Dominion-Provincial Conference, *Record of Proceedings, Ottawa, December 9–13, 1935* (Ottawa: King's Printer, 1936) at 22.

47 British Columbia (1933), Nova Scotia (1933), Ontario (1934) and Prince Edward Island (1935) all saw Conservative governments defeated by Liberals in the first half of the 1930s decade. The 1935 Liberal victory in Prince Edward Island was even more dramatic than the Conservative landslide in New Brunswick, with the Liberals under Walter Lea winning all thirty seats. This prompted a headline in the Conservative-friendly *Charlottetown Guardian*: "Island Votes for Liberal Dictatorship" (24 July 1935: 1). In the other provinces, Alberta's new Social Credit Party under William Aberhart would defeat the incumbent United Farmers in 1935 while the Quebec Liberals, in power since 1897, would be defeated by Maurice Duplessis' Union Nationale in 1936. In Saskatchewan, the Liberals returned to power in 1934 after having been ousted by a Conservative/Progressive coalition following the 1929 election.

48 William Marchington, "Way to Change B.N.A. Act is Being Sought" *The Globe* (11 December 1935) at 2. Taschereau admitted to the conference that he had indeed "changed his mind" regarding his support for an amendment to the BNA 1867 and was no longer concerned that such an amendment would undermine Quebec's cultural independence. *Dominion-Provincial Conference 1935* at 51.

49 *Dominion-Provincial Conference 1935* at 17.

50 Quebec also asked for assistance with job-creation programs.

51 New federal spending on relief in 1930.

52 *Dominion-Provincial Conference 1935* at 53.

53 *Dominion-Provincial Conference 1935* at 50.

54 McNair, a Rhodes Scholar, would succeed Dysart as premier in 1940.

55 Henderson, "A New Federal Vision': Nova Scotia and the Rowell-Sirois Report, 1938-1948," above note 27 at 69–79, n 21. The constitutional questions were discussed first at a sub-conference, which met 10–12 December (1935). McNair represented New Brunswick.

56 The attorneys general of the provinces and the federal government first met to formally appoint the committee, and having done so, adjourned.

57 [Editorial], "Why the Haste?" *The Globe* (3 February 1936) at 4.

58 "Ottawa Power over B.N.A. Act Opposed in East: New Brunswick Flatly Against Proposed Change" *The Globe* (1 February 1936) at 1.

59 See, for example, Santo Dodaro & Leonard Pluta, *The Big Picture: The Antigonish Movement of Eastern Nova Scotia*, McGill-Queen's Studies in the History of Religion, Series Two (Montreal: McGill-Queen's University Press, 2012) at 57; Ian MacPherson, "Patterns in the Maritime Co-operative Movement 1900–1945" (1975) 5 *Acadiensis* 67–83; R. James Sacouman, "Underdevelopment and the Structural Origins of Antigonish Movement Co-Operatives in Eastern Nova Scotia" (1977) 7:1 *Acadiensis* 66–85; R. James Sacouman, "The Differing Origins, Organization and Impact of Maritime and Prairie Co-Operative Movements to 1940" (1979) 4 *The Canadian Journal of Sociology* 199–221.

60 Corey Slumkoski, ". . . a fair show and a square deal": New Brunswick and the Renegotiation of Canadian Federalism, 1938–1951" (2010) 1 *Journal of New Brunswick Studies* 124–42 at 126.

61 Canada, *Report of the Royal Commission on Dominion-Provincial Relations* (3 vols), (Ottawa: King's Printer, 1940). Order-in-Council P.C. 1908.

62 *British North America Act, 1940*, 3-4 Geo VI, c 36 (UK) (now *Constitution Act, 1940*).

63 See D.V. Smiley, "The Rowell-Sirois Report, Provincial Autonomy, and Post-War Canadian Federalism" (1962) 28 *Canadian Journal of Economics and Political Science* 54–69; Robert Wardhaugh & Barry Ferguson, *The Rowell-Sirois Commission and the Remaking of Canadian Federalism* (Vancouver: UBC Press, 2021).

64 Canada, *Report of the Royal Commission on Maritime Claims* (Ottawa: King's Printer, 1926).

65 Nova Scotia, *Report of the Royal Commission, Provincial Economic Inquiry* (Halifax: King's Printer, 1934).

66 Canada, *Report of the Royal Commission on Financial Arrangements between the Dominion and the Maritime Provinces* (Ottawa: King's Printer, 1935). For comment, see W. Keirstead, "The Report of the White Commission" (1935) 1 *Canadian Journal of Economics and Political Science* 368–78.

67 Henderson, "'A New Federal Vision': Nova Scotia and the Rowell-Sirois Report, 1938–1948," above note 27 at 51.

68 H.A. Innis, "The Rowell-Sirois Report" (1940) 6 *The Canadian Journal of Economics and Political Science* 562–71.

69 W.J. Waines, "Dominion-Provincial Financial Arrangements: An Examination of Objectives" (1953) 19 *The Canadian Journal of Economics and Political Science* 304–15.

70 Donald Savoie, *Pulling Against Gravity: Economic Development in New Brunswick During the McKenna Years* (Montreal: The Institute for Research on Public Policy, 2001) at 42.

71 Savoie, *Visiting Grandchildren*, above note 14 at 30 and 311.

72 Stephen Henderson, "A Defensive Alliance: The Maritime Provinces and the Turgeon Commission on Transportation, 1948-1951" (2006) 35 *Acadiensis* 46-63 at 53.

73 *Ibid.* at 63.

74 Margaret Conrad, "The Atlantic Revolution of the 1950s" in Berkeley Fleming, ed, *Beyond Anger and Longing: Community and Development in Atlantic Canada* (Fredericton: Acadiensis Press, 1988) at 55-96.

CHAPTER FOUR | **An Atlantic Revolution?**

1 Harvey Hickey, "Premier States Case: Province Needs Cheap Hydro" *The Globe and Mail* (27 October 1955) at 11.

2 W.S. MacNutt, "The Atlantic Revolution" *Atlantic Advocate* (June 1957) 11-13. See also Margaret Conrad, "The Atlantic Revolution of the 1950s" in Berkeley Fleming, ed, *Beyond Anger and Longing: Community and Development in Atlantic Canada* (Fredericton: Acadiensis Press, 1988).

3 Margaret Conrad, "The 1950s: The Decade of Development" in E.R. Forbes et al, eds, *The Atlantic Provinces in Confederation* (Toronto: University of Toronto Press, 1993) 382-420 at 401.

4 For a detailed and fascinating chronicle of the 1950s in Canada, see Nelson Wiseman, *1950s Canada* (Toronto: University of Toronto Press, 2022). See also Robert Bothwell et al, *Canada Since 1945: Power, Politics and Provincialism* (Toronto: University of Toronto Press, 1989).

5 Unsigned editorial, "1948-1949" *The Globe and Mail* (1 January 1949) at 6.

6 Unsigned editorial, "The New Year" *Financial Post* (1 January 1949) at 1.

7 *Ibid.*

8 *Ibid.*

9 The PC's 1948 leadership convention was won by former Ontario Premier George Drew. John Diefenbaker lost to Drew on the first ballot but was now seen as a person to watch.

10 Prime Minister Louis St-Laurent, radio address (Radio-Canada) marking the beginning of the 1949 federal election campaign: "Le Canada est aujourd'hui une nation adulte. Nous voulons que cela soit reconnu pleinement dans notre constitution et dans nos lois. Et nous voulons également encourager l'expression de notre esprit national. Nous vous demandons maintenant un nouveau mandat — un mandat en vue de continuer à travailler à la paix et à la sécurité, à l'augmentation de notre commerce et de notre prospérité, au

maintien de l'emploi et de la sécurité sociale; à la complète reconnaissance du caractère adulte de la nation canadienne et à encourager davantage le développement de nos ressources intellectuelles, scientifiques et artistiques, en un mot, de notre conscience nationale" (9 May 1949), online: https:// perspective.usherbrooke.ca/bilan/servlet/BMDictionnaire/1938.

11 *An Act respecting Citizenship, Nationality, Naturalization and Status of Aliens*, 10 Geo VI, c 15 (assented to 27 June 1946).

12 Australia followed in 1948 with the *Nationality and Citizenship Act 1948* (Cth).

13 Quoted in W.P.M. Kennedy, "The Office of Governor General in Canada" (1953) 31 *Canadian Bar Review* 994–99 at 999. For discussion, see Marcella Firmini & Jennifer Smith, "The Crown in Canada" in Peter Oliver et al, eds, *The Oxford Handbook of the Canadian Constitution* (New York: Oxford University Press, 2017) at 129–50.

14 *An Act to amend the Supreme Court Act, 1949*, 13 Geo VI, c 37.

15 Frederick Vaughan, *Canadian Federalist Experiment: From Defiant Monarchy to Reluctant Republic* (Montreal: McGill-Queen's University Press, 2003) at 118. See also Zelman Cowen, "Appeals to the Privy Council" (1950) 32 *Journal of Comparative Legislation and International Law*, 3d Ser 73–74.

16 J.W. Pickersgill, *My Years with Louis St. Laurent: A Political Memoir* (Toronto: University of Toronto Press, 1975) at 111–21.

17 13 Geo VI, c 81 (UK). The Act was repealed by the *Constitution Act, 1982* and therefore not renamed. It could be argued that the totality of the powers given the Parliament of Canada under BNA Act 1867, section 91.1 and already possessed by the provinces under section 92.1 now gave Canada (so Parliament and all ten provinces), if not the full constitutional authority for amendments, at least the authority to enact an amending procedure — and for that matter, entrench a charter if they so desired — without the need to request a Canada Act from the British Parliament. However, this does not seem to have been contemplated when the "Patriation Reference" (*Re Resolution to amend the Constitution*, [1981] 1 SCR 753) was considered.

18 The UK bill began in the House of Lords and was adopted 22 November 1949. The House of Commons adopted it 2 December 1949. Royal assent was provided on 16 December 1949.

19 For discussion of the controversies over the constitutionality of BNA 1867 (2) 1949, see F.R. Scott, "The British North America (No. 2) Act, 1949" (1950) 8 *The University of Toronto Law Journal* 201–7; W.R. Lederman, "Notes on Recent Canadian Constitutional Developments" (1950) 32 *Journal of Comparative Legislation and International Law*, 3d Ser, 32 (1950) 74–77; D.C. Rowat, "Recent Developments in Canadian Federalism" (1952) 18 *The Canadian Journal of Economics and Political Science* 1–16 at 11; and Paul Gérin-Lajoie, *Constitutional Amendment in Canada* (Toronto: University of Toronto Press, 1950)

at xiv–xliii. This section of the Gérin-Lajoie book also includes discussion of the 1950 conferences.

20 By virtue of the BNA 1867 (now *Constitution Act, 1867*), ss 91 (3) and 92 (2).

21 *British North America Act, 1951*, 14 & 15 Geo VI, c 32 (UK). The amendment added a s 94A to the BNA Act 1867 ("Old Age Pensions"). It was repealed by the *Constitution Act, 1982*, and so not renamed.

22 12–13 Geo VI c 22 (UK), now *Newfoundland Act*.

23 Conrad, "The 1950s," above note 3 at 404.

24 Corey Slumkoski, *Inventing Atlantic Canada: Regionalism and the Maritime Reaction to Newfoundland's Entry into Canadian Confederation* (Toronto: University of Toronto Press, 2011) at 125.

25 *Ibid.* at 127.

26 James Kenny & Andrew Secord, "Engineering Modernity: Hydroelectric Development in New Brunswick, 1945–1970" (2010) 39 *Acadiensis* 3–26.

27 Harvey Hickey, "Premier States Case: Province Needs Cheap Hydro," note 1 above.

28 [unsigned], "Premiers Outline Provincial Proposals as Significant Conference Begins" *The Globe and Mail* (27 April 1955) at 8. Unemployment would actually drop in 1955 but reached 4.6 percent (5.1 percent for men) in 1954. This was double what it had been in 1951.

29 *Ibid.*

30 [unsigned], "Education Aid Not Sufficient, Premier Argues" *The Globe and Mail* (4 October 1955) at 10.

31 Conrad, "The 1950s," above note 3 at 407.

32 [unsigned], "N.B. Premier Proposes Maritimes Conference" *The Globe and Mail* (1 May 1956) at 12.

33 Quoted in Pickersgill, *My Years with Louis St. Laurent: A Political Memoir*, above note 16 at 126.

34 The election was held 18 June 1956. Flemming's PCs gained one seat (thirty-six PC; sixteen Liberals).

35 Not to be confused with Asia-Pacific Economic Cooperation. For a full history of APEC, its predecessors, its mission, as well as a study of the many efforts at Atlantic cooperation over the years, see H.A. Fredericks, *What Happened to the Blueprint for Atlantic Advance?* (Fredericton: HLG Marketing Ltd, 2003). Fredericks was the Director of APEC, 1956–1960.

36 Nelson Mann, "The Atlantic Provinces Economic Council" (1956) 35 *The Dalhousie Review* 309–22. Planning began in 1953.

37 Quoted in Donald Savoie, *Visiting Grandchildren: Economic Development in the Maritimes* (Toronto: University of Toronto Press, 2006) at 199.

38 *Ibid.* at 198–99. This entire paragraph owes a debt to Savoie's comprehensive summary contained in ch 8 ("Heal Thyself") above note 37 at 199–230.

39 The first Acadian premier is generally acknowledged to have been P.J. Veniot (1923-1925). Veniot became premier after Walter Foster resigned in 1923, and so not as the result of an election.

CHAPTER FIVE | Maritime Union Movement: 1960s and 1970s

1 Paul Stevens & John Saywell, "Parliament and Politics" in John Saywell, ed, *Canadian Annual Review of Politics and Public Affairs 1970* (Toronto: University of Toronto Press, 1971) 155–98 at 184.

2 Market Facts of Canada, *The Maritimes and Maritime Union: An Opinion Study* at 1.

3 Della Stanley, "The 1960s: The Illusions and Realities of Progress" in *The Atlantic Provinces in Confederation*, E.R. Forbes, D.A. Muise & Bill Parenteau, eds, cartography by L.D. McCann (Toronto: University of Toronto Press, 1993) 421–59 at 421.

4 *Ibid.* at 424.

5 In addition to Robichaud, the premiers of Atlantic Canada in 1964 were Robert Stanfield of Nova Scotia (PC), Walter Shaw of Prince Edward Island (PC), and Joey Smallwood of Newfoundland (Liberal). Note that by 1970, all but Smallwood had been replaced: in Prince Edward Island, Alex Campbell defeated Shaw in the 1966 election; Stanfield resigned as premier to become leader of the federal PC party; his successor, George Smith, lost to Liberal Gerald Reagan in 1970; Robichaud lost to Richard Hatfield (PC) in 1970.

6 The full text of Robichaud's speech can be found in Appendix 1 of Luke Flanagan's *The Political Union Debate in Canada's Maritime Provinces, 1960–1980: Why did a Union Not Happen?* PhD Thesis, The University of Edinburgh, 2012 at 254.

7 John J. Deutsch, *The Report on Maritime Union: Commissioned by the Governments of Nova Scotia, New Brunswick and Prince Edward Island. Maritime Union Study* (Fredericton: Maritime Union Study, 1970) at 22.

8 Flanagan, *The Political Union Debate in Canada's Maritime Provinces*, above note 6 at 154.

9 Nova Scotia's resolution was passed 16 February 1965: "Resolved that in the opinion of this House it is desirable that the government of the Province of Nova Scotia and the government of the Province of New Brunswick commission a study to enquire into the advantages and disadvantages of a union of the Province of Nova Scotia and the Province of New Brunswick to become one province within the nation." The New Brunswick resolution, passed 25 February 1965, was identical save for the use of the full name of the New Brunswick legislature, rather than simply "the House." Note that the joint resolutions did not include Prince Edward Island. As well, note that

the resolutions did not call for the study of any option other than full union. Both resolutions passed unanimously. *The Report on Maritime Union* note 7 above at 1.

10 On 22 February 1968, the Prince Edward Island Speech from the Throne included the following: "My government proposes the establishment of a Secretariat to further encourage and facilitate the co-operative efforts of the Atlantic Provinces in dealing with regional problems of mutual concern. A resolution will be submitted seeking the encouragement of further measures for joint governmental action." *Ibid*.

11 Royal Commission on Higher Education (1961–62). Deutsch had also been the assistant director of research on the Rowell-Sirois Commission and first chairman of the Economic Council of Canada (1963–1967). He also held a number of senior policy advising roles in the federal government. See M. C. Urquhart, "In Memoriam: John James Deutsch, 1911–76" (1976) 9 *The Canadian Journal of Economics* 685–88.

12 I discuss the report below.

13 Richard Wilbur, "New Brunswick," *Canadian Annual Review for 1964*, John Saywell, ed (Toronto: University of Toronto Press, 1965) 134–39 at 137.

14 Della Stanley, *Louis Robichaud: A Decade of Power* (Halifax: Nimbus, 1984) at 116.

15 Michel Cormier, *Louis Robichaud: A Not So Quiet Revolution*, Jonathan Kaplansky, trans (Moncton: Faye Editions, 2004) at 155. Tansley, the chair of the Medical Care Insurance Commission of Saskatchewan, was a member of the so-called Saskatchewan Mafia. This was a group of senior civil servants Robichaud recruited from Saskatchewan to reorganize and reform the New Brunswick civil service, but more importantly to build and implement such programs as New Brunswick Medicare. All were senior policy advisers in the NDP government in Saskatchewan but were not welcome when Ross Thatcher's Saskatchewan Liberal Party won the 1964 election. See Lisa Pasolli, "Bureaucratizing the Atlantic Revolution: The 'Saskatchewan Mafia' in the New Brunswick Civil Service, 1960–1970" (2009) 38 *Acadiensis* 126–50. See also Gregory Marchildon & Nicole O'Byrne, "Last Province Aboard: New Brunswick and National Medicare" (2013) 42 *Acadiensis* 150–67.

16 Edward Byrne et al, *Report of the New Brunswick Royal Commission on Finance and Municipal Taxation in New Brunswick* (Fredericton: Government of New Brunswick, 1963).

17 Bert Burgoyne, "NEW BRUNSWICK: Report Advocates Double Taxation" *The Globe and Mail* (1 February 1964 at 8. In general, see R.A. Young, "Remembering Equal Opportunity: Clearing the Undergrowth in New Brunswick" (1987) 30 *Canadian Public Administration* 88–102; Laurel Lewey et al, *New Brunswick before the Equal Opportunity Program: History through a Social Work Lens* (Toronto: University of Toronto Press, 2018).

18 *Constitution Act, 1982*, Schedule B to the *Canada Act 1982* (UK), 1982, c 11, ss
16 & 16.1. The New Brunswick legislation is *An Act Respecting the Official Languages of New Brunswick*, SNB 1969, c 14 (*Official Languages of New Brunswick
Act*). I discuss language issues below in Chapter 11.

19 Michael MacMillan, *The Practice of Language Rights in Canada* (Toronto: University of Toronto Press, 1998) at 149. The difference is that one is, or perceived
to be, based on individual rights (bilingualism) while the other is based on
community rights (linguistic equality).

20 Wilbur, "New Brunswick," above note 13 at 215.

21 Maritime Union Study, *Briefs to the Maritime Union Study* (Fredericton: Maritime Union Study, 1970).

22 Arthur Murphy et al, *Region-Wide Policies for Higher Education* (Fredericton:
Maritime Union Study, 1970).

23 Peter C. Findlay, *Union Maritime : Les Consèquences pour la Langue et Culture
Françaises* (Fredericton: Maritime Union Study, 1970).

24 *The Report on Maritime Union* note 7 above at 73.

25 *Ibid.* at 65.

26 *Council of Maritime Premiers Act*, RSPEI 1988, c C-27; *Council of Maritime Premiers
Act*, RSNB 2011, c 133; *Council of Maritime Premiers Act*, RSNS 1989, c 105.

27 *The Report on Maritime Union* note 7 at 75.

28 J. Murray Beck, "An Atlantic Region Political Culture: A Chimera" in David
Jay Bercuson & Phillip A. Buckner, eds, *Eastern & Western Perspectives: Papers
from the Joint Atlantic Canada/Western Canadian Studies Conference* (Toronto:
University of Toronto Press, 1981) 147–68 at 162.

29 *Ibid.*

30 *Ibid.*

31 *Ibid.*

32 *Ibid.* at 163.

CHAPTER SIX | **The Constitutional Processes**

1 B.L. Strayer, "The Constitutional Processes for Prairie Union" (1970) 13 *Canadian Public Administration* 337–43.

2 In 1974, Strayer would be appointed as Assistant Deputy Minister of Justice,
tasked with writing early drafts of what would become the *Constitution Act,
1982*. Strayer also served as a justice on both the Federal Court of Appeal and
the Federal Court of Canada.

3 Strayer, "The Constitutional Processes for Prairie Union," above note 1 at 339.

4 CA 1867, note 48.

5 Were the abolishment of the three provinces and the creation of a new one
the only option for Maritime Union, then the Constitution would have to

be amended to allow for such an event. This would be similar to the amendment to the Constitution that would be required were Quebec to insist on separation. In *Reference Re Secession of Quebec*, [1998] 2 SCR 217 at para 105, the Court did not specify what amendment formula would be required for such a change, choosing to "refrain from pronouncing on the applicability of any particular constitutional procedure to effect secession unless and until sufficiently clear facts exist to squarely raise an issue for judicial determination" (274). But given the profundity of such an event, it is difficult to imagine any other procedure but the unanimity formula (CA 1982, s 41) would suffice. Similarly, amending the Constitution to allow for the abolishment of provinces would also require s 41, even if the abolished provinces were reconstituted as one.

6   K.C. Wheare, *Federal Government*, 3rd ed (London: Oxford University Press, 1953) at 11.

7   J. Murray Beck, *The Government of Nova Scotia* (Toronto: University of Toronto Press, 1957) at 10.

8   Sessional papers No. 70 (1883) 46 Victoria [Sessional Papers, 5th Parliament, 1st Session: vol. 12 at 6].

9   Paul Romney, "Provincial Equality, Special Status and the Compact Theory of Canadian Confederation" (1999) 32 *Canadian Journal of Political Science* 21–39; and Paul Romney, "In Right of Ontario" in *Mr Attorney: The Attorney General for Ontario in Court, Cabinet, and Legislature 1791–1899* (Toronto: University of Toronto Press, 1986) at 240–81. See also Emmanuelle Richez, "The Possibilities and Limits of Provincial Constitution-making Power: The Case of Quebec" in Emmett Macfarlane, ed, *Constitutional Amendment in Canada* (Toronto: University of Toronto Press, 2016) at 164–84.

10 *Ibid.*

11 Although not quite germane to this book, the constitutional status of Ontario and Quebec — whether they were new provinces or the re-establishment of the old Upper and Lower Canada colonies — was once hotly debated. See, for example, Norman McLeod Rogers, "The Compact Theory of Confederation" (June 1931) 9:6 *Canadian Bar Review* 395–417. For discussion, see W.H. McConnell, *Commentary on the British North America Act* (Toronto: Macmillan of Canada, 1977) 124–25. Nevertheless, in 1892, Ontario issued a proclamation celebrating the centennial of the establishment of "the province of Upper Canada and its system of representative government, as outlined in the Constitutional Act of 1791." See Peter Prince, "Provincializing Constitutions: History, Narrative, and the Disappearance of Canada's Provincial Constitutions," 9 *Perspectives on Federalism* (2017) 33–56 at 33. As for the fact that BNA 1867, s 72 established a new upper chamber for Quebec, this no more created a new constitution for Quebec than the subsequent abolishment of that same chamber did.

12   The *British North America Act, 1871*, renamed the *Constitution Act, 1871* (CA 1982, s 53, Schedule, item 5).

CHAPTER SEVEN | **Sections 42 and 43 (and the Constitution Act 1871)**

1   W.H. McConnell, *Commentary on the British North America Act* (Toronto: Macmillan of Canada, 1977) at 245. McConnell is speaking of the *British North America Act, 1871* (BNA 1971), now the *Constitution Act, 1871* (CA 1871).

2   Peter Hogg, *Constitutional Law of Canada* (Toronto: Carswell/Thomson Reuters, 2020) at 4-24, n 86. Hogg does say that under the Constitution this is not entirely clear.

3   Sir John A. Macdonald explained the reason for not using the title "Kingdom of Canada," and using "Dominion of Canada" instead, in a letter to Lord Knutsford: "it was made at the insistence of Lord Derby, then foreign minister, who feared the first name would wound the sensibilities of the Yankees." Joseph Pope, *Correspondence of Sir John Macdonald* (Toronto: Oxford University Press, 1921) at 451.

4   "It shall be lawful for the Queen, by and with the Advice of Her Majesty's Most Honourable Privy Council, on Addresses from the Houses of the Parliament of Canada, and from the Houses of the respective Legislatures of the Colonies or Provinces of Newfoundland, Prince Edward Island, and British Columbia, to admit those Colonies or Provinces, or any of them, into the Union, and on Address from the Houses of the Parliament of Canada to admit Rupert's Land and the North-western Territory, or either of them, into the Union, on such Terms and Conditions in each Case as are in the Addresses expressed and as the Queen thinks fit to approve, subject to the Provisions of this Act; and the Provisions of any Order in Council in that Behalf shall have effect as if they had been enacted by the Parliament of the United Kingdom of Great Britain and Ireland."

5   British Columbia in 1871 and Newfoundland in 1949. See note 6 of *The Constitution Acts, 1767 to 1982* on the Justice Laws website (Government of Canada) for a complete list, online: https://laws-lois.justice.gc.ca/eng/const/endNotes.html#end6.

6   Paul Gérin-Lajoie, *Constitutional Amendment in Canada* (Toronto: University of Toronto Press, 1950) at 51.

7   *Constitution Act, 1871*. Originally titled the *British North America Act, 1871*, 34-35 Vict, c 28 (UK), the title was repealed and renamed as the *Constitution Act, 1871* (Schedule to the *Constitution Act, 1982* (s 53), item 5).

8   *The Constitution Act, 1871*, SBC No 147. See Campbell Sharman, "The Strange Case of a Provincial Constitution: The British Columbia Constitution Act"

(1984) 17 *Canadian Journal of Political Science* 87–108. Note that the British Columbia Constitution is a statute and so can be, and has been, amended by the ordinary legislative process.

9   Caleb Cushing, for example. Cushing was counsel for the United States at the Geneva Conference for the settlement of the Alabama claims. See his *The Treaty of Washington: Its Negotiation, Execution, and Discussions Relating Thereto* (New York: Harper & Brothers, 1873), particularly 247ff.

10   Statistics Canada, *Census of Canada, 1870–71* (Ottawa: Department of Agriculture, 1873–1878).

11   David Alexander, "Economic Growth in the Atlantic Region, 1880–1940" in David Jay Bercuson & Phillip A. Buckner, eds, *Eastern and Western Perspectives: Papers from the Joint Atlantic Canada/Western Canadian Studies Conference* (Calgary and Fredericton: Joint Atlantic Canada/Western Canadian Studies Conference, 1978) 195–227 at 201.

12   Gérin-Lajoie, *Constitutional Amendment in Canada*, above note 6 at 50–58.

13   Anglin, who initially opposed Confederation, was elected as the Member of Parliament for Gloucester in 1867 and later served as Speaker during the Alexander Mackenzie years (1874–1879). See Donald A. Desserud, "A Stranger in the Chair? Parliamentary Rules and Forms and the Anglin Affair 1877–78" (2023) XVII *Journal of Parliamentary and Political Law* 282–306.

14   Honourable Mr. Holton moved that the resolution be amended by adding the following words: "And this House is of opinion that no changes in the provisions of the British North America Act should be sought for by the Executive Government without the previous assent of the Parliament of this Dominion." House of Commons Debates, 1st Parliament, 4th Session: Vol. 1 at 273 (27 March 1871). Cf. Anglin's remarks just prior at 272. Interestingly, Anglin's view on Confederation had been that the people themselves needed to be consulted first and an election called as a way of determining the people's will. See Phillip Buckner, "CHR Dialogue: The Maritimes and Confederation: A Reassessment," *The Canadian Historical Review* 71 (1990) 1–45 at 43.

15   See also CA 1867, s 146.

16   Section 1 is the title. Section 4 allows the Parliament of Canada to legislate for territories not part of provinces; s 5 confirms the right of Parliament to have established a temporary government in Rupert's Land and the North-Western Territory upon their union with Canada, and to establish a government for Manitoba; s 6 limits the powers of Parliament to continue to legislate for Manitoba after it has been granted its own government.

17   An Act to amend and continue the Act 32 and 33 Victoria, chapter 3; and to establish and provide for the Government of the Province of Manitoba, SC 1870 c 3; An Act to establish and provide for the Government of the

Province of Alberta, SC 1905, c 3; An Act to establish and provide for the Government of the Province of Saskatchewan, SC 1905, c 42. All three were renamed by the Constitution Act, 1982, Schedule B to the Canada Act 1982 (UK), 1982, c 11 (CA 1982), Schedule (s 53): Manitoba Act, 1870 (item 1(1)); Alberta Act (item 12); Saskatchewan Act (item 13).

18   New Brunswick might be said to have extended its boundary in the upper St John River area, but that was more to do with a boundary dispute than an expansion. The New Brunswick boundary in the northwest corner was uncertain, given that it was determined by reference to the source of the St John River, which in turn was disputed (the difference between a tributary and the source of river being a chronic problem in cartography). Beginning in 1798, both the United States and the province of Quebec claimed land that is now considered New Brunswick. The dispute with the United States led to an event known as the Aroostook War of 1939, remarkable for being a war with no actual fighting beyond a few skirmishes. See William Campbell, *The Aroostook War of 1839* (Fredericton: Goose Lane Editions, 2013) and Derek Kane O'Leary, "Archival Lines, Historical Practice, and the Atlantic Geopolitics behind the 1842 Webster-Ashburton Treaty" (2021) 110 *Transactions of the American Philosophical Society* 176–91. See also Geoffrey Matthews & Byron Moldofsky, "National Perspectives" in William G. Dean et al, eds, *Concise Historical Atlas of Canada* (Toronto: University of Toronto Press, 1998) 1–72 (plate 10). It is always useful to recall that these boundary disputes did not consider or consult with the First Nations of the region.

19   Peter Hogg, *Constitutional Law of Canada* above note 2 at 4–34. Reesor concurs. Bayard Reesor, *The Canadian Constitution in Historical Perspective* (Scarborough: Prentice-Hall Canada, 1992) at 400.

20   *Reference re Senate Reform*, [2014] 1 SCR 732 at para 43 (732).

21   For example: Maxime St-Hilaire et al, "The Constitution of Canada as Supreme Law: A New Definition" (2019) 28 *Constitutional Forum* 7–18 at 11. According to the authors of this study, "Any provision elsewhere in the supreme law related to constitutional amendment procedure is implied to have been repealed by Part V of the CA 1982." They include "section 3 of the Constitution Act, 1871" as one of these provisions.

22   *Canada (Ontario Boundary) Act*, 1889, 52-53 Vict, c 28 (UK). See Gérin-Lajoie, *Constitutional Amendment in Canada*, above note 6 at 62–71. Note that the Act is now included in the Schedule (53, item 10) of the CA 1982.

23   Jay Sherwood, *Surveying the Great Divide: The Alberta/BC Boundary Survey, 1913-1917* (Halfmoon Bay: Caitlin Press, 2017).

24   J.A. Klain & M. Levesque, "Revisiting the Labrador Boundary Decision to Include Indigenous Interpretations of the Region" (2019) 53 *Journal of Canadian Studies* 123–51.

25 Note that the CA 1867, s 7 reads: "The Provinces of Nova Scotia and New Brunswick shall have the same Limits as at the passing of this Act." Given that no new territory would be added at the cost of another province and the total area of the Maritimes would not be increased, would this section still apply? How would Prince Edward Island be factored in?

26 W.R. Lederman, "Memorandum on Constitutional Amendment to Consolidate Two or More Provinces of Canada into a Single Province," Appendix C, *The Report on Maritime Union*, (Fredericton: Maritime Union Study, 1970) 93–101 at 99–100.

27 McConnell, *Commentary on the British North America Act*, above note 1 at 245 [emphasis added].

28 Reesor, above note 19 at 398.

29 Stephen Scott, "The Canadian Constitutional Amendment Process" (1982) 45 *Law and Contemporary Problems* 249–81 at 254 and n 29.

30 Hogg, *Constitutional Law in Canada*, above note 2 at 4–24 (4.3(g)).

31 *Ibid.* at note 86. This is a point worth pondering and may be useful regarding the impact of a unified Maritime province on another feature of the Constitution, and that is the office of the Lieutenant Governor, which I deal with below.

32 Hogg does acknowledge that there would be other constitutional implications were new provinces created.

33 For the failure of the Charlottetown Accord, see Kenneth McRoberts & Patrick J. Monahan, eds, *The Charlottetown Accord, the Referendum, and the Future of Canada* (Toronto: University of Toronto Press, 1993); Richard Johnston, "An Inverted Logroll: The Charlottetown Accord and the Referendum" (1993) 26 *PS: Political Science and Politics* 43–48; Michael Stein, "Improving the Process of Constitutional Reform in Canada: Lessons from the Meech Lake and Charlottetown Constitutional Rounds" (1997) 30 *Canadian Journal of Political Science* 307–38; Robert Vipond, "Seeing Canada through the Referendum: Still a House Divided" (1993) 23 *Publius* 39–55. For the failure of the Meech Lake Accord, see below.

34 CA 1871, s 2: The Parliament of Canada may from time to time establish new Provinces in any territories forming for the time being part of the Dominion of Canada, but not included in any Province thereof, and may, at the time of such establishment, make provision for the constitution and administration of any such Province, and for the passing of laws for the peace, order, and good government of such Province, and for its representation in the said Parliament.

 CA 1871, s 2 as amended:

 (1) The Parliament of Canada may from time to time establish a new province in any territory forming for the time being part of the Dominion of Canada, but not included in any province thereof, *at the*

> *request of the legislative authority of the territory*, and may, at the time of
> such establishment, make provision for the constitution and adminis-
> tration of any such province, and for the passing of laws for the peace,
> order and good government of the province, and for its representation
> in the *House of Commons*.
>
> (2) Before a new province is established under subsection (1), a confer-
>   ence of the Prime Minister of Canada and the first ministers of the
>   provinces shall be convened to take into account the views of the
>   provinces [emphasis added].

35 Periodically, if fancifully, the question of the Turks and Caicos Islands
joining Canada crops up. See Ian Stuart, "Canada and the Turks & Caicos
Islands" (1988) 11 *Canadian Parliamentary Review* 18–21.

36 *Black's Law Dictionary*, 5th ed (St. Paul: West Pub. Co, 1979) at 71.

37 *United States v Kilbride*, 2009 US App LEXIS 23722 (9th Cir, Ariz, 28 October
2009).

CHAPTER EIGHT | Section 45

1 Arthur Beauchesne, "The Provincial Legislatures Are Not Parliaments"
(1944) 22 *Canadian Bar Review* 137–46 at 140.

2 Erin Crandall, "Amendment by Stealth of Provincial Constitutions in
Canada" (2022) 45 *Manitoba Law Journal* 172–96. See also Erin Crandall,
"What is a provincial constitution and how do we amend it?" *Policy Options*,
28 May 2021, online: https://policyoptions.irpp.org/magazines/may-2021/
what-is-a-provincial-constitution-and-how-do-we-amend-it. In this piece,
Crandall is writing about Quebec's Bill 96 (An Act respecting French, the
official and common language of Québec, 2022, c 14). See also Warren J.
Newman, "Constitutional Amendment by Legislation" in Emmett Macfar-
lane, ed, *Constitutional Amendment in Canada* (Toronto: University of Toronto
Press, 2016) at 105–25, and James Ross Hurley, *Amending Canada's Constitution:
History, Processes, Problems and Prospects* (Ottawa: Privy Council Office, Policy
Development and Constitutional Affairs, 1996) at 78.

3 The Court's example of such a legal scholar was Peter Hogg: "Many constitutional scholars contend that the federal power of disallowance has been
abandoned (e.g., P.W. Hogg, *Constitutional Law of Canada* (4th ed. 1997), at
p. 120)." *Reference Re Quebec Secession of Quebec*, [1998] 2 SCR 217 at para 55.
For Hogg, see Peter Hogg, *Constitutional Law of Canada* (Toronto: Carswell/
Thomson Reuters, 2020) 5.3(e) [5–19]. However, James Hurley argues
that the provision for disallowance and for that matter, reservation, is not
spent: Hurley, *Amending Canada's Constitution: History, Processes, Problems and
Prospects*, above note 2 at 14–16. In general, see Eugene Forsey, "Disallowance

of Provincial Acts, Reservation of Provincial Bills, and Refusal of Assent by Lieutenant-Governors since 1867" (1938) 4 *The Canadian Journal of Economics and Political Science* 47–59, G.V. La Forest, *Disallowance and Reservation of Provincial Legislation* (Ottawa: Department of Justice: 1955), Richard Albert, "Constitutional Amendment by Constitutional Desuetude" (2014) 62 *The American Journal of Comparative Law* 641–86, and Robert C. Vipond, "Alternative Pasts: Legal Liberalism and the Demise of the Disallowance Power" (1990) 39 *University of New Brunswick Law Journal* 126–57.

4   See also *Resolution to Amend the Constitution*, [1981] 1 SCR 753 at 802, "reservation and disallowance of provincial legislation, although in law still open, have, to all intents and purposes, fallen into disuse."

5   Nelson Wiseman, "Clarifying Provincial Constitutions" (1996) 6 *National Journal of Constitutional Law* 269–94 at 288. See also Margaret A. Banks, "Defining 'Constitution of the province' – The Crux of the Manitoba Language Controversy" (1986) 31 *McGill Law Journal* 466–79, Justice Malcolm Rowe & J. Michael Collins, "What is the Constitution of a Province?" *Provinces: Canadian Provincial Politics*, 3d ed, Christopher Dunn, ed (Toronto: University of Toronto Press, 2016) at 297–314, and Peter Prince, "Provincializing Constitutions: History, Narrative, and the Disappearance of Canada's Provincial Constitutions," 9 *Perspectives on Federalism* (2017) 33–56.

6   Stephen Scott, "The Canadian Constitutional Amendment Process" (1982) 45 *Law and Contemporary Problems* 249–81 at 262.

7   Crandall, "Amendment by Stealth of Provincial Constitutions in Canada," above note 2 at 177.

8   Per Beetz, McIntyre, Le Dain, and La Forest JJ, *Ontario (Attorney General) v OPSEU*, [1987] 2 SCR 2 at para 90.

9   The case before the Court having begun prior to the patriation of the Constitution in 1982.

10   *Schedule to the CA 1982* (s 53), item 1(4).

11   Albeit limited now by *Charter* provisions, such as the requirement to meet yearly and hold elections at least every five years (CA 1982, ss 4 & 5). See Hogg, *Constitutional Law of Canada*, above note 3, 4.7 at 4-33.

12   Louis Philippe Pigeon, "Are the Provincial Legislatures Parliaments?" (1943) 21 *Canadian Bar Review* 826–33.

13   9 App Ca 117 [1883–84] (JCPC).

14   See quotation from Beauchesne in the epigraph, above note 1.

15   *Colonial Laws Validity Act, 1865: An Act to remove Doubts as to the Validity of Colonial Laws*, 28 & 29 Vict, c 63 (UK).

16   Beauchesne, "The Provincial Legislatures Are Not Parliaments," above note 1 at 144.

17   *Ibid.*

18 See Brian Bird, "The Unbroken Supremacy of the Canadian Constitution" (2018) 55 *Alberta Law Review* 755–76. See also Peter Hogg, "Colonial Laws Validity Act, 1865" in *Constitutional Law of Canada* 3.2 at 3-3–3-4.

19 See Jeffrey Haylock, "National Class of Extraterritorial Legislation" (2009) 32 *Dalhousie Law Journal* 253–94.

20 Bayard Reesor, *The Canadian Constitution in Historical Perspective* at 229.

21 Frank MacKinnon, *Government of Prince Edward Island* (Toronto: University of Toronto Press, 1951) at 169.

22 *Executive Council Act*, RSPEI 1988, c E-12.

23 Members of the Legislative Assembly (MLAs) would be elected in eighteen constituencies with nine more added at large, the latter being elected as a proportion of the vote a party received, with some caveats and adjustments.

24 See Jeff Collins & Don Desserud, "The ongoing saga of electoral reform in PEI," *Policy Options*, 11 April 2017, and Donald A. Desserud, "The 2019 Provincial Election in Prince Edward Island" (2021) 13 *Canadian Political Science Review* 123–49.

25 Above note 8 at para 108.

26 With the 1867 division of the Province of Canada into Quebec and Ontario, Quebec re-established its old "Lower Canada" Legislative Council and did not abolish it until 1968 (Quebec's Legislative Council was re-established through BNA 1867, ss 71–79). Ontario did not reestablish its "Upper Canada" Legislative Council. Manitoba, which joined the Dominion in 1870, abolished its upper chamber in 1876.

27 Dicey famously criticized the preamble to the BNA 1867, in which the Canadian Constitution is declared to be similar in principle to that of the Constitution of the United Kingdom as "official mendacity" as the new Dominion's federal structure was clearly modelled on that of the United States. He would later revise his opinion, replacing "official mendacity" with "diplomatic inaccuracy." A.V. Dicey, "Federal Government" (1885) 1 *Law Quarterly Review* 80–99 at 93. The correction was made in Dicey, *An Introduction to the Study of the Law of the Constitution*, 4th ed (London: Macmillan, 1893) at 156.

28 Norman Mackenzie, "Constitutional Questions in Nova Scotia. The Attorney-General of Nova Scotia v. The Legislative Council of Nova Scotia" (1929) 11 *Journal of Comparative Legislation and International Law* 87–95.

29 See Chapter 16, in this book, for an explanation of how Prince Edward Island finally adopted single-member ridings.

30 It is interesting to note in this context that some parliamentary scholars claim without qualification that "The principle that informs responsible government is antithetical to the theory of second chambers." David E. Smith, "Responsible Government" in *The Canadian Senate in Bicameral Perspective* (Toronto: University of Toronto Press, 2003) 131–46 at 131.

31 The issue, however, was not the abolishment of the Legislative Council. The
    Liberals were in disarray with internal splits over New Brunswick's peren-
    nial conflicts over language and religion. See D.M. Young, "Blair, Andrew
    George" in *Dictionary of Canadian Biography*, vol 13, University of Toronto/
    Université Laval, 2003–, accessed 8 May 2023, online: www.biographi.ca/en
    /bio/blair_andrew_george_13E.html.

32 MacKinnon, *The Government of Prince Edward Island*, above note 21 at 211.

33 See Donald A. Desserud, "'He Shall Be Resident in the Province': The Senate
    Residency Requirement and the Canadian Constitution" (2017) XI *Journal of
    Parliamentary and Political Law* 61–98.

34 See MacKinnon, *Government of Prince Edward Island*, above note 21 at 211ff.

35 Colin Grittner, "Constitutional Conservatism, Anti-Democratic Ideology,
    and the Elective Principle in British North America's Upper Legislative
    Houses, 1848–1867" in Nikolaj Bijleveld et al, *Reforming Senates: Upper Legisla-
    tive Houses in North Atlantic Small Powers 1800–Present. Routledge Studies in Modern
    History* (Abingdon, Oxford: Routledge, 2020) 91–105 at 101.

36 MacKinnon, *Government of Prince Edward Island*, above note 21 at 306.

37 *An Act respecting the Legislature; Acts of the General Assembly of Prince Edward Island
    1893* (1893) 56 Vict, c 1, 5–89.

38 J. Murray Beck, *The Government of Nova Scotia* (Toronto: University of Toronto
    Press, 1957) at 231. Legislation was passed in the Assembly 1888, 1890, and
    1894 but none survived the council.

39 W.P.M. Kennedy, *The Constitution of Canada: An Introduction to Its Development
    and Law* (London: H. Milford, Oxford University Press, 1922) at 391.

40 R. MacGregor Dawson, "Forward" in Beck, *The Government of Nova Scotia*,
    above note 38 at vii.

41 Norman Mackenzie, "Constitutional Questions in Nova Scotia. The
    Attorney-General of Nova Scotia v. The Legislative Council of Nova Scotia,"
    above note 28.

42 Although not strictly relevant, it is interesting in this context to recall the
    Supreme Court's decision in *Reference re Senate Reform*, 2014 SCC 32:

    Questions 5 and 6: Abolition of the Senate: Abolition of the Senate is not
    merely a matter relating to its "powers" or its "members" under s. 42(1)
    (b) and (c) of the Constitution Act, 1982. This provision captures Senate
    reform, which implies the continued existence of the Senate. Outright
    abolition falls beyond its scope. To interpret s. 42 as embracing Senate
    abolition would depart from the ordinary meaning of its language and
    is not supported by the historical record. The mention of amendments in
    relation to the powers of the Senate and the number of Senators for each
    province presupposes the continuing existence of a Senate and makes no
    room for an indirect abolition of the Senate. Within the scope of s. 42,

it is possible to make significant changes to the powers of the Senate and the number of Senators. But it is outside the scope of s. 42 to altogether strip the Senate of its powers and reduce the number of Senators to zero. The abolition of the upper chamber would entail a significant structural modification of Part V. Amendments to the Constitution of Canada are subject to review by the Senate. The Senate can veto amendments brought under s. 44 and can delay the adoption of amendments made pursuant to ss. 38, 41, 42, and 43 by up to 180 days. The elimination of bicameralism would render this mechanism of review inoperative and effectively change the dynamics of the constitutional amendment process. The constitutional structure of Part V as a whole would be fundamentally altered. Abolition of the Senate would therefore fundamentally alter our constitutional architecture — by removing the bicameral form of government that gives shape to the Constitution Act, 1867 — and would amend Part V, which requires the unanimous consent of Parliament and the provinces under s. 41(e) of the Constitution Act, 1982.
For discussion of related matters, see Donald A. Desserud, "'Whither 91.1?' The Constitutionality of Bill C-19: An Act to Limit Senate Tenure" in Jennifer Smith, ed, *The Democratic Dilemma: Reforming the Canadian Senate* (Montreal: McGill-Queen's University Press, 2009) at 63–80.

CHAPTER NINE | Section 41

1   Roy Romanow, then Attorney General of Saskatchewan, commenting on the SCC decision on the *Patriation Reference*. Quoted in William R. Lederman, "Canadian Constitutional Amending Procedures: 1867–1982" (1984) 32 *American Journal of Comparative Law* 339–60 at 352–53. Lederman references Romanow, "Reworking the Miracle: The Constitutional Accord 1981" (1982–83) 8 *Queen's Law Journal* 74–98 at 75 and 82–83.

2   *Re: Resolution to amend the Constitution*, [1981] 1 SCR 753.

3   Bayard Reesor, *The Canadian Constitution in Historical Perspective* (Scarborough: Prentice-Hall Canada, 1992) at 395.

4   I deal with the representation question below. The distribution of federal seats (and for that matter, new provincial seats) would be a pressing concern in a new Maritime province, and possibly of sufficient difficulty to thwart any union initiative. But this would be a political issue, important yet only tangentially a constitutional one.

5   Now, of course, "the King."

6   "The Amendment from Time to Time, notwithstanding anything in this Act, of the Constitution of the Province, except regarding the office of Lieutenant Governor."

7   W.H. McConnell, *Commentary on the British North America Act* (Toronto: Macmillan of Canada, 1977) at 245.

8   Stephen A. Scott, "Constituent Authority and the Canadian Provinces" (1966–1967) 12 *McGill Law Journal* 528–74 at 532.

9   Peter Hogg, *Constitutional Law of Canada: 2020 Student Edition* (Toronto: Carswell/Thomson Reuters, 2020) at 14.2(d) [14-11].

10 *Reference re Senate Reform*, 2014 SCC 32 at 733 (para 46).

11 Erin Crandall, "Amendment by Stealth of Provincial Constitutions in Canada" (2022) 45 *Manitoba Law Journal* 172–96 at 183.

12 *Reference re Senate Reform*, 2014 SCC 32; *Reference re Supreme Court Act*, ss 5 & 6, 2014 SCC 21, [2014] 1 SCR 433.

13 Adam Dodek, "Uncovering the Wall Surrounding the Castle of the Constitution: Judicial Interpretation of Part V of the Constitution Act, 1982" in Emmett Macfarlane, ed, *Constitutional Amendment in Canada* (Toronto. University of Toronto Press, 2016) 42–64 at 49.

14 Obviously, the size of the province is irrelevant to the office of the Lieutenant Governor, as provinces in Canada vary considerably in size. Nor is a change in the size pertinent as several provinces have vastly increased their sizes over the years without affecting the office.

15 Although dismissing a Lieutenant Governor under this provision is rare, it has happened and in one case was done with no more of an explanation than the person's "usefulness as a Lieutenant-Governor was gone." R. MacGregor Dawson, "The Independence of the Lieutenant-Governor (1922) 2 *Dalhousie Review* 230–46 at 233.

16 Hogg, *Constitutional Law of Canada*, above note 9 at 14.2(d) [14-11].

17 The CA 1867, s 63, does seem to stipulate that Ontario and Quebec must have their own Lieutenant Governors. For an intriguing debate on this subject, with regard to whether the separation of Quebec would constitute an amendment to the office of the Lieutenant Governor (or to the offices of the Lieutenant Governors post separation), see José Woehrling, "Les Aspects Juridiques d'une Eventuelle Secession du Québec" (1995) 74 *Canadian Bar Review* 293–329 and the response by Patrick J. Monahan, "The Law and Politics of Quebec Secession" (1995) 33 *Osgoode Hall Law Journal* 1–34 at 10.

18 The same language is repeated in the Schedule to the Prince Edward Island Terms of Union.

CHAPTER TEN | **Language and the Constitution (Section 16)**

1   Maurice Simard, New Brunswick, *Journal of Debates* (Hansard), vol 16 (1980) at 7069, quoted in Michael MacMillan, *The Practice of Language Rights in Canada* (Toronto: University of Toronto Press, 1998) at 142.

2   *Reference re Secession of Quebec*, [1998] SCJ No 61, [1998] 2 SCR 217 para 59 at 252.

3   Possibly CA 1867, s 133, could also be included. Section 133 ensures that either French or English can be used in debates in Parliament and in the legislature of Quebec.

4   Reference re Secession of Quebec para 79 at 261.

5   The Court did go on to say that in its ruling in *Société des Acadiens v Association of Parents*, [1986] 1 SCR 549 paras 19–20 at 564–65, it acknowledged the constitutional protection of the French language in New Brunswick by virtue of CA 1982, ss 16–20.

6   Léon Thériault, "Acadia, 1763–1978. An Historical Synthesis" in Jean Daigle, ed, *The Acadians of the Maritimes* (Moncton: Université de Moncton, 1982) at 49.

7   Muriel K. Roy, "Settlement and Population Growth" in Jean Daigle, ed, *The Acadians of the Maritimes*, note 6 above at 125–96.

8   "Papists" (Roman Catholics) were forbidden from owning property (*An Act for confirming Titles to Lands and quieting Possessions*, c II, 1758 [Anno tricesimo secondo George II]). Protestants, "dissenting from the Church of England" were guaranteed rights equal to those of Anglicans (*An Act for the establishment of religious public Worship in this Province, and for supressing Popery*, c V, 1758).

9   Basically, in 1784 for Nova Scotia (which then included New Brunswick) and 1818 for Prince Edward Island. Note that the discrimination here was not language but religion: Catholics were not allowed to own property, and that was a requirement to vote. See John Garner, *The Franchise and Politics in British North America, 1755–1867* (Toronto: University of Toronto Press, 1969) at 143–45. The oath requirement obviously presented problems for anglophone Catholics as well.

10   *An Act relating to Common Schools*, ch XXI 34 Victoria 1871 at 136 [1871 Acts General Assembly, HM Province N.B. iii. The premier was George Hatheway (1871–1872) but the legislation had been drawn up by Premier George King's government the year before.

11   *Royal Gazette of New Brunswick*, vol 29, 23 February 1871 at 55.

12   Few Acadians, or for that matter New Brunswickers in general, would have been able to afford private schools, so that was not an option.

13   *An Act relating to Parish Schools*, ch IX 21 Victoria 1858 at 33.

14   *An Act relating to Common Schools*, above note 10.

15   G.F.G. Stanley, "The Caraquet Riots of 1875" (1972) 2 *Acadiensis* 21–38; Peter Toner, "The New Brunswick Schools Question" (1970) 37 *CCHA Study Sessions* 85–95.

16   See Robert C. Vipond, "Alternative Pasts: Legal Liberalism and the Demise of the Disallowance Power (1990) 39 *University of New Brunswick Law Journal* at 126–57:
>Macdonald indicated that the federal government would consider it appropriate to exercise the veto only in the following cases: if provincial

acts were 'altogether illegal or unconstitutional'; 2) if they were 'illegal or unconstitutional in part'; 3) 'in cases of concurrent jurisdiction, as clashing with the legislation of the general parliament'; or 4) in cases 'affecting the interests of the Dominion generally' [at 129].

See also G.V. La Forest, *Disallowance and Reservation of Provincial Legislation* (Ottawa: Department of Justice: 1955) at 39.

17 "All schools conducted under the provisions of this Act, shall be non-sectarian," *Act relating to Schools*, c XXXII (s 119): 63 Vict 1900: 189.

18 Hugh Thorburn, *Politics in New Brunswick* (Toronto: University of Toronto Press, 1961) at 33.

19 The *Official Languages of New Brunswick Act*, SNB 1969, c 14. See Robert W. Kerr, "The Official Languages of New Brunswick Act" (1970) 20 *University of Toronto Law Journal* 478–85.

20 Also ss 17(2), 18(2), and 19(2).

21 *An Act Recognizing the Equality of the Two Official Linguistic Communities in New Brunswick*, SNB 1981, c O-1.1, Acts of New Brunswick 1981, no. Public Acts (1981) at 1-2. This statute is replaced by *An Act Recognizing the Equality of the Two Official Linguistic Communities in New Brunswick*, RSNB 2011, c 198.

22 But only two in what would properly be called Acadian-dominant ridings. In general, see William Cross & Ian Stewart, "Ethnicity and Accommodation in the New Brunswick Party System" (2002) 36 *Journal of Canadian Studies* 32–58.

23 Preamble [emphasis added].

24 *La Societe des Acadiens du Nouveau-Brunswick Inc and l'Association des Conseillers Scolaires Francophones du Nouveau-Brunswick v Minority Language School Board No 50, 1983 CanLII 3785 (NB QB)*. I deal with this issue at some length in Donald A. Desserud, "The Exercise of Community Rights in the Liberal-Federal State: Language Rights and New Brunswick's Bill 88" (1996) 14 *International Journal of Canadian Studies* (special issue on Citizenship and Rights) 215–36.

25 *Canadian Charter of Rights and Freedoms*, s 7, Part 1 of the Constitution Act, 1982, being Schedule B to the Canada Act 1982 (UK), 1982, c 11 a.

26 MacMillan, *The Practice of Language Rights in Canada*, above note 1 at 143ff. Note that CA 1982, s 16(1) declares French and English as the official languages of Canada while s 16.1(1) refers to New Brunswick's two linguistic communities.

27 One who argued that it did not go far enough was Michel Bastarache, who would soon be appointed as co-chair of the *New Brunswick Task Force on Official Languages*. Bastarache wrote that "the recognition granted in New Brunswick is individual and limited to linguistic status, that the methods of implementation are generally ineffective and inadequate, and that the

province's commitment does not truly extend to measures deemed essential by the Acadians to check assimilation and to ensure the economic and social development of their communities." M. Bastarche, "Dualism and Equality in the New Constitution" (1981) 30 *University of New Brunswick Law Journal* 27–42.

28 New Brunswick, *Vers l'égalité des langues officielles au Nouveau-Brunswick : rapport du groupe d'étude sur les langues officielles* (Fredericton: Direction des langues officielles, 1982).

29 Catherine Mary Steele, *Can Bilingualism Work? Attitudes Toward Language Policy in New Brunswick: The 1985 Public Hearings on the Poirier-Bastarache Report* (Fredericton, NB: New Ireland Press, 1990). See also "N.B. Language Groups Fear Possible Violence in Hearings Next Week" *The Globe and Mail* (9 March 1985) at 5; Claude Arpin, "Language 'Harmony' on the Line Today, Acadians Say" *Montreal Gazette* (12 March 1985) at B1; nevertheless, the hearings proceeded without incident: Claude Arpin, "N.B. Hearings on Bilingualism Begin Calmly" *Montreal Gazette* (13 March 1985) at B1; Catherine Clark, "Quiet Dignity Replaces Violence in First N.B. Language Hearings" *The Globe and Mail* (15 March 1985) at 3.

30 H. Wade MacLauchlan, "Canada's Newest Supreme Court Judge: Hon. Michael Bastarache" (1997) 9 *Constitutional Forum* 25–26; Michel Y. Hélie, "Michel Bastarache's Language Rights Legacy" (2009) 47 *The Supreme Court Law Review: Osgoode's Annual Constitutional Cases Conference* 377–408. See also in this Understanding Canada Series, Michel Bastarache, *The Recognition of Two Official Languages in Canada* (Toronto: Irwin Law, 2023).

31 According to Andrew Cohen, Hatfield's only agenda during the Meech Lake Accord negotiations was the entrenchment of property rights and "self determination for aboriginal people." Andrew Cohen, *A Deal Undone: The Making and Breaking of the Meech Lake Accord* (Toronto: Douglas & McIntyre, 1990) at 48–49.

32 Meanwhile, the Confederation of Regions Party won eight seats in the 1991 New Brunswick election and formed the official opposition. CoR, as it was known, promised to repeal the province's official bilingual status if elected. See Chedly Belkhodja, "Populism and Community: The Cases of Reform and the Confederation of Regions Party in New Brunswick" in *Political Parties, Representation, and Electoral Democracy in Canada*, edited by William Cross (Don Mills, ON: Oxford University Press, 2002) at 96–111, and Geoff Martin, "We've Seen It Before: The Rise and Fall of the CoR Party of New Brunswick, 1988–1995" (1998) 33 *Journal of Canadian Studies* 22–38.

33 *Constitution Amendment Proclamation, 1993 (New Brunswick Act)* SI/93-54: By His Excellency the Right Honourable Ramon John Hnatyshyn, Governor

General and Commander-in-Chief of Canada; To All to Whom these Presents shall come, Greeting: A Proclamation

> Whereas section 43 of the Constitution Act, 1982, provides that an amendment to the Constitution of Canada may be made by proclamation issued by the Governor General under the Great Seal of Canada where so authorized by resolutions of the Senate and House Commons and of the legislative assembly of each province to which the amendment apply;
>
> And Whereas the Senate, the House of Commons and the Legislative Assembly of the Province of New Brunswick have, by resolution, authorized an amendment to the Constitution of Canada to be made by proclamation issued by the Governor General under the Great Seal of Canada;
>
> And Whereas the Queen's Privy Council for Canada has advised me to issue this proclamation;
>
> Now Know You that I do issue this proclamation amending the Constitution of Canada in accordance with the schedule hereto.
>
> In Testimony Whereof, We have caused these Letters to be made patent and the Great Seal of Canada to be hereunto affixed.
>
> At Government House, in the City of Ottawa, this twelfth day of March in the Year of Our Lord One Thousand Nine Hundred and Ninety-three.

34   Interestingly, the House of Commons debate on the resolution, which took place 11 December 1992, involved then leader of the Opposition Jean Chrétien who at the time was the Liberal Member of Parliament (MP) for Beausejour in New Brunswick while he waited for his hometown seat of Saint Maurice to become vacant. The resolution was introduced by Bernard Valcourt, MP for Madawaska-Victoria and minister for Employment and Immigration in the Mulroney government. Chrétien moved that the motion be brought to a vote, seconded by Doug Young, the Liberal MP for Acadie-Bathurst.

35   See, for example, Edmond Aunger, *In Search of Political Stability: A Comparative Study of New Brunswick and Northern Ireland* (Montreal: McGill-Queen's University Press, 1981); Richard Wilbur, *The Rise of French New Brunswick* (Halifax: Formac, 1989); MacMillan, *The Practice of Language Rights in Canada*, above note 1 at 139–62; Robert Leavitt, "Language in New Brunswick" in John Edwards, ed, *Language in Canada* (New York: Cambridge University Press, 1998) at 373–84. See also Paul Howe, Joanna Everitt & Don Desserud, "Social and Civic Attitudes and Beliefs in New Brunswick (Canada)'s Linguistic Communities" (2006) 38 *Canadian Ethnic Studies* 37–57.

36   Cf: "Vitalité Health Network is a regional health authority providing and managing health care and services in an area covering northern

and southeastern New Brunswick. The Network is the only Francophone managed organization of its kind in the country and has nearly 60 points of service providing a range of health care and services to members of the public in the official language of their choice." Online: www.vitalitenb.ca/en/who-are-we.

37   Ian Peach reports that at the time, some analysts claimed that even this amendment should have required the General Amending formula. "Quebec Bill 96 — Time for a Primer on Amending the Constitution" (2021) 30 *Constitutional Forum* 1–8 at 5. See also Deborah Coyne, "New Brunswick Amendment Has Fundamental Flaw" *The Gazette* (13 January 1993) at B3.

CHAPTER ELEVEN | Other Amendments

1   Quoted in Edward MacDonald, *If You're Stronghearted: Prince Edward Island in the Twentieth Century* (Charlottetown: Prince Edward Island Museum and Heritage Foundation, 2000) at 54. Mathieson was speaking to the Prince Edward Island Legislative Assembly with regard to his petition to restore Prince Edward Island's six federal seats. He would be unsuccessful.

2   BNA 1867, s 21: "The Senate shall, subject to the Provisions of this Act, consist of Seventy-two Members, who shall be styled Senators."

3   BNA 1867, s 147: "In case of the Admission of Newfoundland and Prince Edward Island, or either of them, each shall be entitled to a Representation in the Senate of Canada of Four Members, and (notwithstanding anything in this Act) in case of the Admission of Newfoundland the normal Number of Senators shall be Seventy-six and their maximum Number shall be Eighty-two; but Prince Edward Island when admitted shall be deemed to be comprised in the third of the Three Divisions into which Canada is, in relation to the Constitution of the Senate, divided by this Act, and accordingly, after the Admission of Prince Edward Island, whether Newfoundland is admitted or not, the Representation of Nova Scotia and New Brunswick in the Senate shall, as Vacancies occur, be reduced from Twelve to Ten Members respectively, and the Representation of each of those Provinces shall not be increased at any Time beyond Ten, except under the Provisions of this Act for the Appointment of Three or Six additional Senators under the Direction of the Queen."

4   *Attorney-General for Prince Edward Island v Attorney-General for Canada and Attorney-General for New Brunswick v Attorney-General for Canada*, [1905] AC 37 (PC 1904). See B.L. Strayer, *Judicial Review of Legislation in Canada* (Toronto: University of Toronto Press, 1968) at 112–13.

5   Frank MacKinnon, *Government of Prince Edward Island* (Toronto: University of Toronto Press, 1951) at 289–93.

6   *British North America Act, 1915*, 5-6 Geo V, c 45 (UK). The Act was renamed the *Constitution Act, 1915* with the passage of the *Constitution Act, 1982*: Schedule to the *Constitution Act, 1982* (s 53), item 15.

7   Also notable was the fact the title, "the Imperial Parliament," was not used in the Address.

8   Paul Gérin-Lajoie, *Constitutional Amendment in Canada* (Toronto: University of Toronto Press, 1950) at 89. See also David Smith, "Redefinition: The Senate of Canada" in *The Constitution in a Hall of Mirrors: Canada at 150* (Toronto: University of Toronto Press, 2017) at 49–86.

9   CA 1982, Sec 22. Defining the old provinces as districts would still require an amendment to CA 1915, likely by using Section 43.

10 David Smith, *The Constitution in a Hall of Mirrors: Canada at 150*, above note 8 at 54.

11 Elections Canada, "The Representation Formula," online: www.elections.ca/content.aspx?section=res&dir=cir/red/form&document=index&lang=e.

12 This number is larger than the population total provided by the 2021 census, as it is an estimate of the population as of October 2021, accounting for predicted growth to that point. I use the actual Statistics Canada 2021 census population numbers elsewhere.

13 *An Act to amend the Constitution Act, 1867 and the Electoral Boundaries Readjustment Act and to provide for certain matters in relation to the 1981 decennial census* (Representation Act, 1985, SC 1986, c 8).

14 CA 1867, s 51(1)(2):

> If the number of members assigned to a province by the application of rule 1 and section 51A is less than the total number assigned to that province on the date of the coming into force of the *Constitution Act, 1985 (Representation)*, there shall be added to the number of members so assigned such number of members as will result in the province having the same number of members as were assigned on that date.

15 Compared to the national Electoral Quotient, these Maritime ridings would have a variance of -33 percent.

16 *Electoral Boundaries Readjustment Act*, RSC 1985, c E-3, s 15(1). There is no guarantee of that, of course, but the Chignecto Peninsula dividing New Brunswick from Nova Scotia does seem to constitute a cultural as well as a geographic border. See Ian Stewart, "More than Just a Line on the Map: The Political Culture of the Nova Scotia-New Brunswick Boundary" (1990) 20 *Publius* 99–111.

17 Peter Hogg, *Constitutional Law of Canada: 2020 Student Edition* (Toronto: Carswell/Thomson Reuters, 2020) at 4.3(g) [4-22].

18 SC 1996, c 1.

19 Hogg, above note 17, points out that the Act does not prohibit MPs who are not ministers of the Crown from introducing such a motion, nor can it prevent Parliament from passing such a motion (at 4.3(h)).

20 An interesting and provocative discussion of this Act can be found in Andrew Heard & Tim Swartz, "The Regional Veto Formula and Its Effects on Canada's Constitutional Amendment Process" (1997) 30 *Canadian Journal of Political Science* 339–56. The authors argue that a minister who ignores this legislation would run afoul of the Criminal Code, RSC 1985, c C-46, specifically s 126(1), which deals with failure to obey an Act of Parliament. The authors point out that "any minister who introduced a resolution without provincial consent required under the act . . . would be personally responsible." However, ministers of the Crown are not acting in a personal capacity when they introduce legislation. Besides, as Joseph Maingot writes, "the criminal law of Canada applies everywhere in Canada except during a proceeding of Parliament" (Joseph Maingot, *Parliamentary Privilege in Canada* (Toronto: Butterworths, 1982) at 219). A court might declare the resulting resolution unconstitutional (which is doubtful given rulings such as *New Brunswick Broadcasting Co v Nova Scotia (Speaker of the House of Assembly)*, [1993] 1 SCR 3190) but could not find criminality. In any case, the Act can easily be overridden by a simple clause exempting a resolution from this Act. Nevertheless, the authors raise many important points about the political consequences of this Act.

CHAPTER TWELVE | **Not in Our Lifetime**

1   Donald Savoie, *Visiting Grandchildren: Economic Development in the Maritimes* (Toronto: University of Toronto Press, 2006) at ix.

2   J. Murray Beck, *The History of Maritime Union: A Study in Frustration* (Fredericton: Maritime Union Study, 1969) at 46.

3   P.B. Waite, *The Life and Times of Confederation: Politics, Newspapers, and the Union of British North America* (Toronto: University of Toronto Press, 1962) at 51.

CHAPTER THIRTEEN | **Political "Clout"**

1   Robert Ghiz is commenting on Senator Mike Duffy's call for Maritime Union. Paul Wells, "Robert Ghiz on Maritime Union: 'Preposterous'" *Maclean's* (29 November 2012), online: https://macleans.ca/politics/ottawa/robert-ghiz-on-maritime-union-preposterous.

2   Richard Simeon, *Federal-Provincial Diplomacy: The Making of Recent Policy in Canada* (Toronto: University of Toronto Press, 1972) at 228.

3   Bluenose, "The Great Necessity for Maritime Union" *The Evening Mail* (2 May 1908) at 3.

4   In a classroom visit, Premier Dennis King of Prince Edward Island told my students that one great advantage of being a premier is that "people answer the phone when you call." It didn't matter, he continued, whether he was calling a federal Cabinet minister, another premier, or even a governor of an

American state. Being the premier of a province gave you clout. King's point is well taken. But what he did not say — and I did not ask — was whether other leaders answered his calls with the same urgency that they would have, had the caller been the premier of Alberta or Ontario, and whether much came of those calls.

5   Quoted in Henry Srebrnik, "Vandals at the Garden's Gates? Political Reaction to the Maritime Union Proposal on Prince Edward Island" (1998) 28 *American Review of Canadian Studies* 83–101 at 90.

6   Joseph S. Nye, "Power and Foreign Policy" (2011) 4 *Journal of Political Power* 9–24 at 9. In general, power is seen as the epitome of an essentially contested concept in the social sciences. See Stanley Benn, "Power," vol 6 in Paul Edwards, ed, *The Encyclopedia of Philosophy* (New York: Collier MacMillan Publishers, 1967) at 424–26. See also P.H. Partridge, "Some Notes on the Concept of Power" (1963) 11 *Political Studies* 107–25.

7   For example, Stephen Lukes, *Power: A Radical View* (London: MacMillan, 1974).

8   Joseph S. Nye, *The Powers to Lead* (Oxford: Oxford University Press, 2008).

9   Joseph S. Nye, "Get Smart: Combining Hard and Soft Power" (2009) 88 *Foreign Affairs* 160–63 at 160. Nye's book-length treatment of these concepts include Joseph S. Nye, *Bound to Lead: The Changing Nature of American Power* (New York: Basic Books, 1990) and Joseph S. Nye, *Soft Power: The Means to Success in World Politics* (Cambridge: Perseus Books, 2004).

10 Many Canadian prime ministers have, over the years, worked to cultivate a personal relationship with the serving American president, for example, P.E. Trudeau and Jimmy Carter, Brian Mulroney and Ronald Reagan, Jean Chrétien and Bill Clinton, Justin Trudeau and Barack Obama. In other cases, other Canadian prime ministers and their counterpart US presidents have simply not enjoyed a good relationship: Lester Pearson and Lyndon Johnson, P.E. Trudeau and Richard Nixon, Barack Obama and Stephen Harper, Justin Trudeau and Donald Trump.

11 Clout has also been studied as an exercise of power in the workplace. Eric Bolland, *Clout: Finding and Using Power at Work* (New York: Palgrave MacMillan, 2014).

12 Carl Von Clausewitz, *On War* (New York: Penguin Books, 1978) at 119. The original German reads: "Der Krieg ist eine bloße Fortsetzung der Politik mit anderen Mitteln."

13 See Andrew Cohen, *While Canada Slept: How We Lost Our Place in the World* (Toronto: McClelland and Stewart, 2003). See also Evan Potter, *Branding Canada: Protecting Canada's Soft Power Through Public Diplomacy* (Montreal: McGill-Queen's University Press, 2008).

14 For an interesting use of Nye's concepts in a Canadian context, see Chapter 8, "Soft Power: Who Has It?" in Donald Savoie, *Power: Where Is It?* (Montreal:

McGill-Queen's University Press, 2010) at 170–92. Savoie, however, deals primarily with soft power exercised through think tanks, lobbyists, journalists, and civil servants, not interprovincial soft power.

15　The FLQ Crisis (1970) (Front de iberation du Québec) and the Oka Crisis (1990), both of which took place in Quebec or primarily in Quebec, are examples of times when the federal government employed the military to deal with domestic matters, but these were not examples of province versus province or a province in conflict with the federal government. In both cases, the military response was at the request of a Quebec government (and in both cases, Premier Robert Bourassa).

16　This is not to say that hard power, for example, is absent from Canada-US relations. However, it is distinctly one-sided. Brian Bow, "Rethinking 'Retaliation' in Canada-U.S. Relations" in Brian Bow & Patrick Lennox, eds, *An Independent Foreign Policy for Canada? Challenges and Choices for the Future* (Toronto: University of Toronto Press, 2008) 63–82.

17　The standard work in this field remains Kim Richard Nossal et al, *The Politics of Canadian Foreign Policy*, 4th ed (Montreal: McGill-Queen's University Press, 2015).

18　Richard Simeon, *Federal-Provincial Diplomacy: The Making of Recent Policy in Canada*, above note 2 at 208.

19　Of course, some argue that Quebec separation would not be devastating for the rest of Canada. Roger Gibbins, "Speculations on a Canada without Quebec" in Kenneth McRoberts & Patrick J. Monahan, eds, *The Charlottetown Accord, the Referendum, and the Future of Canada* (Toronto: University of Toronto Press, 1993) at 264–74. See also Robert Young, *The Secession of Quebec and the Future of Canada* (Montreal: McGill-Queen's University Press, 1995).

20　Mind you, I warrant that few if any Quebec separatists believe that Canada would be "wrecked" were it to separate. Wrecking Canada is certainly not the goal articulated by any political party currently advocating for Quebec independence.

21　Perhaps it is also politically convenient for some Canadian leaders to buy into the separation threat.

22　Simeon, *Federal-Provincial Diplomacy: The Making of Recent Policy in Canada*, above note 2 at 201.

23　RSC 1985, c C-8: Application and Operation of Act (ss 3–4).

24　Jason Clemens et al, "Albertans Make Disproportionate Contributions to National Programs: The Canada Pension Plan as a Case Study" (2019 April) *Fraser Research Bulletin*; James Bradshaw et al, "CPP Board Disputes Math Behind Alberta's Report Estimating \$334-Billion Entitlement as UCP Trumpets Stand-Alone Plan" *The Globe and Mail* (21 September 2023), online: https://www.theglobeandmail.com/canada/alberta/article-alberta-cpp -pension-danielle-smith. Note that clout is established by the credibility of the threat, not simply whether the party making the threat will suffer more harm than it promises to cause.

25 Kenneth G. Pryke, "The Repeal Movement" in Kenneth G. Pryke, *Nova Scotia and Confederation 1864–1874* (Toronto: University of Toronto Press, 1979) at 60–79.

26 David Cameron & Richard Simeon, "Intergovernmental Relations in Canada: The Emergence of Collaborative Federalism" (2002) 32 *Publius* 49–71.

27 For discussion, see James Bickerton, "The New Federalism and Atlantic Canada," paper presented to a Royal Society conference on "Shaping an Agenda for Atlantic Canada," Saint Mary's University, Halifax, 25–27 March 2010.

28 Equalization payments constitute just one type of federal transfer but is the only one based on a formula under which provinces receive different amounts (or none at all) based on need. The other transfers, which all provinces receive regardless of their economic situation, are the Canada Health Transfer and the Canada Social Transfer. These are payments based on population. Alberta, for example, received $7,694.6 million in federal transfers in 2023–2024, while British Columbia received $9,035.3 million. Using pre-COVID-19 numbers, total federal transfers accounted for 33% of the total revenue of all three Maritime provinces. Prince Edward Island: 37.2%; New Brunswick: 35.4%; Nova Scotia: 31.8%. In 2023–2024, these numbers rose slightly — Prince Edward Island: 41%; Nova Scotia: 38%; New Brunswick: 33%.

29 See online: www.canada.ca/en/department-finance/news/2022/12/ federal-government-announces-record-transfers-to-provinces-and-territories .html.

30 Quebec received $14,037.1 million in equalization payments 2023–2024 while Ontario received $420.9 million. The total "major transfers" to Ontario for 2023–2024 was $26,017 million; to Quebec, $28,652 million.

31 Robert Finbow, "Dependents or Dissidents? The Atlantic Provinces in Canada's Constitutional Reform Process, 1967–1992" (1994) 27 *Canadian Journal of Political Science* 465–91 at 465. Finbow is quoting from J.R. Winter, *Federal-Provincial Fiscal Relations and Maritime Union* (Fredericton: Maritime Union Study, 1970) at 57.

32 Richard Simeon, "Regionalism and Canadian Political Institutions" (1975) 82 *Queen's Quarterly* 499–511 at 500. Also found in "Regionalism and Canadian Political Institutions" in J.P. Meekison, ed, *Canadian Federalism: Myth or Reality?* (Toronto: Methuen, 1977) at 293–94.

33 Harper later claimed that he was quoted out of context and he may have a point. Tom Flanagan provides a fuller version of the interview from which the "culture of defeat" phrase was taken:

I think in Atlantic Canada, because of what happened in the decades following Confederation . . . there is a culture of defeat that we have to overcome. It's the idea that we just have to go along, we can't change it, things won't change. I think that's a sad part, a sad reality the traditional parties have bred in parts of Atlantic Canada.

(Tom Flanagan, *Harper's Team* (Montreal: McGill-Queen's University Press, 2009) at 75.) Harper was leader of the Canadian Alliance Party at the time (2002) and it's possible that he was blaming the PC and Liberal federal governments for hampering the region's economic development through misguided policies and failed regional development programs. The "defeat" was the lost confidence in the ability of the federal government to turn things around.

34 Donald Savoie, *Visiting Grandchildren: Economic Development in the Maritimes* (Toronto: University of Toronto Press, 2006) at 197. As Savoie writes elsewhere, the argument that a region should pull itself up by its bootstraps assumes those straps still exist. See Donald Savoie, *Looking for Bootstraps: Economic Development in the Maritimes* (Halifax: Nimbus Publishing, 2017).

35 Finbow, "Dependents or Dissidents," above note 31 at 490.

36 *Constitution Act, 1982* (CA 1982), s 36(2).

37 Simeon, *Federal-Provincial Diplomacy: The Making of Recent Policy in Canada*, above note 2 at 219.

38 Winter, above note 31.

39 See online: www150.statcan.gc.ca/n1/pub/89-652-x/89-652-x2015004-eng.htm.

40 Samuel LaSelva, *Moral Foundations of Canadian Federalism* (Montreal: McGill-Queen's University Press, 1996). See also Charles Taylor, *Reconciling the Solitudes: Essays on Canadian Federalism and Nationalism*, ed Guy Laforest (Montreal: McGill-Queen's University Press, 1993), particularly on "the universality of particularism" at 139.

41 In fact, this is what has often separated the Maritime premiers from their Newfoundland counterparts, such as Joey Smallwood, Brian Peckford, Clyde Wells, and Danny Williams.

42 Cited in Adam Chapnick, "Lester Pearson and the Concept of Peace: Enlightened Realism with a Human Touch" (2010) 35 *Peace & Change* 104–22 at 106.

43 Godfrey Baldacchino, "Islands: Objects of Representation" (2005) 87 *Geografiska Annaler*, Series B, *Human Geography* 247–51 at 248.

44 For example, Prince Edward Island has presented itself as an ideal place to test a guaranteed basic income program: Atlantic Briefs Desk, "Guaranteed basic income report released," *Charlottetown Guardian*, 23 November 2023 at 2; Kevin Yarr, "Guaranteed Basic Income Could Cut Poverty on P.E.I. by 80%: Report" *CBC News* (22 November 2023), online: www.cbc.ca/news/canada/prince-edward-island/pei-guaranteed-basic-income-report-1.7036102.

45 See Andrew Cohen, *A Deal Undone: The Making and Breaking of the Meech Lake Accord* (Toronto: Douglas & McIntyre, 1990); Patrick Monahan, *Meech Lake: The Inside Story* (Toronto: University of Toronto Press, 1991); David E. Smith et al, eds, *After Meech Lake: Lessons for the Future* (Saskatoon: Fifth House Publishers, 1991); Katherine Swinton, "Amending the Canadian Constitution: Lessons from Meech Lake" (1992) 42 *The University of Toronto Law Journal* 139–69; Alan Cairns, *Charter versus Federalism: The Dilemmas of Constitutional Reform* (Montreal: McGill-Queen's University Press, 1992), particularly 98–126.

46 Cohen, *A Deal Undone*, above note 44 at 190. Filmon was premier of Manitoba; Wells of Newfoundland and Labrador.

47 Donald Savoie, *Pulling Against Gravity: Economic Development in New Brunswick During the McKenna Years* (Montreal: The Institute for Research on Public Policy, 2001); William J. Milne, *The McKenna Miracle: Myth or Reality?* (Toronto: Centre for Public Management, University of Toronto, 1996).

48 Richard Starr, *Richard Hatfield, The Seventeen Year Saga* (Halifax: Formac, 1988). See also Michel Cormier & Achille Michaud, *Richard Hatfield: Power and Disobedience*, Daphne Ponder, trans (Fredericton: Goose Lane Editions, 1992).

49 Bernard Lord's PCs would break his party's record in 1999, winning forty-four of fifty-five seats. However, it is unlikely that the McKenna feat will ever be repeated.

50 "New Brunswick Challenger Wants Meech Lake Pact Changed" *The Globe and Mail* (28 September 1987) at A5; "New Brunswick Could Veto Meech Lake" *Toronto Star* (3 October 1987) at D4.

51 Philip Lee, *Frank: The Life and Times of Frank McKenna* (Fredericton: Goose Lane, 2001) at 144.

52 *Ibid.* at 153–55.

53 "Hearings Give Mckenna Lots of Anti-Meech Ammo" *Toronto Star* (18 February 1989) at D4; "Fans of Meech Lake Appear at New Brunswick Hearing" *The Globe and Mail* (16 February 1989) at A8; "Language Issue Prominent at Meech Hearings (in New Brunswick)" *Montreal Gazette* (2 February 1989) at B1; "New Brunswick Hearing Gets Earful on Meech Lake" *The Globe and Mail*, 26 January 1989 at A8; "New Brunswick Women, Natives Urge Rejection Of Meech Deal" *Toronto Star* (26 January 1989) at A1 & A2; "Meech Critics Ready Arguments for Hearings in New Brunswick" *Toronto Star* (24 January 1989) at A8.

54 New Brunswick, Legislative Assembly, Select Committee on the 1987 Constitutional Accord, *Final report on the Constitution Amendment, 1987* (Fredericton: The Committee, 1989) at 126 and 140.

55 "Accord Reveals Deep Divisions: New Brunswickers Poles Apart On Francophone Minority Rights" *Winnipeg Free Press* (2 February 1989) at 21. See also

Alan C. Cairns, *Disruptions: Constitutional Struggles, from the Charter to Meech Lake*, Douglas E. Williams, ed (Toronto: McClelland & Stewart, 1991) at 257.

56 Lee, *Frank: The Life and Times of Frank McKenna*, above note 50 at 155. The Accord had been ratified by Well's predecessor, PC Premier Brian Peckford.

57 Pierre Fournier, *A Meech Lake Post-Mortem*, Sheila Fischman, trans (Montreal: McGill-Queen's University Press, 1991) at 54. On the other hand, Acadian writer and former advisor to Robichaud, Roger Pichette, refuted these charges: "It is sadly ironic and unfair that McKenna's bold role would be misconstrued within the [SANB] at the time, and by sovereignists in Quebec, because it suited their political agenda." Quoted in Lee, *Frank: The Life and Politics of Frank McKenna*, above note 50 at 160. That Pichette felt the need to refute these charges demonstrates how widespread they were.

58 In the summer of 1997, McKenna hosted his final Premiers' Conference. He used this venue to launch yet another program for constitutional reform which would resolve Quebec's difficulties. Bloc Québécois Leader Gilles Duceppe was quick to dismiss the McKenna initiative: "The leader of the Quebec separatist party told reporters yesterday that Mr. McKenna has zero credibility on saving the country because the Premier was the first to stick a knife into the Meech Lake Accord." Jacques Poitras, "Bloc Leader Says Mckenna Has No Credibility" *Telegraph Journal* (14 August 1997).

59 Prime Minister St-Laurent, Speech to the Canadian Congress of Labour, 24 April 1956, quoted in "The Fredericton Conference of Atlantic Premiers" *The Atlantic Advocate* (September 1958) at 28.

CHAPTER FOURTEEN | Federalism as a Social Contract: Union and Secession

1 Daniel Elazar, *Covenant and Civil Society: The Constitutional Matrix of Modern Democracy* (New Brunswick, NJ: Transaction Publishers, 1998) at 291.

2 *Reference re Secession of Quebec*, [1998] 2 SCR 217.

3 For example, *Reference by the Lord Advocate of devolution issues under paragraph 34 of Schedule 6 to the Scotland Act 1998 Michaelmas Term*, [2022] UKSC 31 at para 88. See Giacomo Delledonne & Guiseppe Martinico, eds, The Canadian Contribution to a Comparative Law of Secession: Legacies of the Quebec Secession Reference (Cham: Palgrave Macmillan, 2019).

4 Cass R. Sunstein, "Constitutionalism and Secession" (1991) 58 *University of Chicago Law Review* 633–70.

5 See Jonathon W. Penney, "Deciding in the Heat of the Constitutional Moment: Constitutional Change in the Quebec Secession Reference" (2005) 28 *Dalhousie Law Journal* 217–60, and the examples he cites. In general, see the

articles compiled in the second issue of *Canadian Journal of Law and Jurisprudence* (2000) 13.

6   Samuel V. LaSelva, *Moral Foundations of Canadian Federalism* (Montreal: McGill-Queen's University Press, 1996).

7   *Reference re Secession of Quebec* above note 2 at 217.

8   *Reference re Secession of Quebec* above note 2 at para 148 [emphasis added].

9   *Ibid.* at para 149.

10 *Ibid.* at para 60.

11 Quoted in Henry Srebrnik, "Vandals at the Garden's Gates? Political Reaction to the Maritime Union Proposal on Prince Edward Island" (1998) 28 *American Review of Canadian Studies* 83–101 at 91.

12 *Referendum Act*, SNB 2011, c 23; *Plebiscites Act*, RSPEI 1988, c P-10. Nova Scotia does not have a general Act and instead has passed legislation providing regulations that dealt with specific issues, such as the *Retail Business Uniform Day Closing Act, Sunday Shopping Plebiscite Regulations*, NS Reg 188/2004. There is often some confusion over whether the terms "referendum" and "plebiscite" mean something different. According to Patrick Boyer, the term "referendum" should not be used unless the resulting vote is constitutionally binding; if it is not, the vote is a plebiscite. Note that Boyer does not say that merely using the term "referendum" makes the vote binding; it is only binding if the nation's constitution requires it to be. No such constitutional requirements exist in Canadian law. See Patrick Boyer, *The People's Mandate: Referendums and a More Democratic Canada* (Toronto: Dundurn Press, 1992) at 25.

13 *Freeman*, 1 November 1864. Quoted in William Baker, *Timothy Warren Anglin:1822–96* (Toronto: University of Toronto Press, 1977) at 64. At the time, Anglin was a member of the New Brunswick Legislative Assembly.

14 Garth Stevenson, *Ex Uno Plures: Federal-Provincial Relations in Canada 1867-1896* (McGill-Queen's University Press, 1993) at 111. In general, see Janet Ajzenstat, "Popular Sovereignty in the Confederation Debates" in *The Canadian Founding: John Locke and Parliament* (Montreal: McGill-Queen's University Press, 2007) at 22–48.

15 Some would argue that the complexity of the rules was designed to ensure the proposals were defeated.

16 The 2016 referendum used a preferential ballot and asked voters to rank five choices.

17 Clearly stated thresholds prevent post-result reinterpretation, as happened in Prince Edward Island after the 2016 vote. Premier Wade MacLauchlan declared the low turnout (36.5%) as too low to justify electoral reform. See Donald A. Desserud, "The 2019 Provincial Election in Prince Edward Island" (2021) 13 *Canadian Political Science Review* 123–49. However, thresholds are not without their downside. A high threshold provides an incentive for those

who support the status quo (usually the "no" option) to refrain from voting in order to lower voting turnout and so defeat the proposal, particularly if they believe the "yes" side has the advantage. See Yoichi Hizen & Masafumi Shinmyo, "Imposing a Turnout Threshold in Referendums" (2011) 148 *Public Choice* 491–503.

18 New Brunswick, Commission on Legislative Democracy, *Final Report and Recommendations* (Fredericton: Queen's Printer, 2004) at 39.

19 "The Government of Quebec has made public its proposal to negotiate a new agreement with the rest of Canada, based on the equality of nations; this agreement would enable Quebec to acquire the exclusive power to make its laws, levy its taxes and establish relations abroad — in other words, sovereignty — and at the same time to maintain with Canada an economic association including a common currency; any change in political status resulting from these negotiations will only be implemented with popular approval through another referendum; on these terms, do you give the Government of Quebec the mandate to negotiate the proposed agreement between Quebec and Canada?"

CHAPTER FIFTEEN | Maritime Union or a Maritime Common Market?

1 Frank McKenna, "A Maritime Common Market: An Evolving Collective Force," (speech) 11 September 1990, Moncton, quoted in James P. Feehan, "Atlantic Provinces Economic Union" (2003) 19 *Canadian Public Policy* 133–44 at 135.

2 P.B. Waite, *The Life and Times of Confederation: Politics, Newspapers, and the Union of British North America* (Toronto: University of Toronto Press, 1962) at 51.

3 Close to 2 million in 2024.

4 Donald Savoie, *Visiting Grandchildren: Economic Development in the Maritimes* (Toronto: University of Toronto Press, 2006) at 330.

5 *The Constitution Act, 1867*, 30 & 31 Vict, c 3.

6 Peter Smith, "The Ideological Origins of Canadian Confederation" (1987) 20 *Canadian Journal of Political Science* 3–29; Andrew Smith, "The Historical Origins of Section 121 of the Constitution Act, 1867: A Study of Confederation's Political, Social and Economic Context" (2018) 61 *Canadian Business Law Journal* 205–26.

7 *British North America Act, 1867*, 30-31 Vict, c 3 (UK).

8 The CA 1867, section 92A, known as the "resource amendment," limited the Parliament of Canada's jurisdiction over the export of non-renewable natural resources (for example, gas, oil, potash), forestry, and electrical energy. This section was included in the "patriation" package, so a part of

the constitutional amendments that brought forth the CA 1982 (section 50: Part VI Amendment to the Constitution Act, 1867). See William D. Moull, "Section 92A of the Constitution Act, 1867" (1983) 61 *Canadian Bar Review* 715–34; Robert D. Cairns et al, "The Resource Amendment (Section 92A) and the Political Economy of Canadian Federalism" (1985) 23 *Osgoode Hall Law Journal* 253–74; Robert D. Cairns et al, "Constitutional Change and the Private Sector: The Case of the Resource Amendment" (1986) 24 *Osgoode Hall Law Journal* 299–314.

9   For an interesting and provocative discussion of the meaning of CA 1867, s 94, see Samuel LaSelva, "Federalism and Unanimity: The Supreme Court and Constitutional Amendment" (1983) 16 *Canadian Journal of Political Science* 757–70.

10 Jared Carlberg, *Interprovincial Trade Barriers in Canada: Options for Moving Forward*, SPP Briefing Paper, School of Public Policy (University of Calgary), 14:23 (2021) at 1.

11 Alvarez et al, *Internal Trade in Canada: Case for Liberalization*, IMF Working Paper WP/19/158, International Monetary Fund (Washington, DC) cited in *ibid.* at 1.

12 Eugene Beaulieu & Mustafa Rafat Zaman, "Do Subnational Trade Agreements Reduce Trade Barriers?" (2019) 45 *Canadian Public Policy* 1–15.

13 *The Citizens Insurance Company of Canada and The Queen Insurance Company v Parsons* [1881] UKPC 49, (1881) 7 App Cas 96.

14 *R v Comeau*, 2018 SCC 15 at para 85. See Malcolm Lavoie, "R. v. Comeau and Section 121 of the Constitution Act, 1867: Freeing the Beer and Fortifying the Economic Union" (2017) 40 *Dalhousie Law Journal* 189–219 (note that this article predates the Supreme Court decision); Kerri A. Froc & Michael Marin, "The Supreme Court's Strange Brew: History, Federalism and Anti-Originalism in Comeau" (2019) 70 *University of New Brunswick Law Journal* 297–332; Shannon Hale, "The Bedford Trilogy and the Shifting Foundations of Vertical *Stare Decisis*: Emancipation from Judicial Restraint?" (2020) 29 *Dalhousie Journal of Legal Studies* 97–134; Scott A. Carriere, "The Emergence of a Normative Principle of CoOperative Federalism and Its Application" (2021) 58 *Alberta Law Review* 897–920. The Comeau ruling depended on the *Gold Seal* ruling (*Gold Seal Ltd v Attorney-General for the Province of Alberta* (1921), 62 SCR 424), in which the Court then held that BNA 1867, s 121, applied only to imposing customs duties at a provincial border. That decision has also been criticized by advocates of free trade within Canada. See, for example, Ian Blue, *Free Trade within Canada: Say Goodbye to Gold Seal*, Canada's Founding Ideas Series, Macdonald Laurier Institute, May 2011, online: https://macdonaldlaurier.ca/mlifiles/pdf/IanBlueSection121FreeTradewith-inCanada.pdf.

15 Charles McMillan, *Standing Up to the Future: The Maritimes in the 1990s* (Halifax: Council of Maritime Premiers, 1989).

16 *Ibid.* at 33. Summarized by Feehan, "Atlantic Provinces Economic Union," above note 1 at 135.

17 Charles McMillan, *Focusing on the Future [Microform]: The New Atlantic Revolution.* Council of Atlantic/Maritime Premiers, 2001.

18 Charles McMillan, "The New Disparity: Atlantic Canada is Booming" *Policy: Canadian Politics and Public Policy* (29 June 2023), online: www.policymagazine .ca/the-new-disparity-atlantic-canada-is-booming.

19 *Ibid.*

20 *Ibid.*

21 For a discussion of the economics of a federal constitution in terms of how resources and public goods are efficiently (or not) distributed, see William G. Watson, "The Economics of ConstitutionMaking" (1982) 45 *Law and Contemporary Problems* 87–108.

22 Robert Martin, "New Atlantic Agency Prompts Skepticism" *The Globe and Mail* (27 June 1987) at A5.

23 Online: www.taxpayer.com/media/20000608ACOA.pdf.

24 "ACOA Mistaken Money Mounts" *CBC News* (12 April 2002), online, https:// www.cbc.ca/news/canada/nova-scotia/acoa-mistaken-money-mounts-1.353148.

25 Barb Sweet, "ACOA WriteOff $38.8 Million" *SaltWire News* (31 June 2010), online, www.saltwire.com/newfoundlandlabrador/news/ acoawriteoff388million125867/.

26 Canadian Press, "Bad Publicity Blamed for Atlantic Agency's Image" *The Globe and Mail* (8 September 1992) at A8.

27 Charles J. McMillan, *The Age of Consequence: The Ordeals of Public Policy in Canada* (Montreal: McGill-Queen's University Press, 2022).

28 *Ibid.* at 147.

29 Fund for Rural Economic Development (FRED), Department of Regional Economic Development (DREE), Department of Regional Industrial Expansion (DRIE), Economic and Regional Development Agreements (ERDAS), and Minister of State for Economic and Regional Development (MSERD).

30 *Senate Journals*, 33rd Parliament, 2nd Session, vol 129, Pt 1 (1986: 12).

31 McMillan, *The Age of Consequence: The Ordeals of Public Policy in Canada* note 27 above at 154.

32 Donald Savoie, "ACOA — Looking East," *Regional Economic Development: Canada's Search for Solutions*, 2d ed (Toronto: University of Toronto Press, 1992) 117–39 at 117.

33 McMillan, *The Age of Consequence*, above note 18 at 153.

34 Quoted in Savoie, *Regional Economic Development*, above note 31 at 121–22.

35 *Atlantic Canada Opportunities Agency Act*, RSC 1985, c 41 (4th Supp).

36 David Stewart-Patterson, "DRIE Overspending Casts Fiscal Blight on Atlantic Agency" *The Globe and Mail* (6 June 1987) at A5.

37 The Accord had yet to fail.

38 On Murray's role, and also the role of regional ministers with regard to such agencies, see Herman Bakvis, "Regional Politics and Policy in the Mulroney Cabinet, 1984–88: Towards a Theory of the Regional Minister System in Canada" (1989) 15 *Canadian Public Policy* 121–34.

39 Robert Martin, "Atlantic Aid Agency Powerless To Spend: PM Refuses To Answer Queries About Where Money Comes From" *The Globe and Mail* (8 June 1987) at A5.

40 James Bickerton, "Regional Development Policy and Labour Markets in Atlantic Canada" in Andrew F. Johnson et al, eds, *Continuities and Discontinuities: The Political Economy of Social Welfare and Labour Market Policy in Canada* (Toronto: University of Toronto Press, 1994) 235–52 at 245. Bickerton references Donald Savoie, *ACOA: Transition to Maturity Report Commissioned by the ACOA Minister* (Ottawa, February 1991).

41 Savoie, *Visiting Grandchildren*, above note 4 at 320.

42 Kate Mattocks, "Looking for Bootstraps: Economic Development in the Maritimes (Donald Savoie, Halifax: Nimbus Publishing, 2017)" (2019) *Canadian Journal of Political Science* 418–19 at 419.

CHAPTER SIXTEEN | **Representation and Other Issues**

1 [unsigned editorial] "Maritime Union?" *New Start Nova Scotia* (4 December 2012), online: https://newstartns.ca/2012/12/04/maritime-union/

2 In general, see Munroe Eagles, "Electoral Reform and Electoral Boundaries in New Brunswick," William Cross, ed, *Democratic Reform in New Brunswick* (Toronto: Canadian Scholars' Press, 2007) 170–203. New Brunswick increased its ridings in 1970 from fifty-two to fifty-eight and in 1974 adopted single-member ridings but kept the same number of seats. In 1995, the number of seats was reduced to fifty-five. In 2014, that number was further reduced to forty-nine.

3 The idea of a riding that would represent the province's Mi'kmaq has been floated but has not yet received serious consideration. Keith Doucette, "Senator Wonders If It's Time For Mi'kmaq Seat in Nova Scotia Legislature" *CBC News* (15 June 2017), online: https://www.cbc.ca/news/canada/nova-scotia/senator-nova-scotia-legislature-mi-kmaq-seat-mla-dan-christmas-1.4162346.

4 Callum Beck, *The Protestant-Catholic Divide on Prince Edward Island, Canada: Its Creation, Growth and Resolution*, PhD Thesis, Religious Studies (Open University, 2010) at 224. See also Frank MacKinnon, *Government of Prince Edward Island* (Toronto: University of Toronto Press, 1951) at 216–17.

5   *Reference re the Final Report of the Electoral Boundaries Commission*, 2017 NSCA 10.
     The result was the adoption of single-member ridings for the 1996 election.

6   Population shifts over the years had left some districts with as much as five
     times and more the number of eligible voters as others. Fifth Kings in 1989
     (which was the most recent election before the court case) had 2,042 eligible vot-
     ers; Fifth Queens (encompassing the eastern half of Charlottetown) had 11,964.

7   *Reference re Prov Electoral Boundaries* (Sask), [1991] 2 SCR 158.

8   *Ibid.* at 160.

9   *Reference re the Final Report of the Electoral Boundaries Commission*, 2017 NSCA 10
     at para 22.

10   *Société des Acadiens et Acadiennes du NouveauBrunswick et autres v Canada*, 1997
     CanLII 23620 (NB QB).

11   Commission, *Final Report and Recommendations* (Fredericton: Commission on
     Legislative Democracy, 2004) at 8.

12   For Prince Edward Island: *Electoral Boundaries Act*, RSPEI 1988, c E2.1 (s
     17(2)); for New Brunswick: *Electoral Boundaries and Representation Act*, RSNB
     2014, c 106 (s 11(5)); for Nova Scotia: *House of Assembly Act*, RSNS 1989 (1992
     Supp), c 1 (s 5B). In general, see Stewart Hyson, "The Electoral Boundary
     Revolution in the Maritime Provinces" (1995) 25 *American Review of Canadian
     Studies* 285–99.

13   Interestingly enough, Charles Tupper's original plan for the united Maritime
     province was to hold an assembly comprising the legislatures of the three
     provinces, which would then decide on the "basis of representation and the
     fundamental laws of a new constitution." W.S. MacNutt, *New Brunswick: A
     History: 1784–1867* (Toronto: Macmillan of Canada, 1963; reprinted, Toronto:
     University of Toronto Press, 1984) at 415.

14   All electoral numbers are based on each province's latest election reports. Fol-
     lowing Munroe Eagles and John Courtney, I am using the number of voters
     rather than citizens for these calculations. See Munroe Eagles, "Enhancing
     Relative Vote Equality in Canada: The Role of Electors in Boundary Adjust-
     ment" in David Small, ed, *Drawing the Map: Equality and Efficacy of the Vote in
     Canadian Electoral Boundary Reform*, vol 11 of the Research Studies for the Royal
     Commission on Electoral Reform and Party Financing (Toronto: Dundurn
     Press, 1991) at 175–220; John C. Courtney, *Commissioned Ridings: Designing
     Canada's Electoral Districts* (Montreal: McGill-Queen's University Press, 2001)
     at 75–76.

15   Henry Srebrnik, "Vandals at the Garden's Gates? Political Reaction to the
     Maritime Union Proposal on Prince Edward Island" (1998) 28 *American
     Review of Canadian Studies* 83–101 at 88.

16   Elections PEI, *2016 Annual Report of the Chief Electoral Office* (Charlottetown:
     Elections PEI, 2016).

17 Commission, *Final Report and Recommendations* (Fredericton: Commission on Legislative Democracy, 2004) at 31–49.

CHAPTER SEVENTEEN | Why Hasn't Maritime Union Occurred: Identity or Parochialism?

1 Maritime Union Study, *Briefs to the Maritime Union Study* (Fredericton: Maritime Union Study, 1970) at 78.

2 Philip Jacob, Karl Deutsch & James V. Toscano, eds, *The Integration of Political Communities* (New York: Lippincott, 1964); Leon Lindberg & Stuart Scheingold, eds, *Regional Integration: Theory and Research* (Cambridge, MA: Harvard University Press, 1971).

3 Ernst B. Haas, "The Study of Regional Integration: Reflections on the Joy and Anguish of Pretheorizing" (1970) 24 *International Organization* 607–46 at 610.

4 For example, Martin Kohli, "The Battlegrounds of European Identity" (2000) 2 *European Societies* 113–37; Percy Lehning, "European Citizenship: Towards a European Identity? (2001) 20 *Law and Philosophy* 239–82; Thomas Risse, "Neofunctionalism, European Identity, and the Puzzles of European Integration" (2005) 12 *Journal of European Public Policy* 291–309; Jeffrey T. Checkel & Peter J. Katzenstein, *European Identity. Contemporary European Politics* (Cambridge: Cambridge University Press, 2009); Kenneth Keulman & Agnes Katalin Koós, *European Identity: Its Feasibility and Desirability* (Lanham: Lexington Books, 2014); Frédéric Charillon, Mario Telò & Stefano Guzzini, "Is There a European Identity in IR?" (2015) 2 *European Review of International Studies* 118–20. The classic texts in this field include Karl Deutsch et al, *Political Community and the North Atlantic Area* (Princeton, NJ: Princeton University Press, 1957) and Ernst B. Haas, *Beyond the Nation State* (San Francisco: Stanford University Press, 1964). See also Raymond Aron, "The Crisis of the European Idea" (1976) 11 *Government and Opposition* 5–19. While not completely sceptical, Aron continuously "exposed the illusions and weaknesses undermining the European supranational experiment." See Raschi Francesco & Piras Elisa, "A Realistic Scepticism: Raymond Aron's Perspective on the European Construction" (2020) 26 *Journal of European Integration History* 267–84.

5 Anthony Smith, "National Identity and the Idea of European Unity" (1992) 68 *International Affairs* 55–76 at 55.

6 Denis de Rougemont, *The Meaning of Europe* (London: Sidgwick & Jackson, 1965).

7 Hans Kohn, "Napoleon and the Age of Nationalism" *The Journal of Modern History* (1950) 21–37.

8 Ernst Haas, "The Study of Regional Integration," above note 3 at 610.

9   See, for example, Henri de Waele, "Disintegration from Within: Independ-
     ence and Separatist Movements, the EU Response and the Role of Solidar-
     ity" in Andreas Grimmel & Susanne Giang, eds, *Solidarity in the European
     Union: A Fundamental Value in Crisis* (Cham, Switzerland: Springer Inter-
     national Publishing, 2017) at 119–29.

10   Haas, a leading neofunctionalist of the time, refuted his own theories in
     1975 with the publication of *The Obsolescence of Regional Integration Theory*
     (Berkeley: University of California, Berkeley, 1975). See also Ernst B. Haas,
     "Turbulent Fields and the Theory of Regional Integration" (1976) 30
     International Organization 173–212. My paraphrase does not do justice to the
     complicated analyses that Haas provided.

11   When the MPHEC was set up in 1974, Dalhousie University held the only
     medical school in the region. University of New Brunswick (UNB) and Dal-
     housie had the only law schools. UNB also had an engineering program as did
     what was then called the Nova Scotia Technical College (renamed Technical
     University of Nova Scotia in 1980, in 1997, Dalhousie University Polytechnic
     (nicknamed Dal Tech). It no longer has a separate title, and its faculties are
     simply faculties of Dalhousie. Since 1974, a medical school campus, albeit
     overseen by Dalhousie, has been added to the Saint John campus of UNB and
     l'Université de Moncton has a medical program in cooperation with l'Univer-
     sité de Sherbrooke. Moncton also has a law school. University of Prince Edward
     Island (UPEI) now has a full degree in engineering and has announced the
     establishment of a medical school (in cooperation with Memorial University).
     Cape Breton University has also announced the establishment of a med-
     ical school campus, also in collaboration with Dalhousie University. Other
     examples would include the growth of MBA programs (one in 1970, five as of
     2024), various graduate programs, nursing programs, and so on.

12   See online: https://cap-cpma.ca/key-initiatives/.

13   Charles McMillan, "The New Disparity: Atlantic Canada is Booming" *Policy:
     Canadian Politics and Public Policy* (29 June 2023).

14   Paul Withers, "N.S. Abandons Atlantic Loop, Will Increase Wind
     and Solar Energy Projects for Green Electricity" *CBC News* (11
     October 2023), online: www.cbc.ca/news/canada/nova-scotia/
     clean-power-plan-abandons-atlantic-loop-1.6992765; "P.E.I. Has To Look
     After Itself As Competition For Clean Energy Increases, Energy Minister
     Says," *CBC News* (15 October 2023), online: www.cbc.ca/news/canada
     /prince-edward-island/pei-atlantic-loop-energy-1.6996803.

15   Quoted in J. Murray Beck, "An Atlantic Region Political Culture: A Chi-
     mera" in David Jay Bercuson & Phillip A. Buckner, eds, *Eastern & Western
     Perspectives: Papers from the Joint Atlantic Canada/Western Canadian Studies Confer-
     ence* (Toronto: University of Toronto Press, 1981) 147–68 at 147.

16 Stephen Tomblin, *Ottawa and the Outer Provinces: The Challenge of Regional Integration in Canada* (Toronto: James Lorimer, 1995) at 63.

17 *Ibid.* at 73.

18 *Ibid.* at 164.

19 Quoted in H. Wade MacLauchlan, *Alex B. Campbell: The Prince Edward Island Premier Who Rocked the Cradle* (Charlottetown: Prince Edward Island Museum and Heritage Foundation, 2014) at 234.

20 J. Murray Beck, "An Atlantic Region Political Culture: A Chimera," above note 15 at 148.

21 Beck, "An Atlantic Region Political Culture: A Chimera," above note 15 at 148. Beck is referencing Mildred A. Schwartz, *Politics and Territory: The Sociology of Regional Persistence in Canada* (Montreal and London, 1974) at 4–5. Schwartz, in turn, is quoting Rupert Vance, "Region" (1968) 13 *International Encyclopedia of the Social Sciences* 377–78.

22 Donald Smiley, *The Federal Condition in Canada* (Toronto: McGraw-Hill Ryerson, 1987) at 22–23 and 156–58. Quoted in Janine Brodie, "The Concept of Region in Canadian Politics" in David P. Shugarman & Reg Whitaker, eds, *Federalism and Political Community: Essays in Honour of Donald Smiley* (Toronto: University of Toronto Press, 1989) 33–54 at 33.

23 Lachlan MacKinnon, "A Region in Retrospective: The History of Atlantic Canada, 2009–2019" (2019) 48 *Acadiensis* 230–40. See also Garth Stevenson, "Canadian Regionalism in Continental Perspective" (1980) 15 *Journal of Canadian Studies* 16–28. See also the collected essays in Lisa Young & Keith Archer, eds, *Regionalism and Party Politics in Canada* (Toronto: Oxford University Press, 2002).

24 Beck, "An Atlantic Region Political Culture: A Chimera," above note 15 at 165.

25 I am not ignoring the vibrant and robust identities of the First Nations. However, these communities most certainly do not owe their identities "to their provincial governments."

26 Smith, "National Identity and the Idea of European Unity," above note 5 at 59.

Conclusion

1 Gray speaking in Prince Edward Island House of Assembly, 18 April 1864.

2 James Johnston, Charles Tupper, Nova Scotia House of Assembly, 28 March 1864. Their sentiments were echoed by others such as Benjamin Davis in the Prince Edward Island House of Assembly: Janet Ajzenstat, ed, *Canada's Founding Debates* (Toronto: University of Toronto Press, 2003) at 262, 328, and 331.

Bibliography

ACHESON, T.W. "The National Policy and the Industrialization of the Maritimes, 1880-1910" (1972) 1 *Acadiensis* 3-28.

[JOHN ALLAN]. "To George Washington from a Citizen of Nova Scotia, 8 February 1776" in Philander D. Chase, ed, *The Papers of George Washington, Revolutionary War Series*, vol 3, 1 January 1776-31 March 1776 (Charlottesville: University Press of Virginia, 1988) 259-65.

ALBERT, RICHARD. "Constitutional Amendment by Constitutional Desuetude" (2014) 62 *The American Journal of Comparative Law* 641-86.

AJZENSTAT, JANET, ed. *Canada's Founding Debates* (Toronto: University of Toronto Press, 2003).

———. *The Canadian Founding, John Locke and Parliament* (Montreal: McGill-Queen's University Press, 2007).

ALEXANDER, DAVID. "Economic Growth in the Atlantic Region, 1880-1940" in David Jay Bercuson & Phillip A. Buckner, eds, *Eastern and Western Perspectives: Papers from the Joint Atlantic Canada/Western Canadian Studies Conference* (Calgary and Fredericton: Joint Atlantic Canada/Western Canadian Studies Conference, 1978) 195-227.

ARMSTRONG, CHRISTOPHER. *Politics of Federalism: Ontario's Relations with the Federal Government* (Toronto: University of Toronto Press, 1981).

———. "Ceremonial Politics: Federal-Provincial Meetings Before the Second World War," ch 7 in Kenneth Carty & W. Peter Ward, *National Politics and Community in Canada* (Vancouver: University of British Columbia Press, 1986) 112–50.

ARON, RAYMOND. "The Crisis of the European Idea" (1976) 22 *Government and Opposition* 5–19.

AUCOIN, PETER et al. *Responsible Government: Clarifying Essentials, Dispelling Myths and Exploring Change* (Ottawa: Canadian Centre for Management Development, 2004).

AUNGER, EDMOND. *In Search of Political Stability: A Comparative Study of New Brunswick and Northern Ireland* (Montreal: McGill-Queen's University Press, 1981).

BAKVIS, HERMAN. "Regional Politics and Policy in the Mulroney Cabinet, 1984-88: Towards a Theory of the Regional Minister System in Canada" (1989) 15 *Canadian Public Policy* 121–34.

BAKER, WILLIAM. *Timothy Warren Anglin: 1822-96* (Toronto: University of Toronto Press, 1977).

BALDACCHINO, GODFREY. "Islands: Objects of Representation" (2005) 87 *Geografiska Annaler*, Series B, *Human Geography* 247–51.

BANKS, MARGARET A. "Defining 'Constitution of the Province' — The Crux of the Manitoba Language Controversy" (1986) 31 *McGill Law Journal* 466–79.

BASTARACHE, MICHEL. "Dualism and Equality in the New Constitution" (1981) 30 *University of New Brunswick Law Journal* 27–42.

———. *The Recognition of Two Official Languages in Canada* (Toronto: Irwin Law, 2023).

BATTISTE, JAIME. "Understanding the Progression of Mi'kmaw Law" (2008) 31 *Dalhousie Law Journal* 311–50.

BEAUCHESNE, ARTHUR. "The Provincial Legislatures Are Not Parliaments" (1944) 22 *Canadian Bar Review* 137–46.

BEAULIEU, EUGENE & MUSTAFA RAFAT ZAMAN. "Do Subnational Trade Agreements Reduce Trade Barriers?" (2019) 45 *Canadian Public Policy* 1–15.

BECK, CALLUM. *The Protestant-Catholic Divide on Prince Edward Island, Canada: Its Creation, Growth and Resolution*, PhD Thesis, Religious Studies (Open University, 2010).

BECK, J. MURRAY. *The Government of Nova Scotia* (Toronto: University of Toronto Press, 1957).

———. "Joseph Howe: Opportunist or Empire-builder?" (1960) XLI *Canadian Historical Review* 185–202.

———. *Pendulum of Power* (Scarborough: Prentice-Hall, 1968).

———. *The History of Maritime Union: A Study in Frustration* (Fredericton: Maritime Union Study, 1969).

———. *Joseph Howe: Vol. 1: Conservative Reformer, 1804–1848; Vol. 2: The Briton Becomes Canadian, 1848-1873* (Montreal: McGill-Queen's University Press, 1983).

———. "An Atlantic region political culture: a chimera" in David Jay Bercuson & Phillip A. Buckner, eds, *Eastern & Western Perspectives: Papers from the Joint Atlantic Canada/Western Canadian Studies Conference* (Toronto: University of Toronto Press, 1981) 147–68.

———. "Rise and Fall of Nova Scotia's Attorney General: 1749-1983" (1984) 8 *Dalhousie Law Journal* 125–42.

BELKHODJA, CHEDLY. "Populism and Community: The Cases of Reform and the Confederation of Regions Party in New Brunswick" in *Political Parties, Representation, and Electoral Democracy in Canada*, edited by William Cross (Don Mills, ON: Oxford University Press 2002) 96–111.

BELL, DAVID. "A Note on the Reception of English Statutes in New Brunswick" (1979) 28 *University of New Brunswick Law Journal* 195–201.

———. *Early Loyalist Saint John: The Origin of New Brunswick Politics, 1783–1786* (Saint John: New Ireland Press, 1983).

———. "Sedition among the Loyalists: The Case of Saint John, 1784–1786" (1995) 44 *University of New Brunswick Law Journal* 163–78.

———. "Maritime Legal institutions under the *Ancien Regime*, 1710–1850" (1995) 23 *Manitoba Law Journal* 103–31.

BENN, STANLEY. "Power," vol 6 in Paul Edwards, ed, *The Encyclopedia of Philosophy* (New York: Collier MacMillan Publishers, 1967) 424–26.

BERCUSON, DAVID JAY & PHILLIP A. BUCKNER, eds, *Eastern & Western Perspectives: Papers from the Joint Atlantic Canada/Western Canadian Studies Conference* (Toronto: University of Toronto Press, 1981).

BICKERTON, JAMES. "The New Federalism and Atlantic Canada," Paper presented to a Royal Society conference on "Shaping and Agenda for Atlantic Canada," St Mary's University, Halifax, 25-27 March 2010.

———. "Regional Development Policy and Labour Markets in Atlantic Canada" in Andrew F. Johnson et al, eds, *Continuities and Discontinuities: The Political Economy of Social Welfare and Labour Market Policy in Canada* (Toronto: University of Toronto Press, 1994) 235–52.

BIRD, BRIAN. "The Unbroken Supremacy of the Canadian Constitution" (2018) 755 *Alberta Law Review* 55-53.

BIRD, J. BRIAN. "Settlement Patterns in Maritime Canada: 1687-1786" (1955) 45 *Geographical Review* 385–404.

Black's Law Dictionary, 5th ed (St Paul: West Pub Co, 1979).

BLAKELEY, PHYLLIS. "The Repeal Election of 1886 in Nova Scotia" (1945) 26 *Nova Scotia Historical Society Collections* 131–53.

BLOKKER, LAURA EWEN & HEATHER A. KNIGHT. "Louisiana Bousillage, The Migration and Evolution of a French Building Technique in North America" (2013) 28 *Construction History* 27–48.

BLUE, IAN. *Free Trade within Canada: Say Goodbye to Gold Seal*, Canada's Founding Ideas Series, Macdonald Laurier Institute, May 2011, online: https://macdonaldlaurier.ca/mli-files/pdf/Ian-Blue-Section-121-Free-Trade-within-Canada.pdf.

BOLLAND, ERIC. *Clout: Finding and Using Power at Work* (New York: Palgrave MacMillan, 2014).

BOLGER, FRANCIS WILLIAM PIUS. "Prince Edward Island and Confederation; 1863–1873" (1961) 28 *Canadian Catholic Historical Association (CCHA) Report* 5–30.

———. *Canada's Smallest Province: A History of P.E.I.* (Charlottetown: Prince Edward Island 1973 Centennial Commission, 1973).

BORROWS, JOHN. "Indigenous Legal Traditions in Canada" (2005) 19 *Washington University Journal of Law & Policy* 167–224.

BOTHWELL, ROBERT et al. *Canada Since 1945: Power, Politics and Provincialism* (Toronto: University of Toronto Press, 1989).

BOW, BRIAN. "Rethinking 'Retaliation' in Canada-U.S. Relations" in Brian Bow & Patrick Lennox, eds, *An Independent Foreign Policy for Canada? Challenges and Choices for the Future* (Toronto: University of Toronto Press, 2008) 63–82.

BOYER, PATRICK. *The People's Mandate: Referendums and a More Democratic Canada* (Toronto: Dundurn Press, 1992).

BREBNER, J.B. *The Neutral Yankees of Nova Scotia: A Marginal Colony during the Revolutionary Years* (New York: Columbia University Press, 1937).

———. *New England's Outpost: Acadia Before the Conquest of Canada* (Hamden, CT: Archon Books, 1965).

BRODIE, JANINE. "The Concept of Region in Canadian Politics" in David P. Shugarman & Reg Whitaker, eds, *Federalism and Political Community: Essays in Honour of Donald Smiley* (Toronto: University of Toronto Press, 1989) 33–54.

BROWNE, G.P., ed. *Documents on the Confederation of British North America* (Montreal: McGill-Queen's University Press, 2009).

BUCKNER, PHILLIP. "Beware the Canadian Wolf: The Maritimes and Confederation" (2017) XLV *Acadiensis*, 177–95.

———. "CHR Dialogue: The Maritimes and Confederation: A Reassessment" (1990) 71 *The Canadian Historical Review* 1–45.

———. *The Transition to Responsible Government: British Policy in British North America, 1815–1850* (Westport: Greenwood Press, 1985).

BUCKNER, PHILLIP A. & JOHN G. REID, eds. *The Atlantic Region to Confederation: A History* (Toronto: University of Toronto Press, 1994).

BUMSTED, J.M. *Land, Settlement, and Politics on Eighteenth-Century Prince Edward Island* (Kingston: McGill-Queen's University Press, 1987).

———. *The Peoples of Canada: A Pre-Confederation History* (Toronto: Oxford University Press, 1992).

———. *Canada's Diverse Peoples: A Reference Sourcebook* (Santa Barbara, CA: ABC-CLIO, 2003).

BYRNE, EDWARD et al. *Report of the New Brunswick Royal Commission on Finance and Municipal Taxation in New Brunswick* (Fredericton: Government of New Brunswick, 1963).

CAHILL, BARRY. "How Far English Laws Are in Force Here: Nova Scotia's First Century of Reception Law Jurisprudence" (1993) 42 *University of New Brunswick Law Journal* 113–53.

CAIRNS, ALAN C. *Charter Versus Federalism: The Dilemmas of Constitutional Reform* (Montreal: McGill-Queen's University Press, 1992).

CAIRNS, ALAN C. *Disruptions: Constitutional Struggles, from the Charter to Meech Lake*, Douglas E. Williams, ed (Toronto: McClelland & Stewart, 1991).

CAIRNS, ROBERT D. et al. "The Resource Amendment (Section 92A) and the Political Economy of Canadian Federalism" (1985) 23 *Osgoode Hall Law Journal* 253–74.

———. "Constitutional Change and the Private Sector: The Case of the Resource Amendment" (1986) 24 *Osgoode Hall Law Journal* 299–314.

CAMERON, DAVID & RICHARD SIMEON. "Intergovernmental Relations in Canada: The Emergence of Collaborative Federalism" (2002) 32 *Publius* 49–71.

CAMPBELL, GAIL. "Defining and Redefining Democracy: The History of Electoral Reform in New Brunswick" in William Cross, ed, *Democratic Reform in New Brunswick* (Toronto: Canadian Scholars' Press, 2007) 273–99.

CAMPBELL, WILLIAM. *The Aroostook War of 1839* (Fredericton: Goose Lane Editions, 2013).

CANADA. *Report of the Royal Commission on Maritime Claims* (Ottawa: King's Printer, 1926).

———. *Report of the Royal Commission on Financial Arrangements between the Dominion and the Maritime Provinces* (Ottawa: King's Printer, 1935).

———. *Report of the Royal Commission on Dominion-Provincial Relations* (3 vols), (Ottawa: King's Printer, 1940). Order-in-Council P.C. 1908.

CARELESS, ANTHONY. *Initiative and Response: The Adaptation of Canadian Federalism to Regional Economic Development*. Canadian Public Administration Series (Montreal: McGill-Queen's University Press, 1977).

CARRIERE, SCOTT A. "The Emergence of a Normative Principle of Co-Operative Federalism and Its Application" (2021) 58 *Alberta Law Review* 897–920.

CARLBERG, JARED. *Interprovincial Trade Barriers in Canada: Options for Moving Forward*, SPP Briefing Paper, School of Public Policy, University of Calgary (2021) 14:23.

CHAPNICK, ADAM. "Lester Pearson and the Concept of Peace: Enlightened Realism with a Human Touch" (2010) 35 *Peace & Change* 104–22.

CHARILLON, FRÉDÉRIC, MARIO TELÒ & STEFANO GUZZINI. "Is There a European Identity in IR?" (2015) 2 *European Review of International Studies* 118–20.

CHECKEL, JEFFREY T. & PETER J. Katzenstein. *European Identity. Contemporary European Politics* (Cambridge: Cambridge University Press, 2009).

CHERNOFF, ALEX. "1871 Productivity Differentials and the Decline of the Maritime Manufacturing Sector" (2014) 43 *Acadiensis* 65–88.

CLARKE, ERNEST A. "Cumberland Planters and the Aftermath of the Attack on Fort Cumberland" in Margaret Conrad, ed, *They Planted Well: New England Planters in Maritime Canada* (Fredericton: Acadiensis Press, 1988) 42–60.

CLEMENS, JASON et al. "Albertans Make Disproportionate Contributions to National Programs: The Canada Pension Plan as a Case Study" (April 2019) *Fraser Research Bulletin*.

VON CLAUSEWITZ, CARL. *On War* (New York: Penguin Books, 1978).

COCHRANE, CHRISTOPHER & ANDREA PERRELLA. "Regions, Regionalism and Regional Differences in Canada" (2012) 45 *Canadian Journal of Political Science* 829–53.

COHEN, ANDREW. *A Deal Undone: The Making and Breaking of the Meech Lake Accord* (Toronto: Douglas & McIntyre, 1990).

———. *While Canada Slept: How We Lost Our Place in the World* (Toronto: McClelland & Stewart, 2003).

COLLINS, JEFF & DON DESSERUD. "The ongoing saga of electoral reform in PEI" (April 2017) 11 *Policy Options*.

CONRAD, MARGARET. "The Atlantic Revolution of the 1950s" in Berkeley Fleming, ed, *Beyond Anger and Longing: Community and Development in Atlantic Canada* (Fredericton: Acadiensis Press, 1988) 55–96.

———. "The 1950s: The Decade of Development" in E.R. Forbes et al, eds, *The Atlantic Provinces in Confederation* (Toronto: University of Toronto Press, 1993) 382–420.

———. *At the Ocean's Edge: A History of Nova Scotia to Confederation* (Toronto: University of Toronto Press, 2020).

CORMIER, MICHEL. *Louis Robichaud: A Not So Quiet Revolution*, Jonathan Kaplansky, trans (Moncton: Faye editions, 2004).

CORMIER, MICHEL & ACHILLE MICHAUD. *Richard Hatfield: Power and Disobedience*, Daphne Ponder, trans. (Fredericton: Goose Lane Editions, 1992).

COSTA, ANDREW. "Interrelated Treaty Orders across the Generations: Autonomy, Obligation and Confederacy in the Wabanaki Compact (1725–26)" (2018) 35 *Windsor Yearbook of Access to Justice* 463–85.

COURTNEY, JOHN C. *Commissioned Ridings: Designing Canada's Electoral Districts* (Montreal: McGill-Queen's University Press, 2001).

COWEN, ZELMAN. "Notes on Constitutional Developments in the Commonwealth: Appeals to the Privy Council" (1950) 32 *Journal of Comparative Legislation and International Law*, 3d Ser 73–74.

CRANDALL, ERIN. "Amendment by Stealth of Provincial Constitutions in Canada" (2022) 45 *Manitoba Law Journal* 172–96.

CREELMAN, DAVID. "Conservative Solutions: The Early Historical Fiction of Thomas Raddall" (1995) 20 *Studies in Canadian Literature* 127–49.

CREIGHTON, DONALD. *The Old Chieftain* (Toronto: Houghton Mifflin, 1955).

———. *The Road to Confederation: The Emergence of Canada, 1863–1867* (Toronto: Macmillan of Canada, 1964; reprinted, Toronto: Oxford University Press, 2012).

CROSS, WILLIAM & IAN STEWART. "Ethnicity and Accommodation in the New Brunswick Party System" (2002) 36 *Journal of Canadian Studies* 32–58.

CRUIKSHANK, KEN. "The Intercolonial Railway, Freight Rates and the Maritime Economy" (1992) 22 *Acadiensis* 87–110.

CUSHING, CALEB. *The Treaty of Washington: Its Negotiation, Execution, and Discussions Relating Thereto* (New York: Harper & Brothers, 1873).

CUTHBERTSON, B.C. "Uniacke and the Struggle for Patronage in Nova Scotia" (1986) 12 *The Canadian Journal of Irish Studies* 148–65.

DAIGLE, JEAN, ed. *The Acadians of the Maritimes* (Moncton: Université de Moncton, 1982).

———. James Crombie, trans, *Acadia of the Maritimes* (Moncton: Université de Moncton, 1995).

DAVIS, HAROLD A. "The Fenian Raid on New Brunswick" (1955) 36 *The Canadian Historical Review* 316–34.

DAWSON, R. MACGREGOR, "The Independence of the Lieutenant-Governor" (1922) 2 *Dalhousie Review* 230–46.

DELLEDONNE, GIACOMO & GUISEPPE MARTINICO, eds. *The Canadian Contribution to a Comparative Law of Secession: Legacies of the Quebec Secession Reference* (Cham: Palgrave Macmillan, 2019).

DEN OTTER, A.A. *The Philosophy of Railways: The Transcontinental Railway Idea in British North America* (Toronto: University of Toronto Press, 1997).

DESSERUD, DONALD A. "Nova Scotia and the American Revolution" in Margaret Conrad, ed, *Making Adjustments: Change and Continuity in Planter Nova Scotia, 1759–1800* (Fredericton: Acadiensis Press, 1991) 89–112.

———. "The Exercise of Community Rights in the Liberal-Federal State: Language Rights and New Brunswick's Bill 88" (1996) 14 *International Journal of Canadian Studies*, special issue on Citizenship and Rights 215–36.

———. "An Outpost's Response: The Language and Politics of Moderation in Eighteenth-Century Nova Scotia" (1999) 29 *American Review of Canadian Studies* 379–406.

———. *The Confidence Convention under the Canadian Parliamentary System* (Ottawa: Canadian Study of Parliament Occasional Paper Series No 7, 2006).

———. "'Whither 91.1?' The Constitutionality of Bill C-19: An Act to Limit Senate Tenure" in Jennifer Smith, ed, *The Democratic Dilemma: Reforming the Canadian Senate* (Montreal: McGill-Queen's University Press, 2009) 63–80.

———. "'He Shall Be Resident in the Province': The Senate Residency Requirement and the Canadian Constitution" (2017) XI *Journal of Parliamentary and Political Law* 61–98.

———. "The 2019 Provincial Election in Prince Edward Island" (2021) 13 *Canadian Political Science Review* 123–49.

———. "A Stranger in the Chair? Parliamentary Rules and Forms and the Anglin Affair 1877–78" (2023) LVII *Journal of Parliamentary and Political Law* 282–306.

DEUTSCH, KARL et al. *Political Community and the North Atlantic Area* (Princeton, NJ: Princeton University Press, 1957).

DICEY, A.V. "Federal Government" (1885) 1 *Law Quarterly Review* 80–99.

———. *An Introduction to the Study of the Law of the Constitution*, 4th ed. (London: Macmillan, 1893).

DODA, HILARY. "Scissors, Embellishment, and Womanhood: The Material Culture of Acadian Sewing to 1755" (2021) 50 *Acadiensis* 62–95.

DODARO, SANTO & LEONARD PLUTA. *The Big Picture: The Antigonish Movement of Eastern Nova Scotia*, McGill-Queen's Studies in the History of Religion, Series Two: Montreal: McGill-Queen's University Press, 2012).

DODEK, ADAM. "Uncovering the Wall Surrounding the Castle of the Constitution: Judicial Interpretation of Part V of the Constitution Act, 1982" in Emmett Macfarlane, ed, *Constitutional Amendment in Canada* (Toronto. University of Toronto Press, 2016) 42–64.

DOMINION-PROVINCIAL CONFERENCE. *Record of Proceedings, Ottawa, December 9–13, 1935* (Ottawa King's Printer, 1936).

DOUCET, PHILIPPE. "Politics and the Acadians," Jean Daigle, ed, *The Acadians of the Maritimes* (Moncton: Université de Moncton, 1982) 219–69.

DUNCAN, ANDREW RAE. *Report of the Royal Commission on Maritime Claims* (Ottawa: F. A. Acland, Printer to the King, 1926).

EAGLES, MUNROE. "Enhancing Relative Vote Equality in Canada: The Role of Electors in Boundary Adjustment" in David Small, ed, *Drawing the Map: Equality and Efficacy of the Vote in Canadian Electoral Boundary Reform*, vol 11 of the Research Studies for the Royal Commission on Electoral Reform and Party Financing (Toronto: Dundurn Press, 1991) 175–220.

———. "Electoral Reform and Electoral Boundaries in New Brunswick, William Cross, ed, *Democratic Reform in New Brunswick* (Toronto: Canadian Scholars' Press, 2007) 170–203.

ELLIOTT, SHIRLEY B. "An Historical Review of Nova Scotia Legal Literature; a Select Bibliography" (1984) 8 *Dalhousie Law Journal* 197–212.

ELAZAR, DANIEL. *Covenant and Civil Society: The Constitutional Matrix of Modern Democracy*, (New Brunswick, NJ: Transaction Publishers, 1998).

ELECTIONS CANADA. "The Representation Formula," online: www.elections.ca/content.aspx?section=res&dir=cir/red/ form&document=index&lang=e.

FEEHAN, JAMES P. "Atlantic Provinces Economic Union" (2003) 19 *Canadian Public Policy* 133–44.

FINBOW, ROBERT, "Dependents or Dissidents? The Atlantic Provinces in Canada's Constitutional Reform Process, 1967–1992" (1994) 27 *Canadian Journal of Political Science* 465–91.

———. "Atlantic Canada: Forgotten Periphery in an Endangered Confederation" in Kenneth McRoberts, ed, *Beyond Quebec: Taking Stock of Canada* (Montreal: McGill-Queen's University Press, 1995) 61–80.

FINDLAY, PETER C. *Union Maritime : Les Consèquences pour la Langue et Culture Françaises* (Fredericton: Maritime Union Study, 1970).

FIRMINI, MARCELLA & JENNIFER SMITH. "The Crown in Canada" in Peter Oliver et al, eds, *The Oxford Handbook of the Canadian Constitution* (New York: Oxford University Press, 2017) 129–50.

FLANAGAN, LUKE. *The Political Union Debate in Canada's Maritime Provinces, 1960–1980: Why Did a Union Not Happen?* (PhD Thesis, The University of Edinburgh, 2012).

FLANAGAN, TOM. *Harper's Team* (Montreal: McGill-Queen's University Press, 2007).

FORBES, E.R. "Misguided Symmetry: The Destruction of Regional Transportation Policy for the Maritimes" in David

Jay Bercuson, ed, *Canada and the Burden of Unity* (Toronto: University of Toronto Press, 1977) 60–86.

FORBES E.R., D.A. MUISE & BILL PARENTEAU, eds. *The Atlantic Provinces in Confederation*, cartography by L.D. McCann (Toronto: University of Toronto Press, 1993).

FORBES, ERNEST. "The Origins of the Maritime Rights Movement" (1975) 5 *Acadiensis* 54–66.

FORBES, ERNEST R. *The Maritime Rights Movement, 1919–1927* (Montreal: McGill-Queen's University Press, 1979).

FORSEY, EUGENE. "Disallowance of Provincial Acts, Reservation of Provincial Bills, and Refusal of Assent by Lieutenant-Governors since 1867" (1938) 4 *The Canadian Journal of Economics and Political Science* 47–59.

FOURNIER, PIERRE. *A Meech Lake Post-Mortem*, Sheila Fischman, trans (Montreal: McGill-Queen's University Press, 1991).

FOWKE, VERNON. *The National Policy and the Wheat Economy* (Toronto: University of Toronto Press, 1957).

FRANCESCO, RASCHI & PIRAS ELISA. "A Realistic Scepticism: Raymond Aron's Perspective on the European Construction" (2020) 26 *Journal of European Integration History* 267–84.

FRANCIS, R. DOUGLAS et al. *Origins: Canadian History to Confederation* (Toronto: Holt, Rinehart and Winston of Canada, 1988).

FREDERICKS, H.A. *What Happened to the Blueprint for Atlantic Advance?* (Fredericton: HLG Marketing Ltd., 2003).

FROC, KERRI A. & MICHAEL MARIN. "The Supreme Court's Strange Brew: History, Federalism and Anti-Originalism in Comeau" (2019) 70 *University of New Brunswick Law Journal* 297–332

FROST, JAMES D. "The Union Bank of Halifax, 1856–1910" (2012) 15 *Journal of the Royal Nova Scotia Historical Society* 82–102.

GARNER, JOHN. *The Franchise and Politics in British North America, 1755–1867* (Toronto: University of Toronto Press, 1969).

GASPAR BROWN, ELIZABETH. "British Statutes in the Emergent Nations of North America: 1606–1949" (1963) 7 *American Journal of Legal History* 95–136.

GÉRIN-LAJOIE, PAUL. *Constitutional Amendment in Canada* (Toronto: University of Toronto Press, 1950).

GIBBINS, ROGER. "Speculations on a Canada without Quebec" in Kenneth McRoberts & Patrick J. Monahan, eds, *The Charlottetown Accord, the Referendum, and the Future of Canada* (Toronto: University of Toronto Press, 1993).

GIRARD, PHILIP. "Themes and Variations in Early Canadian Legal Culture: Beamish Murdoch and His Epitome of the Laws of Nova-Scotia" (1993) 11 *Law and History Review* 101–44.

———. "The Supreme Court of Nova Scotia, Responsible Government, and the Quest for Legitimacy, 1850–1920" (1994) 17 *Dalhousie Law Journal* 430–57.

———. *Lawyers and Legal Culture in British North America: Beamish Murdoch of Halifax* (Toronto: University of Toronto Press, 2011).

GLASSFORD, LARRY A. *Reaction and Reform: The Politics of the Conservative Party Under R.B. Bennett* (Toronto: University of Toronto Press, 1992).

GREENE, STEPHEN. "Time for Maritime Union," *Policy Options*, 1 December 2012.

GRIFFITHS, NAOMI. *From Migrant to Acadian: A North American Border People, 1604–1755* (Montreal: McGill University Press, 2005).

GRITTNER, COLIN. "Constitutional Conservatism, Anti-Democratic Ideology, and the Elective Principle in British North America's Upper Legislative Houses, 1848-1867" in Nikolaj Bijleveld et al, *Reforming Senates: Upper Legislative Houses* in *North Atlantic Small Powers 1800–Present. Routledge Studies in Modern History* (Abingdon, Oxford: Routledge, 2020).

GUILDING, BEN. "The Silent Framers of British North American Union: The Colonial Office and Canadian Confederation, 1851–67" (2018) 99 *The Canadian Historical Review* 349–93.

HAAS, ERNST B. *Beyond the Nation State* (San Francisco: Stanford University Press, 1964).

———. "The Study of Regional Integration: Reflections on the Joy and Anguish of Pretheorizing" (1970) 24 *International Organization* 607–46.

———. *The Obsolescence of Regional Integration Theory* (Berkeley: University of California, Berkeley, 1975).

———. "Turbulent Fields and the Theory of Regional Integration" (1976) 30 *International Organization* 173–212.

HALE, SHANNON. "The Bedford Trilogy and the Shifting Foundations of Vertical Stare Decisis: Emancipation from Judicial Restraint?" (2020) 29 *Dalhousie Journal of Legal Studies* 97–134.

HAMILTON, ROBERT. "After Tsilhqot'in Nation: The Aboriginal Title Question in Canada's Maritime Provinces" (2016) 67 *University of New Brunswick Law Journal* 58–108.

HARRIS, REGINALD. "The Union of the Maritime Provinces" (1906) VI *Acadiensis* 172–84.

HARVEY, D.C. "Confederation in Prince Edward Island" (1933) 14 *The Canadian Historical Review* 143–60.

———. "Uniacke's Memorandum to Windham, 1806" (1936) 17 *The Canadian Historical Review* 17 41–58.

———. "Fielding's Call to Ottawa" (1949) 28 *The Dalhousie Review* 369–85.

———. "A Centenary of Edward Whelan" in G.A. Rawlyk, ed, *Historical Essays on the Atlantic Provinces* (Toronto: McClelland & Stewart, 1967) 207–28.

HAYLOCK, JEFFREY. "National Class of Extraterritorial Legislation" (2009) 32 *Dalhousie Law Journal* 253-94.

HEARD, ANDREW. *Canadian Constitutional Conventions: The Marriage of Law and Politics* (Toronto: Oxford University Press Canada, 1991).

HEARD, ANDREW & TIM SWARTZ. "The Regional Veto Formula and Its Effects on Canada's Constitutional Amendment Process" (1997) 30 *Canadian Journal of Political Science* 339-56.

HÉLIE, MICHEL Y. "Michel Bastarache's Language Rights Legacy" (2009) 47 *The Supreme Court Law Review: Osgoode's Annual Constitutional Cases Conference* 377-408.

HENDERSON, STEPHEN. "A Defensive Alliance: The Maritime Provinces and the Turgeon Commission on Transportation, 1948-1951" (2006) 35 *Acadiensis* 46-63.

HENDERSON, STEVEN. "'A New Federal Vision': Nova Scotia and the Rowell-Sirois Report, 1938-1948" in Dimitry Anastakis & P.E. Bryden, eds, *Framing Canadian Federalism* (Toronto: University of Toronto Press, 2009) 51-74.

HIZEN, YOICHI & MASAFUMI SHINMYO. "Imposing a Turnout Threshold in Referendums" (2011) 148 *Public Choice* 491-503.

HOGG, PETER. *Constitutional Law of Canada: 2020 Student Edition* (Toronto: Carswell/Thomson Reuters, 2020).

HOGG, PETER W. "Formal Amendment of the Constitution of Canada" (1992) 55 *Law and Contemporary Problems* 253-60.

HOROWITZ, GAD. "Conservatism, Liberalism, and Socialism in Canada: An Interpretation" (1966) 32 *Canadian Journal of Economics and Political Science* 143-71.

HOWE, PAUL, JOANNA EVERITT & DON DESSERUD. "Social and Civic Attitudes and Beliefs in New Brunswick (Canada)'s Linguistic Communities" (2006) 38 *Canadian Ethnic Studies* 37-57.

HOWELL, C.D. "W.S. Fielding and the Repeal Elections of 1886 and 1887 in Nova Scotia" (1979) 8 *Acadiensis* 28–46.

HURLEY, JAMES ROSS. *Amending Canada's Constitution: History, Processes, Problems and Prospects* (Ottawa: Privy Council Office, Policy Development and Constitutional Affairs, 1996).

HYSON, STEWART. "The electoral boundary revolution in the Maritime provinces" (1995) 25 *American Review of Canadian Studies* 285–99.

INNIS, H.A. "The Rowell-Sirois Report" (1940) 6 *The Canadian Journal of Economics and Political Science* 562–71.

INNIS, HAROLD. "An Introduction to the Economic History of the Maritimes, Including Newfoundland and New England" in Harold Innis, *Essays in Canadian Economic History* (Toronto: University of Toronto Press, 1956) 27–42.

ISAAC, THOMAS. *Aboriginal and Treaty Rights in the Maritimes: The Marshall Decision and Beyond* (Saskatoon: Purich Publishing Ltd, 2001).

JACOB, PHILIP, KARL DEUTSCH & JAMES V. TOSCANO, eds, *The Integration of Political Communities* (New York: Lippincott, 1964).

JOHNSTON, A.J.B. "The Call of the Archetype and the Challenge of Acadian History" (2004) 5 *French Colonial History* 63–92.

JOHNSTON, RICHARD. "An Inverted Logroll: The Charlottetown Accord and the Referendum" (1993) 26 *PS: Political Science and Politics* 43–48.

KENNEDY, W.P.M. *The Constitution of Canada: An Introduction to Its Development and Law* (London: H. Milford, Oxford University Press, 1922).

———. "The Office of Governor General in Canada" (1953) 31 *Canadian Bar Review* 994–99.

KENNY, JAMES & ANDREW SECORD, "Engineering Modernity: Hydroelectric Development in New Brunswick, 1945–1970" (2010) 39 *Acadiensis* 3–26.

KERR, ROBERT W. "The Official Languages of New Brunswick Act" (1970) 20 *University of Toronto Law Journal* 478–85.

KEULMAN, KENNETH & AGNES KATALIN KOÓS, *European Identity: Its Feasibility and Desirability* (Lanham: Lexington Books, 2014).

KLAIN, J.A. & M. LEVESQUE. "Revisiting the Labrador Boundary Decision to Include Indigenous Interpretations of the Region" (2019) 53 *Journal of Canadian Studies* 123–51.

KOHN, HANS. "Napoleon and the Age of Nationalism" (1950) 22 *The Journal of Modern History* 21–37.

KOHLI, MARTIN. "The Battlegrounds of European Identity" (2000) 2 *European Societies* 113–37.

LA FOREST, G.V. *Disallowance and Reservation of Provincial Legislation* (Ottawa: Department of Justice: 1955).

LASELVA, SAMUEL. "Federalism and Unanimity: The Supreme Court and Constitutional Amendment" (1983) 16 *Canadian Journal of Political Science* 757–70.

LASELVA, SAMUEL V. *Moral Foundations of Canadian Federalism* (Montreal: McGill-Queen's University Press, 1996).

———. *Canada and the Ethics of Constitutionalism: Identity, Destiny, and Constitutional Faith* (Montreal: McGill-Queen's University Press, 2018).

LAVOIE, MALCOLM. "R. v. Comeau and Section 121 of the Constitution Act, 1867: Freeing the Beer and Fortifying the Economic Union" (2017) 40 *Dalhousie Law Journal* 189–219.

LEAVITT, ROBERT. "Language in New Brunswick" in John Edwards, ed, *Language in Canada* (New York: Cambridge University Press, 1998) 373–84.

LEBLANC, B.V. & R. LeBLANC "Traditional Material Culture in Acadia" in *Acadia of the Maritimes*, Jean Daigle, ed, James Crombie, trans (Moncton: Université de Moncton, 1995) 62–95.

LEDERMAN, WILLIAM R. "Notes on Recent Canadian Constitutional Developments" (1950) 32 *Journal of Comparative Legislation and International Law*, 3d Ser 74–77.

———. "Memorandum on Constitutional Amendment to Consolidate Two or More Provinces of Canada into a Single Province," Appendix C, *The Report on Maritime Union* (Fredericton: Maritime Union Study, 1970) 93–101.

———. "Canadian Constitutional Amending Procedures: 1867–1982" (1984) 32 *American Journal of Comparative Law* 339–60 at 352–53.

LEE, PHILIP. *Frank: The Life and Times of Frank McKenna* (Fredericton: Goose Lane, 2001).

LEHNING, PERCY. "European Citizenship: Towards a European Identity?" (2001) 20 *Law and Philosophy* 239–82.

LEWEY, LAUREL et al. *New Brunswick before the Equal Opportunity Program: History through a Social Work Lens* (Toronto: University of Toronto Press, 2018).

LIENESCH, MICHAEL. "Founding: Audacity, Ambition, Adaptability" in *New Order of the Ages: Time, the Constitution, and the Making of Modern American Political Thought* (New Jersey: Princeton University Press, 1988) 138–56.

LINDBERG, LEON & STUART SCHEINGOLD, eds, *Regional Integration: Theory and Research* (Cambridge, MA: Harvard University Press, 1971).

LUKES, STEPHEN. *Power: A Radical View* (London: MacMillan, 1974).

LUSZTIG, MICHAEL. "Constitutional Paralysis: Why Canadian Constitutional Initiatives are Doomed to Fail" (1994) 27 *Canadian Journal of Political Science* 747–71.

MACDONALD, EDWARD. *If You're Stronghearted: Prince Edward Island in the Twentieth Century* (Charlottetown: Prince Edward Island Museum and Heritage Foundation, 2000).

———. "Who's Afraid of the Fenians? The Fenian Scare on Prince Edward Island, 1865–1867" (2009) 38 *Acadiensis* 33–51.

MACDONALD, RON. "Maritime Union — We Rise Again" (Winter 1995–96) *Canadian Parliamentary Review* 2–5.

MACKENZIE, NORMAN. "Constitutional Questions in Nova Scotia. The Attorney-General of Nova Scotia v. The Legislative Council of Nova Scotia" (1929) 11 *Journal of Comparative Legislation and International Law* 87–95.

MACKINNON, FRANK. *Government of Prince Edward Island* (Toronto: University of Toronto Press, 1951).

MACKINNON, LACHLAN. "A Region in Retrospective" (2019) 48 *Acadiensis* 230–40.

MACLAUCHLAN, WADE. "Canada's Newest Supreme Court Judge: Hon. Michael Bastarache" (1997) 9 *Constitutional Forum* 25–26.

MACLAUCHLAN, H. WADE. *Alex B. Campbell: The Prince Edward Island Premier Who Rocked the Cradle* (Charlottetown: Prince Edward Island Museum and Heritage Foundation, 2014).

MACMILLAN, MICHAEL. *The Practice of Language Rights in Canada* (Toronto: University of Toronto Press, 1998).

MACNEILL, CHRISTOPHER MARK. "Canada's Post-Colonial Orphan Province: Cape Breton Island's Quest for Autonomy" (2021) 4 *International Journal of Law Management & Humanities* 52–68.

MACNUTT, W.S. *New Brunswick, A History: 1784–1867* (Toronto: Macmillan of Canada, 1963; reprinted, Toronto: University of Toronto Press, 1984).

MACNUTT, W.S. "The Atlantic Revolution" (June 1957) *Atlantic Advocate* 11–13.

MACPHERSON, IAN. "Patterns in the Maritime Co-operative Movement 1900–1945" (1975) 5 *Acadiensis* 67–83.

MAINGOT, JOSEPH. *Parliamentary Privilege in Canada* (Toronto: Butterworths, 1982).

MANCKE, ELIZABETH. "Early Modern Imperial Governance and the Origins of Canadian Political Culture" (1999) 32 *Canadian Journal of Political Science* 3–20.

———. "Idiosyncratic Localism, Provincial Moderation, and Imperial Loyalty: Planter Studies and the History of 18th-Century Nova Scotia" (2013) 42 *Acadiensis* 169–81.

MANN, NELSON. "The Atlantic Provinces Economic Council" (1956) 35 *The Dalhousie Review* 309–22.

MARCHILDON, GREGORY & NICOLE O'BYRNE. "Last Province Aboard: New Brunswick and National Medicare" (2013) 42 *Acadiensis* 150–67.

MARITIME UNION STUDY. *Briefs to the Maritime Union Study* (Fredericton: Maritime Union Study, 1970).

MARKET FACTS OF CANADA. *The Maritimes and Maritime Union: An Opinion Study* (Fredericton: Maritime Union Study, 1970).

MARTIN, GEOFF. "We've seen it Before: The Rise and Fall of the CoR Party of New Brunswick, 1988–1995" (1998) 33 *Journal of Canadian Studies* 22–38.

MATCHIM, JOHN R.H. "A Bibliography on Indigenous Peoples and the History of the Atlantic Region" (2020) 49 *Acadiensis* 223–64.

MATTOCKS, KATE. "Looking for Bootstraps: Economic Development in the Maritimes (Donald Savoie, Halifax: Nimbus Publishing, 2017)" (2019) *Canadian Journal of Political Science* 418–19.

MATTHEWS, GEOFFREY & BYRON MOLDOFSKY. "National Perspectives" in William G. Dean et al, eds, *Concise Historical Atlas of Canada* (Toronto: University of Toronto Press, 1998) 1–72.

MCCONNELL, W.H. *Commentary on the British North America Act* (Toronto: Macmillan of Canada, 1977).

MCKAY, IAN & SUZANNE MORTON. "The Maritimes: Expanding the Circle of Resistance" in Craig Heron, ed, *The Workers' Revolt in Canada, 1917–1925* (Toronto: University of Toronto Press, 1998).

MCMILLAN, CHARLES. *Standing Up to the Future: The Maritimes in the 1990s* (Halifax: Council of Maritime Premiers, 1989).

———. "The New Disparity: Atlantic Canada is Booming" (29 June 2023) *Policy: Canadian Politics and Public Policy*, online: www.policymagazine.ca/the-new-disparity-atlantic-canada -is-booming.

———. *The Age of Consequence: The Ordeals of Public Policy in Canada* (Montreal: McGill-Queen's University Press, 2022).

MCRAE, KENNETH. "The Structure of Canadian History" in Louis Hartz, ed, *The Founding of New Societies* (New York: Harcourt, Brace & World, 1964) 219–74.

MCROBERTS, KENNETH. "Canada's Constitutional Crisis" (1991) 90 *Current History* 411–16.

MCROBERTS, KENNETH & PATRICK J. MONAHAN, eds, *The Charlottetown Accord, the Referendum, and the Future of Canada* (Toronto: University of Toronto Press, 1993).

MEEKISON, J.P., ed. *Canadian Federalism: Myth or Reality?* (Toronto: Methuen, 1977).

MILNE, DAVID. "Consequences of Quebec Independence on Atlantic Provinces" (2002) 51 *University of New Brunswick Law Journal* 289–96.

MILNE, WILLIAM J. *The McKenna Miracle: Myth or Reality?* (Toronto: Centre for Public Management, University of Toronto, 1996).

MONAHAN, PATRICK. *Meech Lake: The Inside Story* (Toronto: University of Toronto Press, 1991).

MONAHAN, PATRICK J. "The Law and Politics of Quebec Secession" (1995) 33 *Osgoode Hall Law Journal* 1–34 at 10.

MOORE, CHRISTOPHER. *1867: How the Fathers Made a Deal* (Toronto: McClelland & Stewart, 1998).

MORGAN, ROBERT. "Separatism in Cape Breton 1820–1884" in Kenneth Donovan, ed, *Cape Breton at 200: Historical Essays in Honour of the Island's Bicentennial, 1785–1985* (Sidney: University College of Cape Breton Press, 1985) 41–51.

MORTON, DESMOND. *A Short History of Canada* (Edmonton: Hurtig Publishers, 1983).

MOULL, WILLIAM D. "Section 92A of the Constitution Act, 1867" (1983) 61 *Canadian Bar Review* 715–34.

MURPHY, ARTHUR et al. *Region-Wide Policies for Higher Education* (Fredericton: Maritime Union Study, 1970).

NEILL, ROBIN. *A New Theory of Value: The Canadian Economics of H.A. Innis* (Toronto: University of Toronto Press, 1972).

NEW BRUNSWICK. *Vers l'égalité des langues officielles au Nouveau-Brunswick : rapport du groupe d'étude sur les langues officielles* (Fredericton: Direction des langues officielles, 1982).

———. Legislative Assembly, Select Committee on the 1987 Constitutional Accord, *Final report on the Constitution Amendment, 1987* (Fredericton: The Committee, 1989) at 126 and 140.

———. Commission on Legislative Democracy, *Final Report and Recommendations* (Fredericton: Queen's Printer, 2004).

NEWMAN, WARREN J. "Living with the Amending Procedures: Prospects for Future Constitutional Reform in Canada" in Graeme Mitchell et al, eds, *A Living Tree: The Legacy of 1982 in Canada's Political Evolution* (Markham: LexisNexis Canada, 2007) 747–80.

———. "Constitutional Amendment by Legislation" in Emmett Macfarlane, ed, *Constitutional Amendment in Canada* (Toronto: University of Toronto Press, 2016) 105–25.

NOSSAL, KIM RICHARD et al, *The Politics of Canadian Foreign Policy*, 4th ed (Montreal: McGill-Queen's University Press, 2015).

NOVA SCOTIA. *Report of the Royal Commission of Provincial Economic Inquiry* (Halifax: King's Printer, 1934).

NYE, JOSEPH S. *Bound to Lead: The Changing Nature of American Power* (New York: Basic Books, 1990).

———. *Soft Power: The Means to Success in World Politics* (Cambridge: Perseus Books, 2004).

———. *The Powers to Lead* (Oxford: Oxford University Press, 2008).

———. "Get Smart: Combining Hard and Soft Power" (2009) 88 *Foreign Affairs* 160–63.

———. "Power and foreign policy" (2011) 4 *Journal of Political Power* 9–24.

O'LEARY, DEREK KANE. "Archival Lines, Historical Practice, and the Atlantic Geopolitics behind the 1842 Webster-Ashburton Treaty" (2021) 110 *Transactions of the American Philosophical Society* 176–91.

PARKIN, ANDREW, JUSTIN SAVOIE & CHARLES BRETON. "Is One Region Favoured by Ottawa?" (23 May 2023) *Policy Options*.

PARTRIDGE, P.H. "Some Notes on the Concept of Power" (1963) 11 *Political Studies* 107–25.

PASOLLI, LISA. "Bureaucratizing the Atlantic Revolution: The 'Saskatchewan Mafia' in the New Brunswick Civil Service, 1960-1970" (2009) 38 *Acadiensis* 126–50.

PATERSON, ALEXANDER. *The True Story of Confederation* (Saint John: Government of the Province of New Brunswick, 1926).

PEACH, IAN. "Quebec Bill 96 — Time for a Primer on Amending the Constitution" (2021) 30 *Constitutional Forum* 1–8.

PENNEY, JONATHON W. "Deciding in the Heat of the Constitutional Moment: Constitutional Change in the

Quebec Secession Reference" (2005) 28 *Dalhousie Law Journal* 217–60.

PICKERSGILL, J.W. *My Years with Louis St. Laurent: A Political Memoir* (Toronto: University of Toronto Press, 1975).

PIGEON, LOUIS PHILIPPE. "Are the Provincial Legislatures Parliaments?" (1943) 21 *Canadian Bar Review* 826–33.

POPE, JOSEPH. *Correspondence of Sir John Macdonald* (Toronto: Oxford University Press, 1921).

POTTER, EVAN. *Branding Canada: Protecting Canada's Soft Power Through Public Diplomacy* (Montreal: McGill-Queen's University Press, 2008).

PRINCE, PETER. "Provincializing Constitutions: History, Narrative, and the Disappearance of Canada's Provincial Constitutions" (2017) 9 *Perspectives on Federalism* 33–56.

PRINCE EDWARD ISLAND. [Elections PEI], *2016 Annual Report of the Chief Electoral Office* (Charlottetown: Elections PEI, 2016).

PRYKE, KENNETH G. *Nova Scotia and Confederation 1864–1874* (Toronto: University of Toronto Press, 1979).

RADDALL, THOMAS H. *His Majesty's Yankees* (Garden City: Doubleday, Doran and Co, Inc 1942).

RAWLYK, GEORGE. *The Atlantic Provinces and the Problems of Confederation* (St John's: Breakwater, 1979).

RAWLYK, GEORGE, ed. *Joseph Howe: Opportunist? Man of Vision? Frustrated Politician?* (Toronto: Copp Clark, 1967).

RAYMOND, W.O. "New Brunswick: Political History, 1867–1912" in Adam Shortt & Arthur G. Doughty, eds, *Canada and its Provinces: A History of the Canadian People and Their Institutions by One Hundred Associates* (Toronto: Publishers' Association of Canada Limited, 1914) 403–31.

READ, J.E. "The Early Provincial Constitutions" (1948) 26 *Canadian Bar Review* 621–37.

REESOR, BAYARD. *The Canadian Constitution in Historical Perspective* (Scarborough: Prentice-Hall Canada, 1992).

REID, JOHN. "Empire, the Maritime Colonies, and the Supplanting of Mi'kma'ki/Wulstukwik, 1780–1820" (2009) 38 *Acadiensis* 78–97.

RESNICK, PHILIP. "Montesquieu Revisited, or the Mixed Constitution and the Separation of Powers in Canada" (1987) 20 *Canadian Journal of Political Science* 97–115.

RICHEZ, EMMANUELLE. "The Possibilities and Limits of Provincial Constitution-making Power: The Case of Quebec" in Emmett Macfarlane, ed, *Constitutional Amendment in Canada* (Toronto: University of Toronto Press, 2016) 164–84.

RISSE, THOMAS. "Neofunctionalism, European Identity, and the Puzzles of European Integration" (2005) 12 *Journal of European Public Policy* 291–309.

ROBERTSON, IAN ROSS. "Edward Whelan" (16 January 2008) *The Canadian Encyclopedia*. Historica Canada.

ROGERS, NORMAN MCLEOD. "The Compact Theory of Confederation" (June 1931) 9:6 *Canadian Bar Review* 395–417.

ROMNEY, PAUL. *Mr. Attorney: The Attorney General for Ontario in Court, Cabinet, and Legislature 1791–1899* (Toronto: University of Toronto Press, 1986).

———. "Provincial Equality, Special Status and the Compact Theory of Canadian Confederation" (1999) 32 *Canadian Journal of Political Science* 21–39.

DE ROUGEMONT, DENIS. *The Meaning of Europe* (London: Sidgwick & Jackson, 1965).

ROWAT, D.C. "Recent Developments in Canadian Federalism" (1952) 18 *The Canadian Journal of Economics and Political Science* 1–16.

ROWE, JUSTICE MALCOLM & J. MICHAEL COLLINS, "What is the Constitution of a Province?" in Christopher Dunn, ed,

Provinces: Canadian Provincial Politics, 3d ed (Toronto: University of Toronto Press, 2016).

ROY, JAMES. *Joseph Howe: A Study in Achievement and Frustration* (Toronto: The Macmillan Company of Canada Limited, 1935).

RUSSELL, PETER H. *Constitutional Odyssey: Can Canadians Become a Sovereign People?* (Toronto: University of Toronto Press, 1993).

SACOUMAN, R. JAMES. "Underdevelopment and the Structural Origins of Antigonish Movement Co-Operatives in Eastern Nova Scotia" (1977) 71 *Acadiensis* 66–85.

———. "The Differing Origins, Organization and Impact of Maritime and Prairie Co-Operative Movements to 1940" (1979) 4 *The Canadian Journal of Sociology* 199–221.

ST-HILAIRE, MAXIME et al. "The Constitution of Canada as Supreme Law: A New Definition" (2019) 28 *Constitutional Forum* 7–18.

SAUL, JOHN RALSTON. *A Fair Country: Telling Truths about Canada* (Toronto: Viking Canada, 2008).

SAUNDERS, S.A. *The Economic History of the Maritime Provinces* (Fredericton: Acadiensis Press, 1984).

SAVOIE, DONALD. *Pulling Against Gravity: Economic Development in New Brunswick During the McKenna Years* (Montreal: The Institute for Research on Public Policy, 2001).

———. *Visiting Grandchildren: Economic Development in the Maritimes* (Toronto: University of Toronto Press, 2006).

———. *Power: Where Is It?* (Montreal: McGill-Queen's University Press, 2010).

———. *Looking for Bootstraps: Economic Development in the Maritimes* (Halifax: Nimbus Publishing, 2017).

———. *Canada: Beyond Grudges, Grievances, and Disunity* (Montreal: McGill-Queen's University Press, 2023).

SCHEPPELE, KIM LANE. "Aspirational and Aversive Constitutionalism: The Case for Studying Cross-Constitutional Influence Through Negative Models" (2003) 1 *International Journal of Constitutional Law* 296–324.

SCHWARTZ, MILDRED A. *Politics and Territory: The Sociology of Regional Persistence in Canada* (Montreal and London: 1974).

SCOTT, F.R. "The British North America (No. 2) Act, 1949" (1950) 8 *The University of Toronto Law Journal* 201–7.

———. "Political Nationalism and Confederation" in *Essays on the Constitution: Aspects of Canadian Law and Politics* (Toronto: University of Toronto Press, 1977) 3–34.

SCOTT, STEPHEN. "Constituent Authority and the Canadian Provinces" (1966–1967) 12 *McGill Law Journal* 528–74.

———. "The Canadian Constitutional Amendment Process" (1982) 45 *Law and Contemporary Problems* 249–81.

Senate Journals, 33rd Parliament, 2nd Session, vol 129, Pt 1 (1986).

Sessional Papers No. 70 (1883) 46 Victoria [Sessional Papers, 5th Parliament, 1st Session: vol. 12 at 6].

SHARMAN, CAMPBELL. "The Strange Case of a Provincial Constitution: The British Columbia Constitution Act" (1984) 17 *Canadian Journal of Political Science* 87–108.

SHERWOOD, JAY. *Surveying the Great Divide: The Alberta/BC Boundary Survey, 1913–1917* (Halfmoon Bay: Caitlin Press, 2017).

SIMEON, RICHARD. *Federal-Provincial Diplomacy: The Making of Recent Policy in Canada* (Toronto: University of Toronto Press, 1972).

———. "Regionalism and Canadian Political Institutions" (1975) 82 *Queen's Quarterly* 499–511.

SLUMKOSKI, COREY. "'. . . a fair show and a square deal': New Brunswick and the Renegotiation of Canadian Federalism, 1938–1951" (2010) 1 *Journal of New Brunswick Studies* 124–42.

———. *Inventing Atlantic Canada: Regionalism and the Maritime Reaction to Newfoundland's Entry into Canadian Confederation* (Toronto: University of Toronto Press, 2011).

SMILEY, D.V. "The Rowell-Sirois Report, Provincial Autonomy, and Post-War Canadian Federalism" (1962) 28 *Canadian Journal of Economics and Political Science* 54–69.

SMILEY, DONALD. *The Federal Condition in Canada* (Toronto: McGraw-Hill Ryerson, 1987).

SMITH, ANDREW. "The Historical Origins of Section 121 of the Constitution Act, 1867: A Study of Confederation's Political, Social and Economic Context" (2018) 61 *Canadian Business Law Journal* 205–26.

SMITH, ANTHONY. "National Identity and the Idea of European Unity" (1992) 68 *International Affairs* 55–76.

SMITH, DAVID. *The Canadian Senate in Bicameral Perspective* (Toronto: University of Toronto Press, 2003).

———. *The Constitution in a Hall of Mirrors: Canada at 150* (Toronto: University of Toronto Press, 2017).

SMITH, DAVID E. et al, eds. *After Meech Lake: Lessons for the Future* (Saskatoon: Fifth House Publishers, 1991).

SMITH, JENNIFER & LORI TURNBULL, *The Nova Scotia House of Assembly: On the Cusp of Change?* (Ottawa: Canadian Study of Parliament Group, 2008).

SMITH, PETER. "The Ideological Origins of Canadian Confederation" (1987) 20 *Canadian Journal of Political Science* 3–30.

SREBRNIK, HENRY. "Vandals at the Garden's Gates? Political Reaction to the Maritime Union Proposal on Prince Edward Island" (1998) 28 *American Review of Canadian Studies* 83–101.

STANLEY, DELLA. *Louis Robichaud: A Decade of Power* (Halifax: Nimbus, 1984).

———. "The 1960s: The Illusions and Realities of Progress" in *The Atlantic Provinces in Confederation*, E.R. Forbes, D.A. Muise & Bill Parenteau, eds, cartography by L.D. McCann (Toronto: University of Toronto Press, 1993) 421–59.

STANLEY, G.F.G. "The Caraquet Riots of 1875" (1972) 2 *Acadiensis* 21-38.

STARR, RICHARD. *Richard Hatfield, The Seventeen Year Saga* (Halifax: Formac, 1988).

STATISTICS CANADA. *Census of Canada, 1870–71* (Ottawa: Department of Agriculture, 1873–1878).

STEELE, CATHERINE MARY. *Can Bilingualism Work? Attitudes Toward Language Policy in New Brunswick: The 1985 Public Hearings on the Poirier-Bastarache Report* (Fredericton, NB: New Ireland Press, 1990).

STEIN, MICHAEL. "Improving the Process of Constitutional Reform in Canada: Lessons from the Meech Lake and Charlottetown Constitutional Rounds" (1997) 30 *Canadian Journal of Political Science* 307–38.

STEVENS, PAUL & JOHN SAYWELL. "Parliament and Politics," John Saywell, ed, *Canadian Annual Review of Politics and Public Affairs 1970* (Toronto: University of Toronto Press, 1971) 155–98 at 184.

STEVENSON, GARTH. "Canadian Regionalism in Continental Perspective" (1980) 15 *Journal of Canadian Studies* 16–28.

———. *Ex Uno Plures: Federal-Provincial Relations in Canada, 1867-1896* (McGill-Queen's University Press, 1993).

STEWART, IAN. "More than Just a Line on the Map: The Political Culture of the Nova Scotia-New Brunswick Boundary" (1990) 20 *Publius* 99–111.

STRAYER, B.L. "The Constitutional Processes for Prairie Union" (1970) 13 *Canadian Public Administration* 337–43.

STUART, IAN. "Canada and the Turks & Caicos Islands" (1988) 11 *Canadian Parliamentary Review* 18–21.

STUART, REGINALD C. *United States Expansionism and British North America, 1775–1871* (Chapel Hill: University of North Carolina Press, 1987).

SUNSTEIN, CASS R. "Constitutionalism and Secession" (1991) 58 *University of Chicago Law Review* 633–70.

SWINTON, KATHERINE. "Amending the Canadian Constitution: Lessons from Meech Lake" (1992) 42 *The University of Toronto Law Journal* 139–69.

TAYLOR, CHARLES. *Reconciling the Solitudes: Essays on Canadian Federalism and Nationalism*, ed Guy Laforest (Montreal: McGill-Queen's University Press, 1993).

THORBURN, HUGH. *Politics in New Brunswick* (Toronto: University of Toronto Press, 1961).

TOMBLIN, STEPHEN. *Ottawa and the Outer Provinces: The Challenge of Regional Integration in Canada* (Toronto: James Lorimer, 1995).

TONER, PETER. "The New Brunswick Schools Question" (1970) 37 *CCHA Study Sessions* 85–95.

TROTTER, REGINALD G. "An Early Proposal for the Federation of British North America" (1925) 6 *The Canadian Historical Review* 142–54.

UNIACKE, RICHARD. *The Statutes at Large Passed in the Several General Assemblies Held in His Majesty's Province of Nova-Scotia: From the First Assembly Which Met at Halifax the Second Day of October, in the Thirty-Second Year of His Late Majesty Geo. II. A.D. 1758, to the Forty-Fourth Year of His Present Majesty Geo. III A.D. 1804, Inclusive; with a Complete Index and Abridgement of the Whole* (Halifax: John Howe and Son, Printers to the King's Most Excellent Majesty, 1805).

URQUHART, M.C. "In Memoriam: John James Deutsch, 1911–76" (1976) 9 *The Canadian Journal of Economics* 685–88.

VANCE, RUPERT. "Region" (1968) 13 *International Encyclopedia of the Social Sciences* 377–78.

VANDERLINDEN, JACQUES. "French Jurisdictional Complexity on the Fringe, Acadia 1667–1710" (2019) 12 *Journal of Civil Law Studies* 33–52.

———. "Acadie: A la rencontre de l'histoire du droit avant le dérangement" (1995) 23 *Manitoba Law Journal* 79–102.

VAUGHAN, FREDERICK. *Canadian Federalist Experiment: From Defiant Monarchy to Reluctant Republic* (Montreal: McGill-Queen's University Press, 2003).

VIPOND, ROBERT C. "Constitutional Politics and the Legacy of the Provincial Rights Movement in Canada" (1985) 18 *Canadian Journal of Political Science* 267–94.

———. "Alternative Pasts: Legal Liberalism and the Demise of the Disallowance Power" (1990) 39 *University of New Brunswick Law Journal* 126–57.

———. "Seeing Canada through the Referendum: Still a House Divided" (1993) 23 *Publius* 39–55.

DE WAELE, HENRI, "Disintegration from Within: Independence and Separatist Movements, the EU Response and the Role of Solidarity" in Andreas Grimmel & Susanne Giang, eds, *Solidarity in the European Union: A Fundamental Value in Crisis* (Cham, Switzerland: Springer International Publishing, 2017) 119–29.

WAINES, W.J. "Dominion-Provincial Financial Arrangements: An Examination of Objectives" (1953) 19 *The Canadian Journal of Economics and Political Science* 304–15.

WAITE, P.B. *The Life and Times of Confederation: Politics, Newspapers, and the Union of British North America* (Toronto: University of Toronto Press, 1962).

———. *The Man from Halifax Book: Sir John Thompson, Prime Minister* (Toronto: University of Toronto Press, 1985).

WALKER, WILLARD. "The Wabanaki Confederacy" (1998) 37 *Maine History* 110–39.

WALTERS, MARK D. "Common Law Constitution in Canada: Return of Lex Non Scripta as Fundamental Law" (2001) 51 *University of Toronto Law Journal* 91–142.

WARDHAUGH, ROBERT & BARRY FERGUSON. *The Rowell-Sirois Commission and the Remaking of Canadian Federalism* (Vancouver: UBC Press, 2021).

WARNER, DONALD F. "The Post-Confederation Annexation Movement in Nova Scotia" (1947) 28 *The Canadian Historical Review* 156–65.

WATSON, WILLIAM G. "The Economics of Constitution-Making" (1982) 45 *Law and Contemporary Problems* 87–108.

WHEARE, K.C. *Federal Government*, 3rd ed (London: Oxford University Press, 1953).

WICKEN, WILLIAM C. *Mi'kmaq Treaties on Trial: History, Land, and Donald Marshall Junior* (Toronto: University of Toronto Press, 2002).

WILBUR, RICHARD. "New Brunswick," *Canadian Annual Review for 1964*, John Saywell, ed (Toronto: University of Toronto Press, 1965) 134–39.

———. *The Rise of French New Brunswick* (Halifax: Formac, 1989).

WINTER, J.R. *Federal-Provincial Fiscal Relations and Maritime Union* (Fredericton: Maritime Union Study, 1970).

WISEMAN, NELSON. "Clarifying Provincial Constitutions" (1996) 6 *National Journal of Constitutional Law* 269–94.

———. *1950s Canada* (Toronto: University of Toronto Press, 2022).

WOEHRLING, JOSÉ "Les Aspects Juridiques d'une Eventuelle Secession du Quebec" (1995) 74 *Canadian Bar Review* 293–329

YOUNG, D.M. "Blair, Andrew George" in *Dictionary of Canadian Biography*, vol 13 (Toronto: University of Toronto/Université Laval, 2003).

YOUNG, LISA & KEITH ARCHER, eds. *Regionalism and Party Politics in Canada* (Toronto: Oxford University Press, 2002).

YOUNG, R.A. "Remembering Equal Opportunity: Clearing the Undergrowth in New Brunswick" (1987) 30 *Canadian Public Administration* 88–102.

YOUNG, ROBERT. *The Secession of Quebec and the Future of Canada* (Montreal: McGill-Queen's University Press, 1995).

YOUNGBLOOD HENDERSON, JAMES. "First Nations Legal Inheritances in Canada: The Mikmaq Model" (1995) 23 *Manitoba Law Journal* 1–31.

YOUNGBLOOD HENDERSON, JAMES [SAKEJ]. "Constitutional Powers and Treaty Rights" (2000) 63 *Saskatchewan Law Review* 719–50.

Media Reports

"1948–1949" *The Globe and Mail* (1 January 1949) at 6.

"Accord Reveals Deep Divisions: New Brunswickers Poles Apart on Francophone Minority Rights" *Winnipeg Free Press* (2 February 1989) at 21.

"ACOA Mistaken Money Mounts" *CBC News* (12 April 2002), online: https://www.cbc.ca/news/canada/nova-scotia/ acoa-mistaken-money-mounts-1.353148.

ATLANTIC BRIEFS DESK, "Guaranteed Basic Income Report Released" *Charlottetown Guardian* (23 November 2023) at 2.

ARPIN, CLAUDE. "Language 'Harmony' on the Line Today, Acadians Say" *Montreal Gazette* (12 March 1985) at B1.

ARPIN, CLAUDE. "NB Hearings on Bilingualism Begin Calmly" *Montreal Gazette* (13 March 1985) at B1.

BLUENOSE, "The Great Necessity for Maritime Union" *The Evening Mail* (2 May 1908) at 3.

BURGOYNE, BERT. "NEW BRUNSWICK: Report Advocates Double Taxation" *The Globe and Mail* (1 February1964) at 8.

CANADIAN PRESS. "Bad Publicity Blamed for Atlantic Agency's Image" *The Globe and Mail* (8 September 1992) at A8.

———. "Revived Maritime Merger Proposal Gets No Political Support" *CBC News* (2 December 2012), online: www.cbc.ca/news/politics/revived-maritime-merger-proposal-gets-no-political-support-1.1173955.

CLARK, CATHERINE. "Quiet Dignity Replaces Violence in First N.B. Language Hearings" *The Globe and Mail* (15 March 1985) at 3.

COYNE, DEBORAH. "New Brunswick Amendment Has Fundamental Flaw" *The Gazette* (13 January 1993) at B3.

DOUCETTE, KEITH. "Senator Wonders if It's Time for Mi'kmaq Seat in Nova Scotia Legislature" *CBC News* (15 June 2017).

"Education Aid Not Sufficient, Premier Argues" *The Globe and Mail* (4 October 1955) at 10.

"Fans of Meech Lake Appear at New Brunswick Hearing" *The Globe and Mail* (16 February 1989) at A8.

"The Fredericton Conference of Atlantic Premiers" *The Atlantic Advocate* (September 1958) at 28.

"Hearings Give Mckenna Lots of Anti-Meech Ammo" *Toronto Star* (18 February 1989) at D4.

HICKEY, HARVEY. "Premier States Case: Province Needs Cheap Hydro" *The Globe and Mail* (27 October 1955) at 11.

"Language Issue Prominent at Meech Hearings (in New Brunswick)" *Montreal Gazette* (2 February 1989) at B1.

"Language-Rights Fight Divides New Brunswick Acadians" *Montreal Gazette* (16 March 1985) at B5.

MARCHINGTON, WILLIAM. "Way to Change B.N.A. Act Is Being Sought" *The Globe* (11 December 1935) at 2.

"Maritime Union" *The Evening Mail* (Halifax) (13 November 1919) at 9.

"Maritime Union?" *New Start Nova Scotia*, online: https://newstartns.ca/2012/12/04/maritimeunion/.

"Maritime Union a Measure Alike of Economy and Patriotism" *The Evening Mail* (Halifax) (15 March 1918) at 15.

"Maritime Union Must Come; and Cannot Come Too Soon" *The Evening Mail* (Halifax) (29 May 1926) at 4.

MARTIN, ROBERT. "Atlantic Aid Agency Powerless To Spend: PM Refuses To Answer Queries About Where Money Comes From" *The Globe and Mail* (8 June 1987) at A5.

MARTIN, ROBERT. "New Atlantic Agency Prompts Skepticism" *The Globe and Mail* (27 June 1987) at A5.

"Meech Critics Ready Arguments for Hearings in New Brunswick" *Toronto Star* (24 January 1989) at A8.

"NB Braces for Hot Debate as Language Hearings Open" *Winnipeg Free Press* (9 March 1985) at 33.

"NB Language Groups Fear Possible Violence in Hearings Next Week" *The Globe and Mail* (9 March 1985) at 5.

"N.B. Premier Proposes Maritimes Conference" *The Globe and Mail* (1 May 1956) at 12.

"New Brunswick Challenger Wants Meech Lake Pact Changed" *The Globe and Mail* (28 September 1987) at A5.

"New Brunswick Could Veto Meech Lake" *Toronto Star* (3 October 1987) at D4.

"New Brunswick Hearing Gets Earful on Meech Lake" *The Globe and Mail* (26 January 1989) at A8.

"New Brunswick Women, Natives Urge Rejection of Meech Deal" *Toronto Star* (26 January 1989) at A1 & A2.

"Ottawa Power over B.N.A. Act Opposed in East: New Brunswick Flatly Against Proposed Change" *The Globe* (1 February 1936) at 1.

"P.E.I. Has To Look After Itself as Competition for Clean Energy Increases, Energy Minister Says" *CBC News* (15 October 2023), online: www.cbc.ca/news/canada/prince-edward-island/pei -atlantic-loop-energy-1.6996803.

POITRAS, JACQUES. "Bloc Leader Says Mckenna Has No Credibility" *Telegraph Journal* (14 August 1997).

"Premiers Outline Provincial Proposals as Significant Conference Begins" *The Globe and Mail* (27 April 1955) at 8.

STEWART-PATTERSON, DAVID. "DRIE Overspending Casts Fiscal Blight on Atlantic Agency" *The Globe and Mail* (6 June 1987) at A5.

SWEET, BARB. "ACOA WriteOff $38.8 Million" *SaltWire News* (31 June 2010), online: www.saltwire.com/newfoundlandlabrador /news/acoawriteoff388million125867/.

"The New Year" *Financial Post* (1 January 1949) at 1.

WELLS, PAUL. "Robert Ghiz on Maritime Union: 'Preposterous'" *Maclean's* (29 November 2012), online: https://macleans.ca/ politics/ottawa/robert-ghiz-on-maritime-union-preposterous.

"Why the Haste?" *The Globe* (3 February 1936) at 4.

WITHERS, PAUL. "N.S. Abandons Atlantic Loop, Will Increase Wind and Solar Energy Projects for Green Electricity" *CBC News* (11 October 2023), online: www.cbc.ca/news/canada/nova-scotia/ clean-power-plan-abandons-atlantic-loop-1.6992765.

YARR, KEVIN. "Guaranteed Basic Income Could Cut Poverty on P.E.I. by 80%: Report" *CBC News* (22 November 2023), online: www.cbc.ca/news/canada/prince-edward-island /pei-guaranteed-basic-income-report-1.7036102.

Court Cases

Attorney-General for Prince Edward Island v Attorney-General for Canada and Attorney-General for New Brunswick v Attorney-General for Canada [1905] AC 37 (PC 1904)

Citizens Insurance Company of Canada and The Queen Insurance Company v Parsons [1881] UKPC 49, (1881) 7 App Cas 96

Gold Seal Ltd v Attorney-General for the Province of Alberta (1921), 62 SCR 424

Hodge v The Queen, 9 App Ca 117 [1883–84] (JCPC)

MacKinnon v Prince Edward Island (Government of), 1993 CanLII 2906 (PEI SCTD)

New Brunswick Broadcasting Co v Nova Scotia (Speaker of the House of Assembly), [1993] 1 SCR 3190)

Ontario (Attorney General) v OPSEU, [1987] 2 SCR 2

R v Comeau, 2018 SCC 15

R v Hills, [2023] SCC 2

R v Paul, 1993 CanLII 4705 (NB CA)

R v Marshall [1999] 3 SCR 456, 177 DLR (4th) 513

Re: Resolution to Amend the Constitution, [1981] 1 SCR 753

Reference by the Lord Advocate of devolution issues under paragraph 34 of Schedule 6 to the Scotland Act 1998 Michaelmas Term, [2022] UKSC 31

Reference re Prov. Electoral Boundaries (Sask.), [1991] 2 SCR 158

Reference re Secession of Quebec, [1998] 2 SCR 217

Reference re Senate Reform, 2014 SCC 32

Reference re the Final Report of the Electoral Boundaries Commission, 2017 NSCA 10

Société des Acadiens v Association of Parents, [1986] 1 SCR 54

Société des Acadiens du Nouveau-Brunswick Inc and l'Association des Conseillers Scolaires Francophones du Nouveau-Brunswick v Minority Language School Board No 50, 1983 CanLII 3785 (NB QB)

Société des Acadiens et Acadiennes du NouveauBrunswick et autres v Canada, 1997 CanLII 23620 (NB QB)

United States v Kilbride, 2009 US. App LEXIS 23722 (9th Cir, Ariz, 28 October 2009)

Index

About the Author

Don Desserud is a political science professor at the University of Prince Edward Island. He has a BA and MA from Dalhousie University, an MA from the University of New Brunswick, and a PhD from Western University. His research focuses on Canadian constitutional history and parliamentary institutions. He also studies Maritime provincial politics. His recent publications include a constitutional analysis of the unsuccessful attempt to remove Speaker Timothy Anglin from his position in 1878.

About the Editor

Gregory Tardi, BCL, LLB, DJur, is the general editor of the Understanding Canada Collection. He is a member of the Barreau du Québec and serves both as president of the Institute of Parliamentary and Political Law and as editor of the *Journal of Parliamentary and Political Law*. He has served as legal counsel with Elections Canada and at the House of Commons. He has taught at McGill, York, and Queen's universities and at the University of Ottawa, and he is the author of several books, including *The Theory and Practice of Political Law*, *Anatomy of an Election*, and, in the Understanding Canada collection, *Political Law in Canada*.

Printed and bound by CPI Group (UK) Ltd, Croydon, CR0 4YY

07/07/2026

14916223-0003